George B. Prettyman, Sr.

The Cecil Comunity College Foundation, Inc. was founded to support the role and mission of Cecil Community College: to offer educational, cultural and economic development to the citizens of the predominantly rural Cecil County.

Columns and articles reprinted with permission of The Cecil Whig and Chesapeake Publishing Corporation, and with permission of The Record and Homestead Publishing Co.

For My Elizabeth

Author: Prettyman, Sr., George B.
Title: Red top boots and other personal essays : a lifetime on the Eastern Shore / George B. Prettyman, Sr.
Published: [Elkton, Md.] : Cecil Community College Foundation, c1997.

Library of Congress Call No.: F187.E2P74 1997

Table of Contents

In The Beginning

Some Family Notes

Pets

At The Old Ball Game

My Elizabeth

He Was Better Known As "Doc"

People I Cannot Forget

Foreword

If you're a longtime reader of George Prettyman's newspaper column, you may have concluded that he loves two things on this earth: people and baseball. If you are not a longtime reader, you have missed more than you know.

George has been writing for newspapers "off and on" since 1934, he said in a 1995 interview. He's been writing his columns since around 1948 in several newspapers, including the Cecil Whig, where the column still appears weekly.

"George Prettyman has a wondrous way with words," I wrote in a 1993 editorial. "George, a youngish fellow barely turned 81, penned this bit of prose turned poetry for his most recent column:

"'But 1993 has been lived by you and by me, and whatever flaws we notice in our behavior during that time are history.'"

I first became aware of George Prettyman in 1971 through his column in The Cecil Democrat. I was then editor of the Whig, a sister paper. In 1981 the Democrat ceased publication. It was merged into the Whig, which was fortunate enough to acquire its two greatest assets: J. Clark Samuel, the Democrat's editor, and George Prettyman, columnist.

Sadly, Mr. Samuel is no longer with us. He died some 10 years ago. Happily, George Prettyman is very much with us and writing his column.

While many of George's pieces over the years have dealt with the village of Zion and its rural setting, in recent years he has written under datelines such as College Park and Seattle. Recent trips have included a journey across Canada by train and another to Arizona to take in NCAA basketball tournament play and baseball in spring training.

But his most memorable columns are spun from nostalgia. George is at his best in recounting such things as early years on Maryland's lower Eastern Shore and listening to Yankee baseball broadcasts of the 1930s.

From time to time George has asked me as editor if he should continue writing. "Absolutely yes," I respond, and I've never been wrong. The proof is in your reading of the pages to follow.

Don Herring
April 1997

Acknowledgments

I would like to thank the following people who brought this book into being. First of all, Polly Binns, who first suggested this project and convinced me to spend an entire summer selecting from more than 2,400 columns a few I thought best reflected me and my years at the typewriter. Then, my son, the younger of us two Georges, who patiently helped in the selection process and tried to make sure each column included herein "said something," as he put it. Geraldine McKeown, acclaimed Cecil County artist, whose beautiful watercolor graces the cover of this book. Faye Riley-Branca, whose expertise in editing and publishing got us off to a good start. Bonnie Geraldi, who spent untold hours on the computer, putting the columns in order, and who precious enthusiasm lifted my spirits whenever I was ready to forget the whole thing. Kristi Eisenberg and her husband, Donn Birdsall, who brought old, yellowed photographs to life to illustrate the columns. Kristi, whose photograph of me, which appears on the back cover, captured the grin that has been with me since childhood. Boni Nash, who agreed to shepherd the finished manuscript all the way to the printers in her very professional manner. Annette Schuetz-Ruff, Peggy Mason and Janet Parrack from the International Reading Association. My friends at the veterans organizations, who helped finance the publication, especially Neil Eller, a former student of mine at Cecil Community College, who spearheaded that mission. And my newspaper editors, past and present, like Don Herring, who have never, as yet, asked me to stop writing. Also Barbara Ramseaur, Mimi McGuirk, Robert McKeown, Jr., Paul and Ben Chidester, Farrah Dowell, Susie Edwards, Liz McKnight, Mandy Powers, Gerald Vaughn III, American Legion Post #194, American Legion Post #135, and VFW Post #6027.

And finally and most importantly my friends and readers who have encouraged me throughout the half-century my pieces have appeared in local and nearby papers.

G.B.P.
June, 1997

Preface

When I was a youngster growing up in Cecil County, My father practiced three separate and distinct professions. Primarily, he was a high school teacher and administrator. This had certain benefits for me. My father accompanied his students on class trips to Gettysburg, Valley Forge, Washington, and Philadelphia. I went along and developed an interest in American history and government. Several of his teacher friends became my lifelong friends as well.

On Sundays, he filled Methodist pulpits for a variety of rural congregations and then preached regularly for the Cecil United Parish, a group of seven churches. His Methodist colleagues and their families became significant people in my life over the years.

But the third profession was the one that I liked the best. School teachers needed summer jobs in the 1950s, and Dad filled in for editors and other staff on weekly newspapers in Elkton and in Oxford. Everything about newspaper offices appealed to me. I liked the style of the people who wrote for a living. Some were just plain characters. There were print shops with fascinating machinery and just enough ink to make a lasting impression. There was interesting mail—weekly releases from the Orioles and Maryland and Delaware football media guides. There was a sense of deadlines just barely met. Even the lunches with the Courthouse crowd in Elkton were fun for me.

Later, Dad was fortunate and combined two of his professions as Harford County Board of Education's first Director of Public Relations. Then, I got to know newspapermen in Aberdeen and Havre de Grace. By that time, he worked twelve months a year but continued to produce a weekly column. The old Underwood portable was replaced first by an electric typewriter and then by a computer. The columns kept their accustomed flavor.

This volume contains a sampling of those weekly columns with the common thread of observing and commenting on the people and events of Maryland, and the Eastern Shore in particular. His columns reflect a full and rich life on the Eastern Shore. My wife Barbara and I sometimes discuss with him what he plans to write about in advance and look forward to the next column, like many of his other loyal readers. For my part, I will always be grateful that I had the chance to observe and participate in bits and pieces of his third profession.

George B. Prettyman
Ellicott City, MD
April 1997

"Memory is a kind of homesickness." —*Ivan Doig*

In The Beginning

FEBRUARY 28, 1973

Pop Left The Pulpit In A Hurry

While I was writing the tag lines of last week's column, Elizabeth called to me (I have a little corner down in our basement where I attempt to put together my columns, week after week) to let me know that a good friend of mine was on the telephone—so I hustled up the stairs to hold a most welcomed conversation with Mr. Tom Adams of Churchville. You just may recall that I became acquainted with Mr. Adams by the very direct statement I made to him one day over in Bel Air: "Mr. Adams," I said, "you aren't a native of Harford County, are you?" And from the tone of my voice, he knew that I had "located him" as an Eastern Shoreman. I recorded here in this space about three or four years ago that we discovered, through our conversation following my question-statement, that my father had been his family's minister down in Crapo, Dorchester County, a few years prior to my birth—and we have re-formed the ties between the two families. It was that chance chat with Mr. Adams which reawakened my interest in the communities which my father once served as a Methodist minister—and Mr. Adams was most interested in hearing that we had revisited Rock Hall.

To use one of his own expressions—to turn it on him, himself—I can say here, "Tom Adams is one 'crackin' good fellow!"

After he and I chatted up a right good telephone bill, I returned to my typewriter to continue jotting down my thoughts about that

February 14 spent in the town of my birth. (I hasten to inform you that no one has placed a marker on that parsonage lawn signifying that George Prettyman was born there! That'll never happen. I'm just another preacher's kid—nothing special at all—but if you're still reading with me, let's go back to Rock Hall.)

It's an old story to people who have read my columns over the years—so I'll repeat it as briefly as I can.

My father was holding revival meetings—with the aid of a guest evangelist—back in December 1912. The Prettyman family had moved to Rock Hall the previous spring. There were four youngsters in the family before I arrived—my brother, Lank, and sisters, Marguerite, Ruth, and Julia. Another sister, Katie, was already married and living in or near Lincoln, Delaware. (Another sister, Vance, had died of typhoid fever, during my father's pastorate in Crapo.)

As I stated, during that December to which I referred, revival meetings were going on in the Rock Hall Methodist Church. While one of the evening meetings was in progress, the town policeman entered the church, walked up the aisle, whispered something in my father's ear—and my father quickly departed from the church. Something was up. My mother needed Dr. Selby, so my father learned; and pretty soon there was a new baby boy in that parsonage. You may rightly say that my arrival broke up the meeting.

In that same church, I called a halt to the worship service a couple of years later—by squirming my way loose from my mother's grasp and making a bee-line for my father who was, at the moment, exhorting. I took the shortest way to get to him—by attempting to crawl through the altar railing. I got stuck. My father found it necessary to depart from his text and dislodge me from my stuck position. I have been told that I was noisy about the whole thing—and I have no doubt that such was the case.

My initial attempt at oratory occurred in that church. It was Children's Day—say about the year 1915. My "piece" was considered of suitable length for a toddler—four lines. I began:

"Roses are—BLUE!
Violets—are RED!"

And there came an extended pause. I looked to my father for help. Receiving none with sufficient promptness to turn off the humiliation I apparently felt, I burst into childish tears, rushed to my father, crying, "I don't know it, Pop!"

This most recent visit to that church was different. I got out of the car, first of all, to see whether or not the door of the church was unlocked. It was. That was the signal for us four visitors to enter.

While I make no pretense of having remembered in detail the appearance of that church's interior, I did sense that some changes have been made. It has been, over the years, redecorated. The rather ornate, decorative border around the edges of the church-window-shaped chancel has given way to plainness; and the section of the wall directly behind the lectern is no longer ornately papered or painted as it was decades ago—it, too, is plain now. A recessed choir area has been created to more or less be in keeping with the architectural symmetry of the pulpit area. A new red carpet has been placed down the center aisle, and the floor is in excellent condition. It is, indeed, an attractive church. Its memorial windows bore names of families familiar to me. The doors between the main auditorium and the Sunday School rooms appeared to me to be the same as they had been when I was a child—they are in fine condition. I felt "at home"—yet I was aware of the changes.

I'd like to show you what the church looked like on a Children's Day something close to sixty years ago—with flowers which had been brought in to decorate the church for the occasion.

Yes, I did take time to examine the altar railing which had once held me a prisoner for a few moments. And as I observed that railing, I had to smile to myself. Why shouldn't I have wanted to reach my father then? He was—and he remained—the greatest man I ever knew!

I think one of the proudest moments of my entire life came in the spring of 1945. My father was in his last illness. He was bedridden at the time and seemed simply to be "waiting." He called me to his bedside one day, took me by the hand, and, in a steady voice—not one indicating emotionalism—said to me, "Thank you, son, for never having caused me any troubles." I know I did not deserve that word of gratitude, for I am sure there had been times when I did cause him concern. But I took him at his word—silently.

My father at Rock Hall Methodist Church on Children's Day
Circa 1913

DATE UNCERTAIN

Where Life Began—For Me

At this time of the year—in fact, upon this very date—I think back to that wonderful town down on the Chesapeake Bay where life began for me: Rock Hall, Kent County, Maryland. It is not so much the houses or the streets that I look back upon, but, rather, the people. Of course, I was not aware of anything at all until awareness became an inevitable part of my life. I cannot say when I first knew that I was in Rock Hall—but as I grew and became alert to my surroundings, Rock Hall became real. And it has remained a treasured place.

I was five years and about three months old when my father's ministry in Rock Hall was terminated, so I can—and do—remember much about the people there. I do not need photographs to picture in my thoughts the church at Christmas time—no, not that first Christmas when I was but ten days old but the Christmases following that. Old Kris, for example, was in Joe Downey's Store! And Joe Downey's Store was so close to the parsonage that I could hear the sleigh bells ringing. When the time came for Ruthie, Julia, and me to visit the toy department of Downey's Store—or Manny Miller's—there was always a treat.

Mr. and Mrs. Clarence Hersch—Miss Mae and Uncle Buddy, I called them—lived a block or so from the parsonage (if Rock Hall could be said to have "blocks") and their home, along with the Middleton home, were second homes to all of us. Miss Mae did much of Mother's sewing for a time: store-bought clothes were a rarity then, though Blaustein's Store carried a good supply of some items which neither Mother nor Miss Mae could produce. Anytime Ruthie was allowed to take me to Durding's Drug Store that visit was worth a stick or two of penny candy. And, gee, I ate at the Middleton home almost as often as I ate at our table, it seems, though I am sure such was not really the case.

The house in Rock Hall were I was born. (left to right) Marguerite,
Julia, Mother, Ruth, Father, Me
Rock Hall, Maryland

The Orrs, the Hubbards, the Kendalls, the Collyers—I can't remember all the names—made sure the preacher and his family had a continuing supply of oysters all winter long. My father kept them in a burlap bag, just outside the kitchen door; and he shucked 'em whenever Mother thought it time for an oyster pie, a stew, or some fritters. Oh, yes—the Rodneys and the Ayers—and Mr. Thompson, the man who sold Buster Brown Shoes—I remember them. In all my life I have never known anyone with a smile that could match Mr. Thompson's—that's the impression I've carried with me for more then sixty years.

Another sister, Marguerite, together with her husband, Harrison, lived just around the corner, a few hundred yards from the parsonage. It was always good to see her coming past the Miller Store, pushing John Edward in his baby carriage. (I had become an uncle at a very tender age, by George!) As soon as he could see our house, John Edward would start calling, "Ju Ju, Ju Ju!" And that was all Julia needed to make her day complete.

And so it is, whenever I can, I like to go down to that waterman's town, on the shores of the Bay—walk around, visit the Middleton's, go into Durding's Drug Store, chat with "Trigger" Collyer—and, in the summertime, go fishing. I couldn't give a rap whether I catch fish or not so long as I can get a glimpse of the church, see the building where Aunt Kate and Uncle Jim Casey lived—and close my eyes and listen for the long, low whoo-oot of the steamboat coming in to dock.

MARCH 7, 1973

Old Friends Are Reunited

THE OLD DRUG STORE . . . Above the store still hangs the sign— "Durding's," the same name it bore when first the Prettymans moved to Rock Hall in 1912. I can't say that the interior appeared the same as it did when I was a toddler—I don't remember the details to that extent. But atop one of the sections of shelving there were some apothecary jars with hand-printed labels identifying the contents those jars once held. The proprietress I met there is the granddaughter of the man whom I knew as the druggist—Mr. Benjamin Durding.

It was Mr. Durding who had listened to my penniless plea for a post-card picture of the old steamer, "B. S. Ford," when I toddled into his store years ago. And it was on the steps of that store that my mother caught up with me as I was backing down—I had run away in order to secure that treasured picture. My mother aided my reentrance into Mr. Durding's establishment by the simple method of paddling me with the palm of her hand. I was directed to return the picture of the "B. S. Ford" to Mr. Durding—and I felt the smack of my mother's hand on the seat of my pants all the way back to the parsonage. It really wasn't very far, but it was of sufficient distance to impress upon that part of my anatomy, at least, that running away was likely to bring with it a most unpleasant sensation.

My sister and I purchased some "penny candy"—stick candy, for the most part—in remembrance of things past. The candy was later to be delivered to Mr. "Buddy" Hersch in a nursing home in Chestertown.

ON TO THE WHARF . . . Hubbard's Restaurant, on the old steamboat wharf, seemed the likeliest place for us to eat and, at the same time, to get a good view of the activity out on the Bay. We were fortunate to find a table right next to the window facing the water, where we could observe the sea gulls, the wild ducks, and note that the cold weather had left chunks of ice floating here and there among the pilings.

There was a gentleman sitting at a table near us who appeared to be most friendly—so I asked him if he were a native of the area. His response was just as friendly in tone as I had expected. I introduced myself—and he, in turn, responded by giving me his name—Captain "Trigger" Collyer—and he, indeed, is a native of Rock Hall.

If any of you happen to know folks down at Rock Hall, you might have heard of three different "Trigger" Collyers: I'm speaking of Captain Samuel Melvin Collyer—whose father was known as "Trigger" and whose cousin is also known by that same rather intriguing nickname.

Captain "Trigger" Collyer was a most accommodating conversationalist. I asked him whether he had any recollection of a Reverend John Prettyman—and his face took on a very pleasant smile as he answered, "Yes, sir! He christened me!" And he went on to explain that the baptismal certificate, signed by my father, had been the "proof" he had needed to obtain his social security status.

We invited Captain Collyer to have lunch with us; and though he wouldn't grant us the pleasure of having him dine along with us, he did move over to our table—and, my, how we talked! My sister and I must have kept him busy answering questions about people we remembered for close to an hour and a half. If he became bored or weary, he never let us know. We talked about so many different families—and I must say that Captain Collyer refreshed our recollections of family names we had long forgotten—I could go on and on; but just names would mean little to you. It is enough for me to say that, through this very congenial man, we really revisited Rock Hall!

Captain Collyer still "follows the water"—he owns a fifty-foot boat and during the summer weeks, starting around the middle of July, he serves as a fishing guide for people who want the thrill of catching some big ones from the Chesapeake Bay. He pointed out to us his boat—the "Lydia May"—presently in her slip in the North Side Marina, a large marina owned by the Collyers.

Of about average height, not of particularly heavy build—perhaps a bit on the slight side, though not so thin as I am, by any means—Captain Collyer "looks" like a waterman. The winds and the weather have been kind to his face; he's not deeply lined with wrinkles; but he has the apparently perpetual "tan" of a waterman. His eyes are alive with expression. His friendly demeanor "made" our lunch—and that's saying something, for the oysters, the crab cakes, the stew, and the rock fish were, in themselves, a treat.

While we were there, he told us of the fine catches of rock fish his sons were having. (A few days later, Elizabeth and I and the Ben Sauseleins, our neighbors, drove down to Hubbard's again—and Captain Collyer was there. That day we saw the catch his son and grandson brought in and watched them load the fish onto the conveyor riggin' which took the fish to the place of cleaning and sale.)

Captain "Trigger" Collyer is the kind of man a fellow could listen to for hours on end—he's knowledgeable about the Bay and all that goes on there and his personality simply captivates one's attention. I gathered that he spends considerable time in Hubbard's during the winter months, watching the boats come in with their catches and chatting with folks who find him exactly what we found him to be—a fascinating gentleman!

Incidentally, the same doctor—Dr. Selby—brought both Captain Collyer and me into this world.

People of the Port Deposit area and State Troopers here in Cecil and Harford Counties would enjoy knowing that the man about whom I have been commenting is Chaplain Bernard T. Hepbron's uncle. Chaplain Hepbron serves the John F. Kennedy Highway Barrack in that capacity and is also employed by *"The Cecil Whig."* He was formerly pastor of the Tome United Methodist Church in Port Deposit.

Chaplain Hepbron and I enjoyed an interesting conversation concerning his uncle, and we discovered that we share the same birthplace—Rock Hall.

And Captain Collyer spoke with considerable pride about Chaplain Hepbron the day I chatted with him.

The women in the group wanted to see "Gratitude"—a sort of appendage to Rock Hall, located right on the Bay. Years ago, this part of the town was made up of boarding houses. Residents from Baltimore would come over on one of the side-wheelers and spend a week or so. The people who operated the boarding houses knew how to put the seafood on the tables—and the city folks knew how to eat it! "Gratitude" was the resort section of Rock Hall. Now it is strictly residential—some of the homes being year-'round homes and some of them summer cottages (if you can call big, rambling houses cottages).

There's a wild-life area off to one side of Rock Hall. The women wanted to see swans and other evidences of nature along the Bay. I asked to be let out in the center of town; I wanted to walk around, see what I could that looked familiar to me, and find out, if at all possible, if anyone knew the whereabouts of Toby Blaustein.

I inquired in one of the general stores. The lady in charge wasn't, herself, old enough to remember much about the Blausteins—except by hearsay. She called her mother and told her that a George Prettyman was asking a lot of questions she couldn't answer. Her mother immediately told her that my father had performed the wedding ceremony for her (the mother) and her husband—and then she gave her daughter some directions for me to locate Mr. and Mrs. Reuben Rodney who just might be able to tell me something about Toby, his parents, and the other members of the Blaustein family.

I knocked on the door of the Rodney home—and was warmly welcomed even before I had identified myself. Mr. and Mrs. Rodney were surprised to learn that I was John Prettyman's son—the "little boy" who had been born some sixteen days before my dad joined the Rodneys in holy matrimony in the Rock Hall parsonage—January 1, 1913.

A delightful couple, the Rodneys! The few minutes I was there with them, we talked about so many things I can scarcely put the conversation together. They hadn't forgotten a single member of the family: they inquired of Ruth, Julia—and they seemed to know that Ruth, Julia, and I are the remaining members of the preacher's family they knew sixty years ago.

It was indeed gracious of them to say the kind things they did about our parents. And I'm sure they didn't say those things just to make me feel good. They told me they'd seen Toby Blaustein but a year or so ago—and they're going to attempt to get his address for me so that we may, perhaps, pick up a friendship which was interrupted in 1918 when we moved from Rock Hall to Sharptown.

MARCH 14, 1973

While We Were Talking

While we were talking—Mr. and Mrs. Reuben Rodney and I—I inquired about Mr. Clarence Thompson who had been proprietor of the shoe store on the main street in Rock Hall sixty years ago. For some inexplicable reason, Mr. Thompson had been one of my very special friends, and I remember well his seemingly ever-pleasant manner, his warm smile, and his generous affection for little folks. He sold, I recall, "Buster Brown" shoes; and he gave away "prizes" which were probably of insignificant monetary value, but which delighted us children.

The Rodneys told me that Mr. Thompson is deceased. The Thompsons had moved away from Rock Hall years ago. It was with interest that I learned that Mr. and Mrs. Thompson named one of their sons "Buster"—I suppose after the Buster Brown whose picture I can still see on the advertisements in the Thompson shoe shop.

One of the families close to the Prettymans during their years in Rock Hall was the Middleton family. Though of no blood relationship to us Prettyman children, we referred to Mr. and Mrs. Middleton as "Uncle Jim" and "Aunt Sally." Uncle Jim had a fishing shack along the shore which we frequented; and we also frequented their home. Miss Hallie, Miss Maude, and Mrs. Cora Middleton Travers still reside in that home.

Our visit there was shadowed somewhat by the knowledge that Miss Hallie is very ill. We were privileged to see her—and despite her illness, she greeted us with the smile we had so well remembered.

Miss Maude and Miss Cora (we still call them by the names we used years ago) brought out photograph albums from the past, and we enjoyed reviewing old times together. There were pictures of our parents—the Middletons and the Prettymans—as well as those of my brother, Lank, and my sisters Marguerite, Ruth, and Julia. And I was there, too—a little fellow, scarcely as tall as my father's knee-cap.

We chuckled over the styles of that era—the long-skirt years, the hair-ribbon years. And those early automobiles (few of them there were in Rock Hall then) were something to behold!

Miss Maude and Miss Cora had been teachers. Miss Maude, I know, taught under Professor Walter H. Davis, and Julia, Ruth, and Marguerite all attended school under Mr. Davis' principalship. Julia had both Miss Maude and Miss Cora as her teachers.

The Middleton ladies helped us locate, for sure, the house in which our sister, Marguerite, and her husband, Harrison Jones, had lived when John Edward, their first-born, came into this world. John Edward was but a scant three years younger than his "Uncle George," I might add.

Ruth's most demanding assignment during those Rock Hall years was to keep me out of mischief and happy. It wasn't easy—keeping me out of mischief. I was, to begin with, spoiled. Miss Maude recalled with us one adventure Ruth and I experienced. We got our supply of milk from a lady whom I now know only by the name of "Miss Nellie." To get the milk, we had to cross an open field—a meadow. One evening when Ruth and I were going after the milk, one of the cows became more or less incensed over our intrusion into her territory—and she started to chase us. Ruth managed somehow to half-carry and half-drag me across the meadow, and we made it under the fence just as the cow was about to catch up with us. I very vaguely remember the incident, though I have heard it discussed many times; one of us was wearing a red sweater—but I have been informed that the color red has little or nothing to do with a cow's reaction to people. Be that as it may, I'm sure it was a long time before our parents could persuade either Ruth or me to be a party to obtaining the supply of milk for the family.

We left the Middleton home with the promise that we would not stay away so long ever again. I hope we are able to keep that promise, for they are among the dearest of our friends.

I don't really know how old Mr. "Buddy" Hersch is—he's well up into his nineties, I'm sure. His wife, Miss Mae, was the seamstress who outfitted me when I was on the expected list. And the Hersch home became, virtually, a second home to all of us.

Mr. Buddy no longer lives in the little house we knew; that house is vacant now. But, you know, it still looks the same as it did—grape arbor, side porch, front porch, and all—even to the little building set some fifty-to-sixty yards behind the house and surrounded by a lattice screen. When we drove past, it seemed as though Mr. Buddy and Miss Mae should be at the window watching for us.

Mr. Buddy presently resides in the Magnolia Nursing Home; and when I entered the main door of that home, there, sitting by the door, I found Mr. Buddy. He didn't recognize me until I identified myself—but then he was right at home again with the Prettyman family! His comment was, "George, I never thought you'd make it here!" And when Julia entered, it was the same—a warm welcome—the same remark directed to her.

Mr. Buddy was once as much a part of the Bay and its tributaries as the tides, it seemed. I doubt that there is an area connected with the Bay that he wasn't familiar with. If we were to give him a proper title in today's language, we would probably call him a marine engineer. He was overseer during the construction of jetties; he was foreman of dredging crews. He knew the channels and those places along the harbors which needed man-made protection from the hazards of storm.

Once, I recall, when he was on a dredging operation near the mouth of the North East River, he used to spend some free time with us in Zion—and Miss Mae visited us then, too.

Mr. Buddy is understandably lonely. There are times when his eyes light up and a flicker of a smile crosses his face; but most of the time he is wanting to return to his home in Rock Hall. It is difficult to see an old friend saddened by the passage of time and the absence of his relationships with yesterday.

Oh, he can think back upon happier days—and does. He wanted to know, for example, if I were as full of mischief now as I was when I used to toddle around in their house. I assured him that I had outgrown some of my impishness, but that I knew Elizabeth could cite innumerable instances to indicate I hadn't entirely outgrown mischief.

SO—THERE YOU ARE . . . You have, if you have wanted to, revisited Rock Hall with me. I plan to go back again—and that, soon. Captain "Trigger" Collyer has already agreed to a tentative fishing excursion which will include several of my friends and neighbors here in Zion. Hubbard's Restaurant on the wharf is not too far to go for a seafood platter. Having been back in touch with folks such as Miss Helen Durding, the Rodneys, and the Middletons, I want to remain in touch.

One thing I especially want to do is to attend church service in Rock Hall—and that I'm going to do before too many months slip by . . . By the way, Captain Collyer has said he would be our "guide" there, too.

One more thing I want to say—I don't think there was ever a day during the six years my father served the Rock Hall congregation that the Prettyman family was without some seafood brought to the parsonage by the generous people who populated that town. That's where my appetite for rock fish, oysters, crabs, and soft-shelled clams was whetted. That's where my appreciation of people began to develop. It was a good place to live; it was a wonderfully human environment.

I found it great—just great—being able to "go home" without finding myself lost—for I was right among friends, by George!

That's me in the yard of the Middleton Family in Rock Hall 1914

SEPTEMBER 1, 1987

I Feigned A Cough To Be Given Tar Balsam

Back before the horseless carriages and the flying machines revolutionized America's way of living and dying, too—oil was primarily used for medicinal purposes. I wasn't around then, though highways, such as were in use during pre-World War I days which I do remember, certainly weren't crammed with bumper-to-bumper automobile traffic. And I don't think I saw my first airplane in flight until several years after our boys had come home from "over there." But to get back to my first thought when I began this piece: oil of the kind that Colonel Drake was trying to coax from the depths of the earth had medicinal value—and probably still does for all I know.

And that raises a question in my mind: Was the tar balsam which Dr. Selby prescribed as a cough remedy when I was a toddler derived from oil or from a tree? I am hoping that some pharmacist or doctor can provide me with the answer. Not that I'm about to be in the market for any of that black stuff; I hope that I've outgrown the need for it.

You see, when I was six weeks old, I contracted whooping cough. Old Dr. Selby, down in Rock Hall, watched over me during the long winter when whooping spasms were rendering me scrawny like a bird. For the next six years the good doctor made sure that something was on hand as soon as I gave the slightest indication of a wheeze or a whoop. He prescribed tar balsam. I became an addict of sorts. I'll explain.

Tar balsam was given a drop or so at a time on a heaping spoonful of sugar. Sugar is sweet and I was born with an enormous sweet tooth. Whatever bad taste the medicine may have had was wonderfully camouflaged by the sugar. Thus it was that mischievous me learned to fake a mean cough, just to get another dose. Gee whiz! It was like candy!

And now, I would like to know whether tar balsam was a product of coal tar or the old pine tree or whatever.

Sometimes a simple recollection will cause one to want to know more about the ingredients of an experience of yester-years. I couldn't get tar balsam off my mind the whole time I was doing a bit of research on Colonel Drake. Seeing a picture of the Colonel standing alongside his oil well, sporting that Prince Albert coat and a stovepipe hat, I kept wondering: Was I swallowing liquid tar from the oil-rocks when I eagerly opened my mouth for Dr. Selby's cough remedy?

By the way, whale oil burned in the lamps of America before coal oil came into use. No charge for that information, by George! Captain Ahab wasn't altogether fictional, you know; he was a part of virtually every New England coastal town in the days before kerosene became a household word.

Let's not forget acetylene—you know, gaslight? And then came electricity which has been here forever but wasn't harnessed for centuries on end.

How did I get into this?

DATE UNCERTAIN

We Moved To Sharptown

With the return-to-school thought still very much in the air, I did a little recollecting. In the fall of 1918, I got off to my own start in the first grade. That was down in Sharptown—Wicomico County.

I remember very well my first teacher—Miss Hattie Twilley, since married and since lost to my acquaintance. She lives in my recollection only as a very kind, patient lady, whose voice was never raised in wrath at the youngsters she had gathered there on the top floor of a hall that housed the first two grades.

During the year my dad bought me a rather inexpensive pen knife, I recall. My first official act with that knife was to lose the thing.

When I returned in the afternoon minus the new treasure, my parents hiked me right back to the school grounds to look for it.

If Miss Hattie was annoyed at my childish carelessness, she never made a display of that annoyance. A thorough search of the playground brought its reward—and I ran home pleased at having retrieved my shiny knife.

Miss Hattie helped immeasurably in getting me adjusted to being outside the protection of home. Here was the same sort of task which confronts the first-grade teachers today, despite modification of method and varying psychological approaches.

Speaking of Sharptown, which I have learned to place in the proper county at long last, there's a lady down that way who is doing me a truly fine honor. I am not boasting when I report this, for I do not feel worthy of that which she is doing, to tell you the truth.

Mrs. Alice Hastings keeps a scrap-book of this column. She has clipped and saved my pieces for some little time, I have just learned.

My folks tell me I don't actually remember her, but I think I do. Unless I am very badly mistaken, she is the wife of Billy Hastings, whom I remember as a rather large man. Too, I am under the strong impression that Mrs. Hastings served as a Sunday School teacher—and that I was in her class for a time.

Perhaps she can set me straight on that.

At any rate, Mrs. Hastings, I sincerely appreciate your interest in what I try to do here in this column—through I'm afraid much of the time "Rural Ramblin's" is not what it should be.

There's another little incident concerning Sharptown that was brought to my attention recently. It concerned my father and one of his ministerial duties.

Now let's get this straight—my dad was not a marryin' parson in the sense that he set out to snag any and all couples that came around with that strange twinkle in the eye. He performed wedding ceremonies upon request, as per the usual Methodist custom. And, then too, Sharptown was not, to my knowledge, noted as a mecca for those longing for marital ties.

It was a snowy winter evening. The Prettyman children and friend, Miss Hilda Taylor (known to Cecil Countians now as

Mrs. Walter Cooling, Chesapeake City) were deeply engrossed in a new set of books that had come to the household via Santa's most recent visit. (Were I not afraid I'd be accused of "plugging," I'd tell you the set was entitled "The Book of Knowledge.")

I've always liked browsing through books on cold winter nights—and liked it even then, as a six-year-old youngster.

A knock came to the front door of the parsonage. My father answered the knock—and there stood a couple of hopefuls awaiting the well-known knot.

But there was a catch to the whole thing: their license was of another county and the ceremony could not be performed in Wicomico unless a new license were obtained. This would cause delay. Yet, nothing would suffice except that my dad do the solemnizing of the wedding. Thus, the problem.

My father did not cater to playing in the snow—not even when his children plagued him into construction of a snow-man. However, at the insistence of the bridegroom-to-be, he eventually consented to accomplish the ceremony—on the bridge, across the county line, of all places!

Those of you who recall my father can picture him, I'm sure, the collar of his over-coat turned up tightly around his neck—and perhaps, a slight trace of chill in his voice, as he stood there, on the bridge, the snow whipping in the wind and stinging against his face—pronouncing the couple man and wife.

Witnesses there were to the ceremony, though none of us recalls them now.

My father returned, after the wedding, and was chuckling to himself as he entered the door and stamped the snow from his over-shoes on the front mat, just inside the hallway.

Mrs. Cooling, who remembers the scene more vividly than I, relates that he was chuckling with his accustomed good humor as he said, "The bride-groom tells me he'll pay me next Saturday!"

"Next Saturday," as he well knew, was never to arrive.

That was one wedding fee that failed to materialize—and you all know, wedding fees go to the preacher's wife, customarily.

Lest you get the idea that weddings are strictly commercial, insofar as preachers go, that is not true. But the variety of wedding fees in years gone by were, to say the least, amusing—ranging from the usual financial show of gratitude, to chickens, alive and kicking and cackling.

This cold, cold wedding was one for the records, though.

MARCH 5, 1985

Sentimental Journey

One thing leads to another. I was peeling an apple one day not so long ago when I was suddenly taken back in time, say, sixty-seven years ago. That put me in the Sharptown parsonage. World War I had not ended. Sammy Calloway, a young soldier from Sharptown, was "over there" and had been wounded. Shot through the leg. I remember asking my father if Sammy's leg had a hole in it. Since I received an affirmative answer, I supposed that the hole went right through—that anyone could see daylight on the other side of the wound, knothole fashion. A youngster can certainly have weird ideas.

BUT GETTING back to my apple, I was peeling it and my knife slipped a little, causing my knife to scrape instead of peel. That bit of scraped apple reminded me of something my father did for me when I was a little tot.

My father almost always kept a basket of apples for us to eat during the winter evenings. He liked to make the apple last a while, so he would feed me scraped apple on occasion. He'd peel the skin off a small area of the apple, then gently scrape the pared surface. The resulting pulp was juicy—and delicious. Sort of an uncooked apple sauce.

Yes, he would accumulate about a spoonful on the end of his wide-bladed knife, and pop the scrapings into my mouth.

Oh, I should have prefaced all this by pointing out that I was ill much of the two years we lived in Sharptown. Pestered by scarlet fever, a cranky heart (I had already passed the measles, chicken pox, whooping cough stage). My dad's scraped-apple bit usually came while I was under the doctor's care.

THE DOCTOR? Yes. He was Dr. Gordy. I can't recall much about Dr. Gordy's physical appearance. That's all pretty vague to me. However, I do remember that he was mighty kind—soft-spoken, friendly, and gentle.

Dr. Gordy had two sons, Lee and Lyle. Lee was about three years my senior; Lyle, a bit younger than I. I don't think I ever saw any of the Gordy family after we left Sharptown in 1920. Only recently I learned from Mr. Richard Cooper, of Salisbury, that Lee Gordy is living in Hebron, Maryland. I'll have to get in touch.

The Gordy dog was named Bruce. One day, Mrs. Gordy showed me a picture of Bruce and there were little specks which seemed to be flying around the dog's head. I offered the opinion that Bruce had fleas. That's when I was told that fleas don't fly. (A child learns by his bloopers.)

LYLE WAS IN AND OUT of our house from early morning until bedtime. He was a spunky kid, ready to defend me from real or imagined enemies. I think his father must have told him that I needed a defender.

My! From apple peelings to a sentimental journey back to Sharptown. Now and then I seem to reach back for a yesterday. Not that my todays aren't satisfying. They are! But, after all, we are, in a very real sense, what your yesterdays dictated. I'll admit to back-tracking—maybe more than I should. But, there again, I like my memories. They keep me in touch with who I am and give me reason for holding on to my attitudes and values which shape my behavior. And without which I am not myself at all, by George!

In My Father's Shoes

This past Sunday I, together with several folks who wanted to be among those present, went back to Sharptown, Maryland, to participate in the Homecoming services at the Asbury Methodist Church. I had not been in the church for something like 35 years. Needless to say, my recollection of the building was absolutely negligible—I was just past seven when we left there for a new home on another charge. Yet the entire experience was delightful and heart-warming.

A couple of years ago I, in this column, tried to put Sharptown in Dorchester County—an error in geography which promptly brought response from that area. It is located in the northwestern-most part of Wicomico County—just across the Nanticoke River.

I was admittedly thrilled to be asked to substitute for my father, in a sense, at the Homecoming services. I make no pretense at being a minister of his stature or quality—I merely lay-preach, with emphasis on the merely. But I tried to be an acceptable substitute—and the folks were gracious enough to express appreciation.

Our traveling party was made up of Beth, young George, Mom, Beth's father (Pop), Dick, Julia, Hilda and Walter Cooling and Toby—and me; that makes ten of us. In a sense, I was assuring myself, I suppose, of some congregation. We ten were treated royally—and that's no exaggeration. No one suggested by manner or word that I suspend my delivery prior to the completion of my remarks, which is a courtesy I have come to appreciate. Following the service in the morning, we were fed—the word is sumptuously. To some of the party of Cecil folks, the Eastern Shore corn bread was something new; some of them approved heartily and some with reservations—and that was to be expected.

Everyone of us noted the devastation caused by Hurricane Hazel more than a week ago—much debris is yet to be cleared away. We, here in Cecil, got by with much less damage than the people further down the Delmarva Peninsula.

The flatness of the terrain always fascinates me, though I have known the lower Shore to be flat and shouldn't be particularly impressed by that fact now.

The Rev. and Mrs. Frederick Truitt (former pastor and wife up here at Lewisville) were fine hosts; they showed the Prettyman clan through the parsonage. I tried hard to remember some of the various rooms in the house—but few things about the place struck a recollective chord with me. The front stairway, the side sun-porch, the window at the bottom of the stairs, and the twisting back stairs—they were the items that I remembered. The sun porch seemed much lower to the ground than it was back when World War I was ending. Actually, my legs are longer now—and that's how we measure distances and recall them, by our own personal relationship.

I walked through the town with several others—and it was strange coming up to Dr. Gordy's house but knowing that the Gordy family has long since moved away. I could imagine Bruce, the big bird dog, lying by the front bay window, waiting to romp with Lyle and me (Lyle was my particular little buddy who was always ready and willing to be a part of our family life and to welcome me into his).

It was strange, too, noting that houses and other buildings aren't nearly so far apart today as they were in 1920! The school, above the Twilley store, was a good piece from home the day I started there—and it's actually less than a block away!

And so it was—everything I could recall was "not exactly" at all—and a bit disconcerting it is to realize the tricks time plays on what we think we remember.

I was sincerely happy to see Mr. Taylor, his wife, the kind neighbors (one of whom admitted to me that she often thinks of my dirty little hands that frequently soiled her clean white paint!), the people who made Sharptown "home" to us years ago.

You know, I could go back there, I think, and feel at home again! That's how warmly we were received.

I have been asked is it difficult to be taking my father's place—trying to play his role. The answer is yes, when I consider how much he meant to other people and to me; the answer is no, when I think that the privilege is indeed rare—getting to know people again and getting to have a part in perpetuating people's remembrance of him. Without conceit, I can truly say—what a marvelous opportunity to repay those who made his life good and beautiful and full!

It was a tremendous pleasure to be greeted by my Sunday School teacher of 1919-1920—Mrs. Alice Hastings. It was she who met me at the door of the church.

It was a good day!

MAY 3, 1995

10-Year-Old Column Reinforces Memories

A couple of weeks ago, when words wouldn't come when I called them, Marie Webb of the *Whig* staff pulled one of my old columns from the files and took me off the hook, you might say. The column she pulled was one I had written in March, 1985, a little more than ten years ago.

When I opened the *Whig* on Wednesday, April 19, I was surprised; she had unknowingly created a coincidence, for the town of Sharptown had been on my mind for many days.

Mrs. Walter Cooling was once upon a time our neighbor in that Wicomico County town. Only two days prior to the 19th, my sister and I, along with a host of people, had attended the funeral service which celebrated her life.

It was during World War I when we—my parents, my sister Julia, and I—moved from Rock Hall in Kent County to Sharptown. My dad was a Methodist minister and Methodist ministers were not always consulted 70-plus years ago as to where they were to do their preaching and pastoring; so my father obeyed the bishop.

With the aid of my mother, he packed our belongings, saw that they were loaded aboard a steamboat, and moved to his new charge.

THE PARSONAGE we were to live in for the next two years was situated next to a plot of land which was cultivated by an elderly gentleman by the name of Mr. Taylor. He and his wife lived in the house adjacent to the plot. Their granddaughter, Hilda, a very pretty high school girl, lived with them.

Almost from day one after our arrival in Sharptown, Hilda became a virtual member of the Prettyman family. She and my sister Julia became lifelong "best friends" and I, a pesky little 5-year-old boy, thought we ought to make it a threesome. I've always felt that we did.

Hilda spent much of what time she had available, after helping her hearing-impaired grandparents with their chores, over in the parsonage with us, often seeking information for her school work from our 20-volume set of "The Book of Knowledge." She often played the board game, "Pollyanna," with us. (That game was created following the success of Eleanor H. Porter's sentimental novel by the same name.)

In a very real sense, Hilda was my "baby-sitter," though I don't believe the word had been coined at that time. Julia was deemed old enough to fend for herself.

My mother and father sometimes permitted Julia and me to go to the movies on the second floor of the town hall if Hilda were along to watch over me and keep Julia company. On one occasion, a violent storm came up while we were at the picture show, as folks called it then. The lights went out and Julia and I, for reasons which we've never fathomed, decided to strike out for home.

That was a foolish and dangerous thing to do. We were unaware that the strong wind had blown limbs from trees and downed telephone and electric wires. We lost Hilda in the darkened auditorium, so we rushed down the steps, out onto the street, and headed home, picking our way through the debris.

How we managed to reach the parsonage without serious mishap I'll never know.

Our parents were alarmed, to put it mildly, and they were especially concerned that we had deserted Hilda without her knowing we were leaving the building. Not long after we had arrived at the parsonage, however, an almost hysterical Hilda came, too. She was almost inconsolable, fearing that something might have happened to Julia and me.

SHE WAS RELIEVED when she saw we were safe, but I'm sure she was distressed, if not a little angry, because we had run away from her. (To let you know how severe that storm was, the buildings on the wharf collapsed, pinning one of my father's parishioners, Mr. Lev Cooper, beneath the rubble, injuring him severely.)

Mr. Taylor and my father had a sweet potato patch in that sandy lot between the Taylor house and the parsonage. (I still have the potato fork Pop used for digging the succulent tubers; it hangs in my garage as a memento of our two years in Sharptown.) I can recall reaching down, picking up a sweet potato, brushing off the sandy soil, and eating it raw—right there in the patch. The potatoes weren't yams; they were a paler yellow and were drier than yams—not so syrupy.

In the spring of 1920—World War I had ended and the terrible influenza epidemic had subsided—we moved again, this time from Sharptown to Chance, in Somerset County. Hilda visited us at least once during the three years we were living there. The visit I remember came during camp meeting time on Deal's Island.

It was customary that young girls promenade outside the tabernacle prior to service, and Julia and Hilda joined the other young ladies in that ritual. Hilda was most attractive and the young men viewing the walk-around would call out to her, "Hello, Rock Hall!"—thinking she was from that town, not Sharptown.

Hilda and Julia often sequestered themselves in one of the bedrooms as they engaged in what they called "girl talk." I was warned by my mother not to pester them—which was like daring a 7-year-old boy to do just that. I kept peeping through the partially-open door to the bedroom and making some kind of silly jabber. Finally Hilda grabbed me, took the hairbrush from the bureau, and paddled me. It didn't really hurt, but it did startle and embarrass me to the point that I stopped annoying the girls—at least for that day.

Hilda worried about what Miss Grace (my mother) would say. She needn't have, for Mother knew Hilda wouldn't have spanked me had I not deserved such a warming. In later years, Hilda often made reference to that incident. We laughed many times when we relived some of our experiences of "back then."

After she had completed her two years at Towson Normal School and two years of teaching in Howard County, not far from Ellicott City, Hilda expressed the desire to be near us again and near her father, Mr. Ermon Taylor, a widower, who worked and lived in the Wilmington area. My dad talked with Mr. Hugh Caldwell, then superintendent of schools in Cecil County, about the possibility of her getting a teaching assignment here.

Hilda was hired and was assigned to teach in the elementary school in Chesapeake City. The rest is history. While she was boarding with the Howard family there, Walter Cooling, an area resident, began paying attention to the pretty school teacher.

I'VE HEARD RUMORS—and I believe them to be true—that Mrs. Howard, who was like a mother to Hilda, encouraged her to accept Walter's courtesies. And in August of 1936, Hilda became Mrs. Walter F. Cooling.

My father and mother, along with Julia and Dick Touchton, and Elizabeth and I, rode down to Sharptown for the wedding ceremony which my dad performed.

Hilda's relationship with our family never changed. And Walter became a member of our family right along with Hilda. A few years later, Toby, their son, was born. My father christened him just before Walter and Hilda migrated from Elkton to Kentucky where Walter's work took him. Their stay in Kentucky was not of long duration, and when they returned to Cecil County it was, as the saying goes, for good.

The passage of time takes its toll. One by one we take leave of those whom we have loved and who have loved us. That is the natural flow of life. Henry Wadsworth Longfellow, in his poem "Resignation," I think it was, said:

This is life of mortal breath
Is but a suburb of the life elysian,
Whose portal we call Death.

Oh, my, yes! The little boy who lives within me still remembers that beautiful girl next door who remained beautiful always. And just as kind and talented as she was beautiful. She was one of life's blessings, by George!

Take a look, sometime, if you haven't already seen it, at her painting of Jesus in Gethsemane; it hangs in Trinity United Methodist Church in Chesapeake City. A lasting testimony, given something like 40 years ago, to her faith.

AUGUST 30, 1972

A Memory Of Augusts Past

IT WAS ABOUT THIS TIME OF YEAR—when I was a youngster, living down in the village of Chance (also known as Rock Creek), just a bridge away from Deal's Island—that the water of the Tangier Sound took on special meaning, it seemed. For quite often the married members of the Prettyman family would come "home." And with them, nieces and nephews not too many years my junior. One of my nephews, in particular, was close enough to my age to be a real buddy during his summer visits—John Edward Jones, now a resident of Baltimore.

John Edward (we always called him by his "double name," for another nephew was also named John—John Lank, Jr.) and I would don our bathing suits early in the morning and keep at my father until he agreed to take us over to one of the numerous sandy beaches so that we might go bathing. Neither of us had then learned to swim. The Tangier Sound could be very angry at times, but on a hot, humid August day, the tiny waves simply lapped at the shore; the sand extended well out so that we had good, solid footing even when we were in water up to our necks. Once in a great while we would be fortunate enough to have an old inner tube which my father had inflated for us, and we could float and paddle in the warm, salt water.

When my sister Ruth would visit, she and I often took long walks along the beach, just west of the bridge which connected Deal's Island and Rock Creek—on the Rock Creek side we did our nature stroll. Ruth had been about ten years old when I was born, and she had adopted me, so to speak, as her very own project. She was always able to make me feel very much wanted and cared for; and my mother utilized this relationship much in the manner today's mothers make use of children's "favorite" baby-sitters.

I recall very vividly one August afternoon. Ruth and I had walked along the shore, and we came upon a sand bar which extended well out into the Sound. We were not more than fifty yards from shore when we reached the farthest point of the sand bar. But we had neglected to take into account the tide. It had begun to come in—and, much to our surprise, we found ourselves stranded on a little island of sand. And that little island was rapidly diminishing. We were surrounded by water.

It was not quite sundown yet, and there were still some watermen out on the Sound. We could see the white sails of their boats—and, as I have indicated, we were not really too far from shore. Nonetheless, we began to feel just a bit skittish about the predicament we were in, for Ruth couldn't swim, either, and we were both fully clad except for the fact that we were barefooted.

Back in that year, women's dresses were almost to the ankle, and even on a hot summer's day, there were petticoats and other cumbersome bits of apparel. As the water kept rising, Ruth kept lifting her skirts higher and higher. I was still in short pants, but before long, the water began to threaten to lap around my knees when we gingerly attempted to wade back to the shoreline.

Our island had been submerged by the flooding tide by the time help finally arrived—a neighbor fisherman, coming in with his day's catch, brought his small boat close enough to take us aboard and safely back to dry land.

SPEAKING OF NEIGHBORS—one of those neighbors I will never forget: Mr. Ira Webster. Mr. Webster was not rich in terms of worldly goods; and, to the best of my knowledge, he made no profession of great faith—I never saw him in my father's congregation on Sunday morning, for instance. But never a day passed, had he been out fishing, crabbing, or tonging for oysters, that he didn't stop by our back door and leave off a part of his day's haul. And what counted even more than that to me was that he always had time for a little boy—me! Soft-spoken, kind in manner, he often whittled "catty" plugs for me, and showed me how to drive the plug, once I had tipped it properly so that it was hittable. He possessed a wealth of humanness—and real goodness.

If you never have heard of "catty," let me explain as best I can. A "catty" plug was usually a piece of broomstick, about five-to-six inches long, tapered to a point at both ends. The object of the game was to tap a tip of the plug with a paddle (also homemade) so that the plug would flip up high enough to be struck with the paddle and whacked a right good distance. I forget exactly how we "kept score"; but it seems to me we established a point some hundred or so yards away, and the person who could reach that designated point with his plug and return it to the starting place in the fewest number of strokes was the winner. Mr. Webster fashioned many, many "catty" plugs for me—and paddles, too. Sometimes he would join in the game with us youngsters.

Sometimes we human beings long to "go home"—to see those who made our childhood days happy and memorable. I've tried that on a few occasions—going home to those towns and villages in which my father served as a minister. But I always came away somewhat saddened. The people I had longed to see, more often than not, weren't there any longer; they had either moved or had lived out their days on this earth.

Like Mr. Webster, there were others who had, in their own special ways, made my summer days—all the days of the year, for that matter—better, simply because they were there. Dr. Simpson—tall, white-haired, gentle, genteel in every respect—I can see him now, coming into the parsonage, carrying his black satchel that day when I had carelessly kicked a pitch fork as we were gathering pine shats for my father's chicken house and had run one prong of the fork deep into my foot, between my great toe and the toe next to it. I didn't know how worried Doctor was about me until some weeks after his medication had healed my wound. He had, as any doctor would have, feared tetanus. But he never let me see anything on his countenance but a heartening smile whenever he came to see how I was coming along.

A few years ago, we visited Rock Creek for a day. I was particularly interested in seeing my boyhood chum, Raymond France, whom I hadn't seen for some thirty-five to forty years. I went to his mother's house, knocked on the door, and was greeted with wonderful warmth. But I knew just as soon as I saw her that my quest was in vain; her face was lined with sorrow. Very matter-of-factly she told me I had arrived too late; Raymond had died that previous winter.

Happily, I did see some of my one-time friends and neighbors that day. And I enjoyed the recall of the yesterdays of years ago. But I couldn't stay—not long, I couldn't. There was no Ira Webster, sitting beneath the tree in his yard, waiting to help a little boy whittle a paddle or a "catty" plug. Dr. Simpson's house had other occupants. And the white-headed little boy who had been my playmate had grown to be a man—a waterman, like his father before him. And the Sound had claimed him; he had fallen victim of a heart attack while working his boat out on the Sound.

The old parsonage in which we had lived was still there—but the yard seemed so small! And someone had decided that the parsonage would look better painted white instead of red. The school house—which had been just a hop, step, and a jump from the parsonage—was gone and not a trace of it remained . . . only the pine-tree woods, the great expanse of marshland, the Tangier Sound seemed really responsive to my being there. I fancied I heard the long, deep-throated whistle of the steamboat approaching the Deal's Island wharf. I closed my eyes and thought of the mornings when "The Virginia" would be slipping up to the wharf—and my brother would be coming off, ready to ride across the rattling wooden bridge to our home where Mother would have an oven full of oysters steaming for him. As I rode past the church in which my father had preached, it seemed as though I could see him—tall, immaculately attired in his Prince Albert coat, his black hair styled by himself with a bit of a swirl on the right side; I thought he was the most distinguished man I had ever seen!

Rock Creek Elementary School At Chance in 1921
That's me sporting the white collar (front row)

I didn't care to talk much as we drove back across the marsh toward Princess Anne. I was trying hard to recapture something that was lost—and would be forever lost, save for the recollections that keep those days and years alive from time to time . . . August was a great month then. I didn't seem to mind the heat, the mosquitoes, the approach of the school year . . . Every day was a holiday when John Edward . . . or Ruth . . . or Lank . . . or Marguerite joined Julia, Mother, and "Papa," as we called him—all "at home."

I am glad I can remember, by George!

JANUARY 20, 1979

A Real Neighbor, By George!

Even before we had moved to Rock Creek, my father had been informed that our next-door-neighbor could very well be intolerable. His reputation for neighborliness toward ministers had been more than a little tarnished, so it seemed. He was reputed to be irascible—even vicious. But my father took such forewarnings with tongue-in-cheek and was determined to refrain from passing even the slightest judgment upon any individual insofar as personal relationships were concerned until he, himself, had reason to assess another's behavior. I am glad that he possessed that kind of wisdom, for it not only saved him from falling prey to pre-notions about people who would be a part of new ministerial assignments, but it also provided him with a kind of open-mindedness which, by his actions and voiced attitudes, rubbed off on the entire family whom he influenced as a parent.

We arrived in Rock Creek during the early spring of 1920. The chill of winter had not completely given way to the soft breezes of spring, though the fig trees and the other deciduous trees and shrubs were beginning to show signs that warm weather was not many weeks away. Mosquitoes were beginning to pester people now and then, but the veritable swarms of those blood-suckers had not yet taken over the lawns and the fields;

they were shoring up their forces for the summer's onslaught across the adjacent marshlands which seemed to stretch forever on the eastern side of the village.

Since "little pitchers have big ears," as the old saying goes (and that trite expression is entirely apropos in my case, literally, I mean!), I had listened to conversations relating to that next-door-neighbor and I was wondering what kind of person he would really turn out to be. From the parsonage windows I looked across the vacant lot which separated what was to be our new home grounds for the next three years to Captain Kelley's house and environs. I was impressed by the stately trees which filled the Kelley front yard and the privet hedge, neatly trimmed, which outlined that lawn. The big white house had what was to my inexperienced eye an unusual appendage—an uncovered back porch which led to a small, white, story-and-one-half building equipped with neat windows and a chimney. And I saw the neighbors moving about their premises; I wondered how our relationships with them would really turn out.

I DID NOT HAVE TO WAIT LONG. My father was an outgoing person. He made it his business to take the initiative in establishing neighborliness. I was not privy to the first meeting between Cap'n Will Kelley and "the preacher," as they came to call my dad; but from the way things turned out, I can only judge that no blows were struck, no harsh words were exchanged, that good feelings were mutual after the initial handshake. For, as garden-planting time came, my dad was aided by Cap'n Will—and the youngest of the Kelley daughters began calling across the open space between the two properties, "Preacher, can Julia come over?"

That Cap'n Kelley had once been a waterman I have no doubt. In fact, it may well have been that he still went out on the Sound now and then for a catch of fish or to tong a few oysters; I can't rightly remember his day-to-day routine. I do know that from him the Prettyman family received more than its share of seafood now and then. I also know that Cap'n Kelley had what seemed to me a strawberry patch, as they called it, that was endless! School was out as soon as strawberry season was in—very early in May, if my memory serves me correctly—and, even though I was not yet more than seven or eight years old, I was one of the "hands" in the strawberry patch.

Picking strawberries for Cap'n Kelley was a joy! For me, at least. We all received some little pay—by the quart box or the crate—and we were not admonished to curb our appetites for those delicious fruits. Mom's strawberry short cakes were something else! The "cake" wasn't cake at all, you know; it was short bread—pipin' hot, split open, buttered, and sandwiched with strawberries and topped with 'em, too! And they were free for the picking; Cap'n Kelley saw to that for the preacher's family.

The Kelley residence became something of a second home for me. I discovered that the little house at the end of the back porch was a summer kitchen out of which came the most delicious food one could ever imagine. Mrs. Kelley was a brisk, sharp-tongued person, but altogether lovable. And Cap'n Will was the next thing to a grandfather to me—not the cuddling sort, at all, but patient and soft-spoken and generous.

I never saw Cap'n Will in church—not to my recollection, that is. I feel pretty certain that my father never pushed religion down the Cap'n's throat; I don't think Cap'n Will would have taken kindly to evangelism by words. Even so, I am very sure that my dad's life style, his refusal to set himself up as the possessor of all the keys to the Kingdom, had an impact upon Cap'n Will. Whatever orneriness Cap'n Will had demonstrated to my father's predecessors never showed up in his relationships with any of us. In our book, he was a good man! I'd be hard put to name anyone who "took us in" with greater warmth when we were virtually total strangers than Cap'n Will and his wife and family.

I haven't been down to Rock Creek for fifteen or twenty years. The last time I did visit there, Lois Kelley was still living in the old family home—her parents long since deceased. She had been a very little girl when we moved there—the little tot who called, "Preacher, can Julia come over?" It was good to have seen her again, to talk with her about the days when her father and mine planted sorghum together in one of the fields, harvested their potatoes grown cooperatively; and to learn of the whereabouts of her sisters, Norma and Alma.

Somehow we tend to get out of touch with folks along the way—and we shouldn't! A Cap'n Will Kelley and family, after all, come but once in a lifetime, by George!

JANUARY 27, 1979

Pirates And Pitchforks

One Christmas my brother Lank gave me copies of two well-known books—"Black Rock" and "Treasure Island." While I had had good examples set before me in the matter of reading—Ruthie and Lank had been avid readers ever since I could remember—I had not yet learned to imitate them; I was content to be read to, rather than to read by myself, for I was yet in the second or third grade. But I treasured those two volumes highly and made an effort to get into Robert Louis Stevenson's classic story about pirates. I got about as far into that story as to where Jim Hawkins discovered that the old sea captain was a pirate and that he was being beset by former comrades who were out to get the map of Treasure Island when I became so frightened that I shut the book and tried as hard as I could to get pirates, the Admiral Benbow Inn, and the cove infested by wicked men out of my mind.

You see, within a quarter of a mile of our house in Rock Creek was a cove which was, to my thinking, almost identical to that fictitious cove in Stevenson's novel. And since my playmates and I had heard stories of pirates having once visited the waters of the Tangier Sound, I was certain that any time I might run into someone akin to Black Dog or old Blind Pew. After all, there was supposed to be a buried treasure in the woods between our house and Dr. Simpson's—on the winding oyster shell road which led to the cove. The gold was available, so the stories went, to anyone who would dare dig for it at midnight. It reportedly rested near the largest holly tree, deep into the woods.

MY BUDDIES AND I WERE BRAVE ENOUGH to visit the spot during daylight hours, but, so we had been told, no one had yet possessed the courage to attempt to obtain that treasure when the moon was high and the hour would be striking twelve.

"Treasure Island" remained a closed book for me for several years, for I had gone through too many nightmares, trying to outrun pirates and avoid their cruel swords. It was not until I became a teacher, years later, that I actually completed reading the adventures of Jim Hawkins, Dr. Smollett, and the protagonists Stevenson pitted against Long John Silver and his wicked companions.

BUT THAT COVE: it was close by Captain Bill Carroll Todd's large, rambling house and the store where watermen purchased their provisions prior to setting out for long weeks of tonging for oysters. We youngsters liked to have our games within and around that cove—so long as it was daylight. One special feature of that cove remains very clear in my memory. To cross one portion of the soggy marsh just off the white, narrow roadway, we had to negotiate a kind of bridge built of the discarded remains of small boats placed end to end. In our follow-the-leader games we would run with wild abandon from one crumbling old boat to another, sometimes having only the narrowest of boards on which to find footing. I can't remember exactly where that improvised bridge led to, but I think it took us to a sandy bit of shore not too distant from the big bridge which connected Rock Creek to Deal's Island.

Sometimes our play became very hazardous, for much of the time we went barefooted; sneakers were not yet in vogue and leather-soled shoes would make for slipping and taking a tumble upon rusty nails, old tin utensils, or the like.

One afternoon my father sent several of us into the nearby pine woods to gather some brown needles for his hens' nests and for bedding for the twenty-eight Belgian hares I had in pens. We had pitchforks and wheel barrows and were having a great time romping in the slick pine needles. For some reason, I kicked into a pile of needles—and felt the prong of a pitchfork penetrate my rubber overshoes, my leather shoe, and enter my foot. Hastily I yanked the prong from my foot, took off my shoe, and examined the wound. The fork had buried itself several inches into my foot, between my great toe and its nearest neighbor-digit. I let out a howl that so startled my playmates that they hustled to get my dad.

Dr. Simpson, a genteel, white-haired man, was summoned to the parsonage to take a look at my foot. Tetanus shots had not yet become a way of treating a puncture wound—not, at least, in that area—so Dr. Simpson prescribed soaking my foot in almost scalding hot water into which a pill, which turned the water purple, had been dissolved. He warned my parents against the possibility of lockjaw, but to me he said not a word concerning that killing disease. Obviously the treatment he prescribed did the trick, otherwise I wouldn't be sitting here at my typewriter doing weekly pieces.

THE SORE FOOT TOOK ME OUT of the follow-the-leader romps around the cove; but within a week or so I was on foot again, ready to go wherever Raymond France, Wilson Shores, John Parks, and my other buddies led—even to that enormous holly tree where, as the folk-tale would have us believe, a pirate treasure remains buried to this very day.

Yes, you guessed it: reading "Chesapeake" truly stirred my recollections of the years close to the Sound where skipjacks and old bay steamers provided much of the access to the world beyond the Eastern Shore.

NOVEMBER 29, 1995

Red Top Boots

Red top boots! To fit the feet of a very small boy who didn't need 'em at all, but who wanted them very much because Mr. Ira Webster, who lived next-door, wore red top boots every day. And Mr. Webster was a very nice man.

That was the Christmas of 1920 when we lived at Chance, down in Somerset County, across the bridge from Deal's Island. (It's DEAL Island, now. Why do the old names have to be fiddled with?)

Ira Webster and his wife, Essie, and their children, Loretta, Vaughn, and Little Ira, lived sort of behind and, yet, next-door to the Methodist parsonage. They were most wonderful neighbors, if I may wax superlative—and I mean that!

They were poorer than the mice that occasionally skittered along the aisles in my father's church; but they were kind and generous with what they had. Mr. Webster kept the Prettymans in fish, crabs, and oysters in due seasons. He was, obviously, a waterman.

To a little boy, he was tops! And so were his boots which he wore every single day. Black boots with red tops. They came up as far as his knees. His trousers were stuffed within his boots.

Mr. Webster's face was kind of leathered by the weather. Tanned and with many wrinkles, though he wasn't really an old man at all. He was shorter than my dad—say, 5-8—and of muscular build. His hair was graying—what you could see of it beneath his cap. It had once been black.

There was a path alongside a ditch behind our house. Mr. Webster walked that path, morning and evening, going to and coming from his boat which he tied up somewhere near the bridge in the water of the Tangier Sound. He was a whistler, which indicated that he was happy, seemingly, in spite of his rather low place on the economic totem pole.

About the only thing I remember Mr. Webster actually doing for me was whittling. Whittling a whistle that really worked when I blew it.

I think I can rightly say that he had a kind voice—not at all harsh or gruff. (Why isn't that word spelled g-r-o-u-g-h, just like r-o-u-g-h and t-o-u-g-h? Our mother tongue ain't easy to figure out sometimes.)

Well, I found my red top boots beneath the Christmas tree, alongside the plate I had set out the night before and which had been filled with candy, an apple and an orange, and some nuts. (We didn't hang stockings because we never lived in a house where there was a fireplace and because we pretty much did what our parents said they had done when they were children.)

I could hardly wait to get my feet into those boots. My trousers weren't long enough to be tucked within the boots; little boys weren't wearing long pants at that point in time. Otherwise, I felt as though I was dressed like Mr. Webster, and I ran to his house to show him my new boots.

On my way back the 60 to 70 yards to the parsonage, I thought I might just as well try the boots out in real water. So, I jumped into the ditch I mentioned a while back. I shouldn't have! That ditch was deeper than it appeared. The marsh water was mighty cold. And my boots runneth over!

It was one sorrowful little boy who went back into the house that Christmas morning—and heard his mother say, "No more boots! Not for several days. Not until they've thoroughly dried out and you promise you'll stay out of that ditch!"

WHAT DID I THEN DO? I went into the parlor and ate all the chocolate-covered peanuts my stomach would hold and became as sick as I've ever been—in the stomach, that is. I received little or no sympathy from anybody the rest of that Christmas Day.

I soon outgrew those boots; but I never outgrew my affection for the Websters. There are some folks you just never forget, by George!

(P.S. The last time my sister Julia and I visited Chance, we went to the cemetery, trying to locate the graves of some of the people we had known. And, yes, there were four graves marked Ira Webster; Essie, His Wife; Loretta Webster; and Vaughn Webster. You know something? That family comes back to me in my dreams sometimes, and it's as though I'm back in that parsonage again with my parents and my sister. And my red top boots!)

DECEMBER 20, 1995

As Though Time Had Simply Been Rolled Back

This is exactly what I said: *"It would be a wonderful Christmas were I able to shake his hand and tell him, face to face, just how much his daddy and mother meant to a little 10-year-old boy, 73 years ago, in that village that, once upon a time, we both called home."*

And here is more of that story: On December 7, just a couple of weeks ago, it happened! And it was great! We met each other for the first time in more than seven decades, shook hands, even embraced, and it was as though time had simply been rolled back.

YOU MUST UNDERSTAND that neither of us could have conceivably recognized the other, for Howard Prettyman Webster was about 7 months old when last we saw each other and I was only 10 years old. By the way, I'm going to call him Doc, for that was the name which was fastened on him when he was a little fellow and that's what the folks who know him best call him now.

He came by that name because of a physician who, at different times, treated both of us in Chance. That was Dr. Simpson, a tall, white-haired man with a healing voice and gentle manner. When Doc was born, he, too, was white-headed. Not blonde, but white. (As was my last great-grandson, Neil, when he was born.)

Dr. Simpson called him Doc right off! That name has stuck with him. It was expanded to Doxology, which was how I addressed him when I first called him after Leland Corbett had given me his telephone number. Someday I'll get the story on that nickname, too.

Doc is 73; I am 83. Not exactly youngsters, wouldn't you say? He looks hale and hearty—could easily be taken for a man in his early 60s. (I can't tell you how I look—that's a matter of opinion of those who know me. And it depends on how tired I am when that opinion is expressed.)

PERHAPS SOME PEOPLE MAY WONDER why seeing him again was so important to me—important enough to, figuratively speaking, *make* my Christmas. I can only say that I saw immediately that he bears a most striking resemblance to his father, the man who was a little boy's role model even before that expression came into general usage.

Being with him, I sensed the presence of both his father and his mother in his personality—his manner of speaking, his walk, the kindness and warmth with which he accepted me. After all, I was, in essence, a stranger. *And he took me in!* Just as Ira and Essie had done in 1920 when we Prettymans moved next door to them.

Yes, my wish was granted. Make it more than a wish. It was a prayer—an answered prayer.

I have always been a firm believer in the notion that the past casts a long and seemingly lasting, hallowed light on the present. I could not forget Ira and Essie Webster if I tried to do so; they were special neighbors when the preacher's sickly little boy needed their love. I feel as though it has all come back to me. Oh, my yes! red top boots and all.

The reunion came about when Mrs. Fran Fiore, Doc's good friend, invited my sister Julia and me to share dinner with her and Doc. That gracious lady treated us to rock fish, from Doc's fishing expertise, and steak and tomatoes stewed the Eastern Shore way.

We sat around the table for a good hour and a half—maybe longer—enjoying the food and conversation. It was all so very comfortable and comforting.

NO, I WON'T BE WRITING a letter to Santa Claus asking for boots come Christmas Eve. I already have them stored away in memory where they will always remind me of members of the Webster family, those of years long gone by and of the present.

The human touch! That's what we need at Christmas time. But that touch should be tempered by a visit to Bethlehem. Like the shepherds who star in the Gospel of Luke—and the Wise Men who saw and followed a star, as Matthew told it—we can go to the manger if we really want to; and there, in our hearts, we can celebrate His birth. Then we can reach out and lead someone else to the Christ Child.

I wish each and every one of my readers a wonderful Christmas! A blessed one! A happy one for all the little children! You bet! Merry Christmas, by George!

1975

Life On The Shore Way Back When

ABOUT THIS TIME OF YEAR, say, fifty-odd years ago, when the Prettyman family was living down the 'Shore in Somerset County, it was a real delight to doff the fleece-lined winter underwear, feel the fresh air blowing off the Tangier Sound, and know that within a few short weeks—perhaps even days—Cap'n Will Kelley's strawberries would be coming on. And if our parents weren't keeping too close a vigil on our out-of-doors activities, we'd sneak our shoes and stockings off and run about the parsonage lawn; my, did the cool, green grass ever feel good to the bottoms of our feet!

The marsh seemed to stretch for miles and miles directly behind the parsonage and the other houses on the side of the oyster-shell road on which we lived. That made a perfect place for us kids to fly our home-made kites. We had saved store-string all winter long, waiting for the days when we could send our kites up almost out of sight. As I said, the kites were fashioned by our own hands, with patient help from both Mother and Dad. Heavy brown wrapping paper, some appropriate sticks, flour-and-water paste, and some of Mom's old bits of cloth for a tail-and we had a kite that was really a kite. Since we had a rabbit hutch, and since some of the rabbits found their way to the dinner table, I'd often fasten a rabbit tail to my kite and let out all the string as I watched the creation soar above the marsh grasses, up toward the clouds.

GOING BARE-FOOT ON THE MARSH was not the fun it might have appeared to us to be, for those grasses which covered the low lands were harsh and brittle. We saved the barefoot business for the lawns—and all went well until we happened to step on a honey bee or a bumble bee. That hurt! But it was all a part of springtime then. And it was fun!

Airplanes were not exactly the looked-for thing back then, and I can remember that all of us kids—there must have been a dozen of us who played together—were held spellbound one day when a single-engine plane roared over the marshland. Suddenly there was a shower of sparkling particles falling from the plane, like silver pennies from heaven. We raced across the marsh as fast as we could go to gather some of the glittering objects. They turned out to be round pin-buttons, advertising something—perhaps they had something to do with a political campaign. I don't exactly recall. I think that was my first view of an airplane (we called them "flying machines").

Come to think of it, we were living at a time when yesterday, today, and tomorrow were all closing in on us—and we didn't quite take it all in. For example, the hearses of that area and era were horse-drawn; cord-wood was often hauled by ox cart; there were very few automobiles either in Chance or on Deal's Island; steamboats made nightly crossings to Baltimore, carrying passengers and freight—some of the freight in the form of livestock; the boats on the Sound were, for the most part, sail boats—only a few had engines as auxiliary forces should the wind die down; the word "radio" was scarcely thought of, much less did it have object meaning to us; there were few telephones in the community, and those few were used by any and all who came to request their use; the school and the church—and church-related activities, such as camp meetings—made up the religious and social aspects of life. Home was where the family worked together, played together during the evening hours—and "Rook" was our particular family game—and read together. The reading was for sheer pleasure, though I defy anyone to read without learning something useful, then and later. The coal-oil lamps went out well before what is now called prime time in today's television-oriented life.

I DO NOT RECALL ever attending a motion picture showing throughout the three years that we lived in Chance. Now, I had become acquainted with the silent screen when I was very young—four or five, let's say—down in Rock Hall. I knew all a youngster could know about Charlie Chaplin, for instance—and Buffalo Bill movies had thrilled me considerably. While we resided in Sharptown, which is in Wicomico County, we often attended the movies in the fire hall—on the second floor, that is. But down in Somerset the movies just didn't exist for us. Nor did we seem to miss them.

We boys played our own brand of baseball. We even made our own baseballs! Balls of string, they were, covered with tar tape. Babe Ruth was the big hero in Chance and on the Island. He was a Baltimore Boy, you know, and we regarded Baltimore as "our" city—though folks such as H.L. Mencken chose to regard us who lived on the 'Shore as a species of the human race not yet fully civilized. I was all ears, as the saying goes, whenever anyone turned the conversation to the exploits of baseball's newest idol, Babe Ruth. He was opening up a whole new brand of baseball—he was, in fact, a one-man murderer's row for the New York Yankees who had just bought him from the Red Sox.

Several lighthouse keepers attended my father's churches. They lived a solitary life, you know, for weeks on end. And when they had shore leave, they really enjoyed conversation. We were often entertained in the home of one lighthouse keeper whose name I happen to remember—Watt Carew. Mr. Carew was a baseball fan if I ever knew one! It was he who, quite unknowingly, led me to follow Babe Ruth's career through the daily papers—and I became a Yankee fan for life!

I wish I could remember all the interesting conversations I sat in on when Mr. Carew and my father would be together. I'm sure that the famed—or ill-famed—Tea Pot Dome scandal was as lively a topic of conversation as the Watergate mess was for those of us who talked politics this past year or so.

Watt Carew had a brother, Tom. We visited the Tom Carews frequently, too. How about this for a menu—at either of those homes: ham, fried chicken, oysters (if in season), some kind of fish, crab cakes (if in season), all kinds of vegetables—and I mean a real variety!—relishes, preserves, home-canned peaches, and coconut cake. We had to eat to keep up our strength against the onslaught of swarms of mosquitoes!

By George, I really rambled, didn't I? From long underwear to a feast! Blame my ramblin' on this time of year.

FEBRUARY 3, 1979

The Old Canning House

The canning house was situated on a sandy beach of the Tangier Sound, which, as you know, is really a part of the great Chesapeake Bay. Mr. Granville P. Webster owned and operated the canning house. He was one of my father's friends and also attended my father's church. As I recall, he was a rather stocky man with a ruddy complexion and had an abundant, but neatly trimmed, mustache. And while he was all-business during working hours, he was in no sense of the word a hard task master; nor was he ever unpleasant toward those whom he hired to work for him—never in my presence, at least.

His middle initial had special meaning for us; it denoted that his middle name was Prettyman. No, he did not come by that through any connection with my father. You see, another Rev. Prettyman had served as a Methodist minister in that Eastern Shore area back in the early-to-middle part of the 1800s—say, around 1840. Joshua Thomas, the famed "Parson of the Islands," had cruised the waters thereabouts in his sailing canoe which bore the name, "Methodist." It is probable that Granville Webster's forebearers had used the name Prettyman as a kind of testimony to the Rev. Levin M. Prettyman's service to his congregations down in Somerset County. That particular Prettyman preacher had undertaken to write the life story of Joshua Thomas, whom he knew well; but since Mr. Prettyman was given an appointment up in Philadelphia, I believe it was, he left off his writing of Thomas's amazing cruising-for-Christ evangelistic ventures. His unfinished manuscript was thereafter used by the Rev. Adam Wallace in the biographical account, "The Parson of the Islands," virtually word for word as far into Thomas's life as the Prettyman work carried him.

At any rate, Granville Prettyman Webster became, for a brief period of time, a part of my childhood years—however he came to have our family name as his middle one. My sister Julia and I were among his employees when we were about twelve and eight years of age respectively. (Don't get riled up about child labor! We weren't being exploited! The whole deal was fun!)

Our job was a very simple one: we scoured the ends of tin cans containing tomatoes. The scouring process removed rust from the cans and made them shine as tin cans should. If by chance we came across a can with bulged ends, we passed it to an adult who, in turn, relegated it to a trash heap, since bulging cans indicated spoilage.

The salt air coming off the Sound caused anything metal to oxidize almost overnight. Rust was a problem to anyone engaged in working on or using metal. My father, I recall, had the underside of the fenders of his Moon (an automobile long since extinct) coated with red lead paint to help prevent the rusting out of said fenders. Even red lead did not deter the eroding process brought on by oxidization, however. The metal screen netting which enclosed our front porch was forever being eaten away by rust. Mr. Webster's tin cans were constant targets for that same plague.

I remember so well that the steel wool we used to scour the tins ground into our fingers and made our clothing prickly. That was a part of the process and none of us complained.

My parents were obviously pleased to have Julia and me gainfully employed, though I am sure our productivity was scant and whatever pay we received certainly could not have amounted to much. At lunch time, our mother and father would bring us a hot lunch and a special treat of sorts. One of Mom's most tasty dishes was fresh green pea soup, made with peas, milk, butter, diced potatoes, and delicious little "slippery" dumplings. When I talked with Julia about this, she reminded me that on one occasion Mother brought great slices of mahogany cake—a specialty of hers. It was a kind of chocolate-colored cake and some of the ingredients were a bit unusual: a certain amount of coffee; black walnut meats; thin slices of citron; a dash of salt and a bit of vinegar—along with other things that go into almost any cake. The icing was white—not made with 4-X sugar and shortening (10X sugar was not even on the market yet)—but carefully concocted according to a recipe which required boiling.

There on the sandy beach, the four of us had lunch together during our short time of employment. And it was good!

Granville P. Webster's grandson, Leland F. Corbett, and his wife are now residents of Cecil County. They live in Bayview Springs, not far from the village of Zion. One of these days I want very much to bend Lt. Corbett's ear and chat with him about Rock Creek (Chance) and Deal's Island and the good people who were, more than a half-century ago, my neighbors, by George!

JANUARY 29, 1991

Ship-Grounding Made Shopping An Adventure

Running a-ground doesn't qualify as a shipwreck, I'm sure; but when the bay steamer is stuck on a sand bar, passengers are right there for the duration unless otherwise removed from the vessel.

It was in the winter of 1921 or 1922 that my father put me in his greatcoat pocket and took me aboard The Virginia for an over-night journey from Deal's Island to Baltimore. He had some family shopping to do and he took me along to be fitted for some new clothing. It had been decided that I had grown beyond that stage where Mother could make my blouses—that's what a little boy's shirts were called back then—at least in that part of the country.

The shopping went well enough and Pop had a couple of nice dresses for Mother, one of which would be returned to the store after she had made her choice. Ditto for Julia. In a suit box with The Hub label plain to be seen was my first store-bought suit, complete with a shirt with a Buster Brown collar and a little four-in-hand necktie. (The Hub is a furniture store now and I have no idea where it is located in relation to the old Hub.)

Pop and I boarded the steamer for the return trip to Deal's Island in the evening. We had our supper in the dining room and retired shortly thereafter to the stateroom where I was to occupy the upper berth. I was unaware of a storm which had blown up on the Bay—I always slept well on any of the bay steamers.

Along about two or three o'clock the next morning I was awakened by my father's shaking me. He told me to get into my clothes right away. Soon we were down below where the crates of various goods were piled and the livestock was being held. I saw the black, angry water and was duly alarmed as a youngster would normally be—I think. Since that time I have never enjoyed watching the wake of a vessel at night, with the white foam accentuating the blackness of the water.

The boat had run a-ground. Strong wind and an unusually high tide had contributed to a miscalculation on the part of the captain and there we were, some miles out in the Bay, stuck on a sand bar. And we remained there for more than a day—I forget the exact amount of time. I know that I was the only little fellow aboard and was treated royally by all hands. I even got to ride in the elevator-like contraption which sent food from the galley up to the dining room. And I had more than my share of ice cream during our enforced stay aboard the stranded ship.

We were rescued, if that is the proper word, by means of a motor boat—taken ashore at some port like Bivalve, for example, where we awaited the next steamer for the conclusion of the trip. Mom's dresses—Julia's, too—arrived with us upon our return to Chance, just a bridge away from Deal's Island. Their selections were made and the unchosen garments returned to the Julius Gutman store where Aunt Lily was a saleslady.

I was one proud character when I wore my new suit and that shirt with its stiff collar to church the following Sunday. The only fault I could find was that my long johns made grotesque lumps on my legs when stuffed beneath my brown lisle stockings. You see, I was still in knickers and high-top shoes; little boys hadn't graduated into long trousers back then.

Yes, by George, that was an experience. I liked being my father's traveling companion. You could bet on that!

"There are moments of life that we never forget, which brighten and brighten as time steals away."

—J.G. Percival

Some Family Notes

MARCH 3, 1979

Grandpop—As I Recall Him

I was too young when he died to have gotten to know him well. Therefore, my recollections of him are necessarily ones which date back to the late 'teens and early 'twenties of this present century and are those of a child, in a sense. But hanging on the wall of our son's home in Columbia is a political poster which bears my grandfather's picture along with pictures of other candidates running on the GOP ticket seventy-nine years ago. George B. Clendaniel was his name. I inherited his first name and his middle initial, though his middle name was "Benjamin" while I was given the middle name of "Barker," a family name from the Prettyman line.

Just as Grandpop, as I called him, was known as "George B.," so I have been called "George B." by most of my Delaware relatives—and my son has been known by that same combination of name-and-initial for much of his lifetime to distinguish him from me, especially within the family circle.

Before I have more to say about Grandpop Clendaniel, I should tell you how fortunate I feel to have come by his first name. It seems that when I arrived on the scene, my father would have preferred that I become Bagwell Barker Prettyman, II—after my Grandfather Prettyman. I can understand his desire, but I have been eternally grateful that my mother talked him out of fastening upon me that "Bagwell" bit! I doubt that either of my parents was aware that I had been endowed with oversized ears—ones which were fitted to my head at an almost ninety degree angle. With a name such as Bagwell, I most probably would have been tagged with the sobriquet, "Bagears," and that would have been enough to discourage me from social intercourse during the tender years of childhood and youth. So, I say, "Thank heavens for Grandpop George B. Clendaniel and my mother's insistence that I bear his name!" Grandfather Prettyman was, I am sure, a fine gentleman—but his name just had to be something of a social millstone.

Now, Grandpop Clendaniel, following his ventures into politics in which he was successful, I must add, serving Sussex County, Delaware, in the State legislature for a couple of terms, unless I am mistaken, became a storekeeper in the town of Lincoln. He had been a miller earlier in his day, but by the time I was added to the family he was selling Brown's Mule, groceries, and candy! (The exclamation point is triggered by the word "candy.") Candy appealed to me. Still does, in fact.

I remember Grandpop as a very quiet person. He was not demonstrative; that is to say, I cannot recall any special overt affection directed toward me. Nor can I recall any rebuffs from him. Since we didn't live in Lincoln, I saw him only when we visited there during the summer weeks or when some family event took my parents back to my mother's home town.

When I did have contact with him, it was pleasant. I never went to his store, however, without carrying with me my penny or my nickel. I would tell him what I wanted in the way of candy—or cookies, perhaps—and he would put my "purchase" into a brown paper bag, take my money, and then, gently press that money back into my little hand. Quite naturally, Grandpop's store became a place I pestered my parents to permit me to frequent; but there was restraint. I was not allowed to take advantage of Grandpop; my visits to his place of business were held down to a conservative number.

Grandpop was off to his work before I was up and around in the mornings and he kept the store open far past my bedtime at night, so I saw little of him, actually. I am sure that the mental picture I carry of him comes largely from photographs rather than from real memory. But somehow I remember his gentleness, his kind smile, and his generosity.

My mother told the story that concerned a reception or some such social event in Lincoln which she took me to when I was barely able to toddle and was not yet talking in the most acceptable manner. My sentences were still quite babyish, though definitely understandable. During the course of the evening, I spied the refreshment table, and I began literally to chant, "I see cakie! I see cakie!" And my chanting embarrassed my mother to the extent that she took me by the hand, none too gently, so she related to me later, and marched me the equivalent of two or three city blocks to Grandpop's store and told him of my misbehavior, as she viewed it.

Without raising his voice, she said, Grandpop responded, "Now, Grace, he's just a little boy—and you made him walk all that distance simply for 'seeing cakie'?" And he reached into a cookie box and saw to it that I had something to stop the wailing.

Grandpop died in 1920. I regret that I didn't get to know him better than I did. I have in my possession one of the glass candy jars which was on the counter in his store—something to remember him by. And I am glad that I was given his first name, by George! Otherwise this might have ended, by Bagwell!

OCTOBER 16, 1996

There Was Once A Romance

A year or so into this century, my father was appointed to serve the Lincoln, Delaware, charge. He moved his family, which consisted of a wife, four daughters, and one son, into the parsonage.

Not long into his ministry there, his wife died. He was left with a motherless family of five children, ranging in age from the late 'teens to little more than a year. His deceased wife was buried in the Lincoln cemetery. Many times in later years, I was with him as he placed wild flowers on her grave.

In due course of time, my father took a fancy to a pretty miss who sang a beautiful soprano in the choir. That pretty miss was Grace Clendaniel, daughter of George B. and Julia M. Clendaniel. George B., an official in Dad's church, was postmaster in Lincoln, and he also operated a small grocery store. Grace quite often helped him sort the mail or wait on customers in the store. Of course, the preacher found it necessary to frequent both places where Grace might be found at work.

Social life in Lincoln at that time centered around choir practice, spelling bees, debates, and mid-week prayer meetings, all under the auspices of the church. Gentlemen had the privilege of walking their ladies home following such events. And my dad chose Grace, some seventeen years younger than he.

By the time Dad's term of service in the Lincoln church had ended, the romance was almost at the stage of fruition. Thus it was that John William Prettyman and Grace Clendaniel were married shortly after he had moved his family to his next appointment. The wedding took place on June 25, 1907, in the Clendaniel home, with my father's brother, the Rev. A.P. Prettyman, performing the ceremony.

I often heard it said—perhaps in jest, or perhaps as a matter of fact—that Grace had in her mind to become a missionary. Her role in life came close to being just that. She became the mis-

My father,
The Reverend J. W. Prettyman

My mother,
Grace Clendaniel
They were married on June 25, 1907

tress of the parsonage, step-mother to five children (who, with affection, called her Miss Grace throughout their lives), and, eventually, the mother of additional members of the family, a girl and a boy.

I have heard it said that, while my grandfather voiced no serious objection to the marriage, he did say, "Grace, you know you'll never have a home of your own." That was in reference to the itinerant nature of the Methodist ministry. Insofar as I know, he and "JW"—as he called my father—got along fine. But Grandpop was wrong. Grace did get to have her own home—years later. In 1937 she and my father moved into a new Sears, Roebuck story-and-a-half house in Zion.

My father enjoyed their new home for almost eight years. He had about a quarter-acre garden in which he grew every kind of vegetable this area would produce. On his 75th birthday, he saw, for the first time, our son, born November 11, 1939.

MY FATHER VISITED THE BABY every morning at bath time, holding and amusing him while Elizabeth got a bottle ready for the baby's nap. George was my father's 18th grandchild.

Born November 14, 1864, my father lived to be 80 years and six months old. He slept away, May 14, 1945, following a lengthy illness during which Mother watched over him, day and night. Throughout the several months he was bedridden, she took great care in feeding him things he particularly liked, such as plump lima beans, fresh from their garden, cooked in milk, with a modicum of tomato tossed in. When he was in the hospital in Baltimore during the summer of 1944—at the outset of his illness—she was accorded use of a kitchen where she would prepare that favorite dish.

Mother became our next-door neighbor in 1950 when we moved into our new home, built on the lot adjacent to hers. My father had designated that piece of ground for that purpose. Her house became something of a haven for our son who would often take the pillow from his own bed and announce that he was spending the night with "MomMom."

We were neighbors for 18 years—until the night of January 1, 1968. She had become seriously ill two weeks before Christmas, and the doctor told us the end was near. On Christmas morning, she sang the first verse of "Silent Night" at the request of Dr. F.B. Robinson. Her voice was clear and sweet. My sister Julia and I were there with her. One week thereafter, she slipped into that lasting slumber. She was 87 years of age.

She and my father are at rest, side by side, in the Rosebank Cemetery. . .

Yes, there was once a romance in the town of Lincoln, Delaware. It all started with my father walking his lady home. I have reason to be happy about that, by George!

APRIL 30, 1985

The Iron Horse

My love affair with trains goes back as far as I can remember. Since my grandparents' house in Lincoln, Delaware, faced the railroad tracks, I had what amounted to a grandstand seat from which to watch the trains go by. Or stop at the freight or passenger station, whichever was appropriate, trainwise. Or stop at the miniature stockyard where cattle bawled while being held in waiting prior to being herded into a cattle-car.

The sights and sounds occasioned by trains fascinated me. And sometimes frightened me. The passenger trains gave off a kind of deep-throated, "woo-oo-oo-oo, woo-oo-oo-oo, woo-woo!" A bit mournful, but pretty to the ear. The freight trains seemed to emit a high-pitched scream which caused me to hold my hands over my ears lest my eardrums burst. I was, as a small child, terrorized when an engine let off steam; the hissing was deafening, indeed.

As a locomotive began to renew its journey toward Ellendale and points beyond, it seemed to huff and puff outlandishly and then stutter—the huge wheels spinning on the steel rails—before that final convulsive jerk which signaled the eventual get-on-with-it. Then, in a moment or so, the clackety-clack of the train could be heard gradually fading away as the train disappeared far down the track.

The prettiest sight of all was the night train, a three-to-five coach passenger train, lighted up to appear as an elongated jewel of varying colors. At the top of the brilliantly illuminated windows were stained-glass strips of green or amber. The white head-cloths on the dark plush seats were visible and gave contrast to the overall golden glow. How warm and beautiful that sight was! And how a little boy stood in awe of the giant locomotive as it belched black smoke into the darkened night sky, its Cycloptic eye blazing a glistening path down the track!

It was always fun to count the freight cars as they rumbled by. Grandmom's house seemed to tremble in the wake of their passage. At night, my mother would often take me out on the back porch and let me watch the lights on the rear of the caboose move farther and farther away until, at last, they were extinguished by both distance and the black of night.

I have yet to fulfill a dream which had its origin almost 70 years ago as I stood by my mother and saw the caboose disappear: I wanted to be in that caboose as it drifted into infinity. Many years later, as a teacher, I took a vicarious journey in such a caboose along with the man Owen Wister, called "The Virginian," and his fellow cowpokes as they rattled along from Wyoming to the Chicago stockyards with Judge Henry's cattle.

Yes, I have really ridden on trains many times—not just through books. Perhaps my most exciting ride on the rails came in the late 1950s when I traveled from Baltimore to Detroit on a night train. I asked the porter to call me when we came to the famed horseshoe curve up at Altoona, Pennsylvania. He did and I saw ourselves going the other way, so to speak. Very strange sensation.

Another train ride I won't forget came in 1973. Elizabeth and I took Susan Beth up to Boston for a few days. It was fun giving that granddaughter a vacation by rail, by George! She's grown up now—away out in San Francisco!

NOVEMBER 14, 1979

His 115th Birthday

While he appeared to be very tall as I saw him when I was a youngster, he was, in reality, no more than five-feet-ten—and he never tipped the scales beyond the 110-pound mark. Perhaps his thinness made him seem taller than he was.

Despite his frail appearance, he was not a physical weakling. Even in his later years he and a neighbor, Doc Hall, chopped wood for the winter with considerable vigor; and right up to his last illness, when he was approaching eighty, he tended a fairly good-sized vegetable garden. Settled the poles for his bean crop, pushed his hand cultivator to clear out invading weeds, and used his hoe with real authority. I can remember that his red-skinned white potatoes often took first prize at the then annual "fair" held in the old Calvert Agricultural High School. Once, I recall, he let me put my name on the basket of potatoes he had for the fair, though I'm sure I had little to do with that crop. Oh, he would let me help him plant the potatoes; and when it came time to dig them, he called on me for assistance. But the garden was his: that was his hobby. How many sermons he thought up while working in his beloved garden I'll never know.

It was one of his goals to have new potatoes and green peas ready to eat by June 25 every year. That was his and Mother's anniversary. Mom diced the potatoes, made little slick dumplings, and served that tasty dish as something akin to a soup—plenty of milk and butter. Just about that time, his chickens would be of the right size for frying. It was something of a feast day he looked forward to. That and July 4th when the menu would be repeated.

When the weather got extremely warm, he would put some cooling leaves from the grape vine within the crown of his wide-brimmed straw hat as he worked outside. He always managed to get most of his chores in the garden done before the hottest part of the day; then he would sit under the shade trees on the parsonage lawn and chat with a neighbor or, maybe, just sit and read the daily newspaper.

I came into his life when he was 48—something of a postscript, I was. I have been told that during my first summer, in 1913, after I had fully recovered from whooping cough which I contracted at the age of six weeks, he took me down to the edge of the Chesapeake Bay and, with his hands supporting me, let the salt waves lap over me. That gave me my first taste of the Bay, the wonderful body of water which has provided food and wealth for so many of the people lucky enough to live close by its shores.

As I have said many, many times, it was my good fortune to fit into his greatcoat pocket, so to speak, when I was a little fellow, and I accompanied him on innumerable over-night trips from the wharf at Deal's Island across the Bay by steamer to Baltimore. Actually I was more than a toddler then; I was already in school and his taking me along with him probably gave the truant officer something to growl about. Whatever I lost by being absent from the classroom, I know I more than made up for it just by being with him.

I do not presume to have been his favorite in any way. I'm certain that each of his seven children found in him someone special—someone personally theirs. To each one of us he was an individual somewhat apart from his relationship to the others. I recall that when I was attending the University of Delaware, one of the students whom I had never met came up to me and said, "Your father is well-known as quite a philosopher." Of course that made me feel good—to know that he was highly regarded outside the family circle, and it also emphasized the fact that he was able to relate to a variety of people.

He never accumulated a fortune. Methodist ministers seldom do. He never served a so-called "big" church. But I can attest to the fact that the churches or charges he served knew he had been there, for over the years friends throughout the Eastern Shore frequented our home from time to time. I was partial to his preaching. To me he was one of the very best I have ever heard. Not eloquent in the sense of having been a Bishop Hughes, perhaps; but his sermons related to life here on earth among people—and I liked that!

He could be strict when the occasion called for discipline. He was not cruel, but when he thought I needed a lesson punctuated by a bit of physical sting, he would break a little switch from a tree and more than tickle my bare legs with it. Or he could dismiss me from the table for unnecessary giggling or jabber. I always knew why I was being punished and I accepted his corrective measures with no resentment.

His potato fork—used for turning up luscious sweet potatoes in that patch between the church in Sharptown and Hilda Taylor Cooling's grandfather's house—and two of his precious hoes are among the mementos resting in my garage. Some of his sermon notes, written on the back of envelopes, are tucked between the pages of books he once used and passed on to me. I have never attempted to utilize his notes for a sermon of my own because they were his and his only, and I could not plagiarize them.

He saw our son for the first time on November 14, 1939, when he—not our son—was seventy-five years old. He seldom missed a day coming to our house about the time the baby's bath had been given, and he held him while my wife got the bottle ready so that young George could be fed and take his morning nap.

My niece, Joanne Touchton Tosh, probably characterized his preaching best, if I may back-track for a moment. One day, when she was quite young, she went home from church and said, "Dad Dad preached hard this morning!"

And Howie Goodrich, I recall, caught him in one of his pensive moods. He was walking in the fields just outside of Zion with our dog, Rover—probably meditating upon next Sunday's sermon. He noted that Rover was getting too far ahead of him or maybe the dog was about to take off after a neighbor's cat. At any rate, Rover evidently interrupted his train of thought and needed some scolding.

Howie ran into my sister's kitchen wearing a perturbed look upon his little face. He exclaimed, "Ju Ju, I think you ought to know that your father is talking harshly to Rover!"

You know, the publication date of this issue is November 14, 1979. If he were still alive, we would be marking his 115th birthday!

My brother-in-law, Dick Touchton, keeps telling me I'm getting more like my father every day. If that is true, Dick, it's one of the finest compliments I've ever had thrown my way, by George!

AUGUST 23, 1995

Fireflies Light The Way Back To Long Ago

Not long ago I read in a daily-devotion book about a person from one of the Far Eastern countries who was delighted to find that here in the United States lightning bugs are free!

Where that individual had come from, lightning bugs were scarce and relatively expensive should a host family want a few live ones to add to the ambiance of a twilight garden party. And here the little fireflies flash on and off by the thousands in the summer evenings! They light up life!

Now, here I go! Back several decades—and you don't have to follow me if you are tired of my back-tracking. I'm warning you. I have no idea where this is going to take me—and you, if you choose to go along . . .

LINCOLN, a village in Delaware's Sussex County (which my mother always thought of as home, even though she'd been up and down Maryland's Eastern Shore as a pastor's wife and settled down to spend more than 40 years of her life in Cecil County)—Lincoln, as I started to say, was my vacationland from birth until I was a teenager. And as a little fellow, I chased lightning bugs on my grandparents' spacious lawn many, many summer evenings.

Grandmom was accommodating. She kept a supply of Rumford's Baking Powder bottles, corks included, for me, my sister (who had outgrown chasing fireflies by the time I was just getting started), and my several cousins. It was fun for me to stuff some of nature's miniature sparklers into the bottle and see them turn on their tiny, but brilliant, lights.

I was always cautioned to uncork the bottle when it was time for me to go to bed so that my captives could go free. When morning came, the bottle was almost always empty.

It was such a simple game to play, yet it stays in my mind as one of the pleasures of childhood. You see, there was a certain wonder about those creatures which had tail-lights of their very own; and when they drifted in flight as darkness shrouded out the daylight, they gave the scene a kind of ethereal—almost spiritual—quality.

SOMEHOW THERE WAS a certain sense of peace, to be interrupted only by the somewhat muted whistle of the last passenger train leaving Milford and soon to be coming down the rails to stop at the station directly across the dusty road from Grandmom and Grandpop's house.

When the train pulled in at the station, I stopped catching fireflies and watched the brightly lighted coaches with that narrow rim of green above windows. And I dreamed of the day when I could board a train with my father and go far, far away—say down past Ellendale and maybe as far as Georgetown. The big engine gave a few short puffs; its giant wheels began to turn. That was the signal for approaching bedtime.

The old iron pump at Grandmom's was on the back porch. I mentioned dust a moment ago. Yes, the unpaved street in front of the house was dusty—a soft, yellow dust which managed daily to encrust itself on my bare feet so that I had to undergo a special foot bath as well as a pretty good scrubbing of hands, face, and body.

Mother pumped cold water on my feet. It was cold enough to cause me to gasp at the moment of impact. She pumped and pumped until my feet were white again.

Very often, while my feet were being flushed, a freight train would rumble past and, while I could not see it, I heard its shrill whistle at the crossing and I waited eagerly to get a good view of the light on the caboose fade as it disappeared down past the canning factory, down Ellendaleway.

I don't understand the railroad business well enough to know the reason, but I'm told the old cabooses have outlived their usefulness and are no longer bringing up the rear of a freight train. Owen Wister's "The Virginian" wouldn't have been half the fun to read had there not been that episode of tall tales in the caboose on the way to the stock yards.

After saying good-night to my captives and making sure the cork was out, I went into the house and probably was directed to the couch in the dining room, which also served as a living room. (Not a parlor! That was off limits save for special occasions.) There I fell asleep and would be roused only when all members of the family mounted the stairs and called it a day.

THAT PARLOR. One of the few times I was in that room I had my first close contact with death. Grandpop, who at the age of 70 had been found dead on the floor of his grocery store, was asleep, as they told me, in his casket in the parlor. I remember feeling strange and uneasy seeing him there until Uncle Harry came into the room, my cousin Edgar in his arms; the three of us stayed there a few moments looking at Grandpop.

I didn't quite know why Uncle Harry was wiping tears from his eyes, but as time went on and my awareness of the mortality of man materialized, I discovered what it was like to lose a dad or a friend or a life-long companion.

I'm named after Grandpop. He was a gentle man—and a gentleman, too! In 1900, he ran for the House of Delegates in Delaware and won. He's where I get my "George" from, by George!

JANUARY 12, 1994

Remember Those Old On-The-Wall Phones?

There are, I presume, some of my readers who can remember the on-the-wall, hand-cranked telephone. No dialing. No area codes. Operators on duty day and night to ring a number for you if you wanted to call someone not on your own party line. Or to help you get a long-distance call through. Or to give you the correct time if your clock had run down.

Pleasant ladies, those operators were. No doubt they knew more about what was happening in the community than anyone else. But who cared? They were there by the switchboard and they did their work with something of a personal local touch.

I HAVE AN especially warm spot in my heart for telephone operators for my sister Ruth was one, down in Washington, D.C. I always thought she had a perfect telephone voice. Gentle, soft, and kind of soothing to the ear. (Of course, now that I'm getting deafer every day, Ruth would have to raise her voice to a virtual shout for me to understand her.)

The recent break-up of AT&T reminded me of the days when telephoning was something of an adventure and a socializing event. Almost every operator I had occasion to crank for immediately recognized my voice and exchanged a friendly greeting. Even inquired as to my health now and then.

THERE WAS A chummy relationship, it seemed, between those of us who cranked the phone at home and the lady who assisted us. Much more fun than listening for dial tone or a busy-buzzing.

Even after I had migrated, professionally, across the Susquehanna and made calls from the office in Bel Air, there were operators who knew me by voice—Mary Gifford and Julia Carcirieri, both former students of mine. I liked that. Kind of made my day—and helped me get my call through to the right place and/or person.

AT ONE POINT in time, we on the old Farmers' system out of Rising Sun had pretty neat telephone numbers. Two digits with a letter added for specific identification.

We were for a time on a four-party line with my mother, whose number was 39-C; my sister and brother-in-law, 39-B; Dick's store, 39-X; and Elizabeth and me, 39-O. The letters indicated, say, two longs and a short—rings, that is, or some other combination, such as four shorts or three longs.

On occasions when Julia and Dick and Elizabeth and I were away, Mom was our answering service. I don't recall her ever being nosey; she didn't listen-in on conversations unless she knew there was some sort of excitement stirring within the family circle. She simply took care of our calls when we were not at home. It was a much more personal sort of arrangement than having a caller receive a recorded message and wait for a beep or a tone in order to leave a message.

ONE DAY DICK and Julia's telephone rang, and Mom, knowing that they were not there to answer it, did her usual thing. She lifted her receiver and said, "Hello!" Mom's hellos were cheery and bright, let me tell you!

"Hello," came the reply. "Is this 39-B?"

"No," Mom said, "but it's 39-B's mother!"

I never was filled in on the wind-down of that conversation. I'm certain that Mom's response cracked the funny-bone on the other end of the line. It had to! Better than a beep by a long shot!

SOMETIMES I FEEL so computerized and electronicized that I actually yearn for an on-the-wall telephone to crank. Sure, there were times when it was difficult to tell longs from shorts, and there would be clicks on the line to let you know someone was listening in.

Conversations weren't so private as we might have wanted 'em to be. Once in a while you could hear a dog bark or someone sneeze—a dead give-away that what you were saying would be scattered about the community. All in all, though, it was pretty folksy.

Well, that was the long and the short of the old crank phone. Wasn't so bad, by George!

JULY 28, 1981

Talking Turkey

My mother liked to raise turkeys. Now, as you know, we never lived on a farm, though very late in his life my father did hold the deed on one. I say he held the deed because that's about all it amounted to; the bank held the mortgage. My dad did manage to keep up interest payments, however, and a few years after he had "bought" it, he sold the 100-plus acre farm for a sufficient profit to pay off the mortgage and buy their retirement home from Sears, Roebuck & Co.

That's a fact. A Sears, Roebuck precut frame house. My father lived in their modest little white house from 1937 until his death in May, 1945. My mother kept right on living there until she died, January 1, 1968. That was the only home they ever actually owned, although they made every parsonage we ever lived in "home" for all of us . . .

But let's get back to turkeys, which I started to write about.

I remember the year Mom had a setting of turkey eggs—we were living in the old Zion parsonage, sometime in the early '20s it was. The mortality rate among young turkeys was pretty high, especially if they were not raised in a wire pen—off the ground. Mom nursed those little turkeys from the day they were hatched. She lost a few, but it certainly wasn't because they weren't cared for as best my mother knew how to coddle them.

I remember sitting beside her under the old apple tree in the back yard, watching her as she crumbled bread and carefully chopped hard-boiled eggs. She mixed the crumbs and the eggs well and then let the baby turkeys peck away at the delicacy she had prepared for them. Eventually, of course, they out-grew baby food and were given something more substantial in the way of nourishment.

I don't know how many of those turkeys made it to maturity. I do know that our Christmas turkey came from that hatching. And Mom sold some turkeys—maybe five or six—and that was her Christmas money which she used to purchase gifts. You could call those turkeys "Mama's Bank Account," for that's what they amounted to.

Several years later she was still raising turkeys in a wire pen, several feet off the ground. She lost very few turkeys over several seasons. Always at Christmas time she had her turkey money, she used to say. I recall that my wife and I bought our first Christmas turkey from her in 1937—the first year she and my father lived in their new home. That turkey was a 20-pounder! It served us well as we entertained members of the family and friends over the holidays in our apartment which Dick Touchton had fashioned in what had once been a barn. (My first employer, the late Murray J. Ewing, Editor of *The Cecil Whig* back then, used to tell me I was sleeping right where his horse used to have his stall!)

My mother used to "talk turkey" quite often. You see, when she was a young girl, back before the turn of the century, her father was a miller and she really did raise a few turkeys. On Christmas, with some of her turkey money, she bought her mother a beautiful globed oil lamp for the parlor—just a beautiful lamp, as I have said. After my grandmother died, Mother got the lamp. She had paid four dollars for it, she told us—and that's hard to believe. The price I mean. That lamp was my mother's pride and joy. She had it electrified and kept it on a drum-top table the remainder of her life.

Strange—what triggered my recollection of Mother and her turkeys. I was chopping up a hard-boiled egg the other day for an egg salad sandwich and I thought about Mom and her baby turkeys. Gee whiz, the way she pampered those little feathered creatures! Their bread crumb and egg mixture looked good enough for me to eat! As good as my egg salad!

Wonderful, isn't it, how easily memories can become so vivid that today seems like only yesterday, by George!

JULY 24, 1984

It Was An Oakland

My father bought our first automobile in 1919 or 1920. It was an Oakland—a big touring car. We lived in Sharptown (Wicomico County) at the time. The two big towns closest to Sharptown were Salisbury and Cambridge. My dad chose to visit Cambridge more frequently then he chose to make Salisbury his destination.

The roads were rather narrow at that point in time. Scarcely wide enough to accommodate two cars in passing. And it was an exceptional trip if we made it to Cambridge without having a tire blow out. Getting a tire loose from the wheel was a big job; and patching the inner-tube wasn't the most simple task, either. I was too young to help. While my father wasn't particularly gifted as a mechanic, he did well wielding the tire-iron and keeping the lugs and nuts from rolling away while he replaced the tube and got the tire back on the rim.

On occasion, Uncle Al, my father's oldest brother, would be visiting us and he would ride along with us to Cambridge. During the time-out for tire repairs, Uncle Al would entertain me by building a little pyramid out of loose stones on the shoulders of the highway. Uncle Al was not given to assisting Brother John with manual labor.

The garage at the parsonage in Sharptown was hardly wide enough—or long enough—to house the Oakland. My mother discovered that parking that car in the garage or on the street could be a hazardous undertaking. In fact, parking the long and unwieldy vehicle almost caused her to fail to get her license. As it was, it took two tries for her to pass the driver's test.

Mother took her test in Salisbury. She did a fine job of the oral quiz. And the driving, too, until it came to parking. My father accompanied her and the officer on the ride around several blocks. Unfortunately, my dad had to put in his two cents as Mother went to park.

There was a vacant spot on the left-hand side of the two-way street and my father suggested that mother pull in there. She did and she was promptly told by the attending officer that she had flunked the test. (You see, mother was a dutiful wife. She was not liberated, she minded my father admirably, and adopted his name following her marriage to him.)

The second time 'round, mother did her own thing. She parked on the right side of the street. My father did not ride with her then.

Some weeks later, mother discovered a way to add length to the garage. It wasn't the prettiest method, but it worked.

She was putting the Oakland to rest one day. She carefully nosed the car into the garage. Suddenly the car darted forward at increased speed and, before mother could apply the brakes, the car crashed right through the end of the garage, splintering lumber as it tore its way out of the building.

The car was not damaged. No dents on the fenders. Oh, maybe a broken headlight. Cars were sturdy in those days. Mother wasn't hurt. Just embarrassed. She took the subsequent teasing from members of the family quite well. My dad fell at once to the task of putting a new end on the garage. It wasn't the fanciest bit of carpentry work but it served its purpose. He used coffin crates which he obtained from the undertaking establishment across the street from the parsonage.

The Oakland was traded in on a Moon shortly thereafter. That Moon was one mighty fine car! A sports coupe with real leather upholstery. Its engine roared like a lion. Just a beautiful automobile! Bucket seats, though no one called 'em that back in the 'twenties.

The Moon roared into Zion one afternoon in the spring of 1923. We four Prettymans were passengers. My father had engaged the driving services of a man in Lincoln, Delaware, since we had been advised that Zion was nestled among hills. Neither of my parents was accustomed to hilly highways. We were from the flat country, you see.

That was the fanciest car we Prettymans ever owned. Unfortunately, it proved to be too heavy for the sodden roads of spring. Cecil County had few stretches of hard-top roads in those years. So, after having been stuck in the yellow mud of the gravel roads leading to Union, Ebenezer, and Rosebank Churches, my father decided to trade the Moon for a lighter automobile, a Studebaker—purchased in 1925.

You know, I still have to chuckle when I think of my mother's misadventure with the Oakland. She practiced demolition before that sport became popular. She was some sport herself, by George!

JUNE 28, 1995

Fourth Of July Brings Back Memories

Harrison didn't have much time off. He was a carpenter working on the construction of the Conowingo Dam. My sister Marguerite, his wife, was in the Maryland General Hospital down in Baltimore and their children, John Edward, Geraldine, and Ruthie, were staying with us in the Zion parsonage. When Harrison did have time to visit, he was right here in Zion with them. The year was 1924, I think.

It was a memorable Fourth of July for me. Harrison brought John Edward and me each a paper-cap toy—a bit different from the usual imitation handgun which shot caps. Our new toy consisted of a little wooden hammer-like contraption; a cap was inserted in the hollow of the head and a gadget similar to a badminton shuttlecock fit in that hollow atop the cap.

When one of us hit his hammer on the concrete walk, the cap went off and the shuttlecock took flight—and I mean the thing really took off! Unfortunately, it got caught in the wind and landed in the belfry of the church adjacent to the parsonage lawn. Since each of us had one of the cap-toys, we still had one shuttlecock left. I don't remember how soon the second shuttlecock joined the first one in the belfry but it eventually did. Many years later one of the little bird-like doodle-funnies was recovered by someone—probably someone painting up there.

Harrison came into our family when we lived in Rock Hall. His father was a waterman—Cap'n Jones. If you wonder why John Edward had two names, he inherited John from his grandfathers Jones and Prettyman, his uncle, John Lank Prettyman, my brother, and the Edward, from my sister Katie's husband, Ed Fitzgerald, of Lincoln, Delaware. John Edward grew to be a fine man.

Unfortunately he contracted Lou Gehrig's disease when he was in his late 60s and had a long, lingering illness, immobile from his shoulders down for what seemed to us who watched him an eternity. He would be 80 were he alive today.

This summer the three youngsters spent with us in the parsonage sticks in my memory as one of the best during my childhood years. Ruthie was the baby, barely old enough to talk plainly. One of her favorite expressions was, "Din'ready Miss G'ace?" Any time of the day she asked that. That's the clue to her appetite; it was a big one! Even so, she was tiny enough that she could stand up straight in the palm of her daddy's outstretched hand. She still lives down in Baltimore.

Geraldine was forever getting in John Edward's hair, fussing him up no end. If he had a toy or a piece of candy—anything at all that she could grab—she grabbed it. And John Edward would run to Miss Grace (my mother), saying, "Geraldine 'tuck' it and it wasn't her'n!" Ever so often, my sister Julia and I come over that expression—we haven't the slightest idea whose language the little boy was imitating. Geraldine died some years ahead of John Edward.

A year or so later, Jimmy Renn and I were deemed old enough to set off a few fireworks on the Fourth. Each of us would save up a dollar or so—from mowing Dr. Gifford's lawn or weeding his garden—and we'd lay in a small store of firecrackers, sparklers, Roman candles, and spit devils. My parents and Mrs. Renn were careful not to let us buy what would be similar to the cherry bombs of today. We could hardly wait until it became dark enough the evening of the Fourth to apply a lighted match to the fuses.

Speaking of fuses, my cousin Jean Clendaniel was just learning to read this one Fourth down in Lincoln, Delaware, when we were getting ready for our fireworks display in Grandmom's yard. Jean picked up a firecracker of some sort and demonstrated her reading skill by letting us all in on the directions. Very slowly she read: "Set on end and light the fuss!" She was a precious little girl—and she grew to be a fine lady!

I GOT TO RUMMAGING through some of my old sermons—hand written, they were, and for reasons of which I know not there was a Valentine tucked in one of them from my son. He was experimenting with cursive writing. He addressed it to me and signed it in his childish hand. Being the sentimental old man that I am, I promptly gave it a prominent place among the photographs of and cards sent me by my great-grandchildren.

OK. So I'm on a looking-back kick today. Maybe someday you will be, too. It's not at all painful and it's relatively harmless. Makes me seem a bit wacky, but I'm really not. Not any more wacky than I've always been. I'll give this computer a rest while I check my grammar, by George!

By the way, I hope you have a happy firecracker, wherever you are—Elkton, North East, or in your own back yard.

MARCH 21, 1973

Childhood Dream Almost Comes True

A PICTURE-PUZZLE STARTED IT . . . The first picture-puzzle I ever owned depicted, after I had put the pieces together, a circus scene: clowns; acrobats; elephants; horses and bare-back riders; trapeze artists; monkeys; dancing bears; and the king of all beasts—the magnificent African lion. As picture-puzzles go, it was not too difficult for a youngster to assemble; and it was, for years, one of my most cherished possessions.

When I was somewhere between nine and eleven years of age, one of my uncle's asked me what I wanted to be when I grew up. I expressed two choices—to be a performer in a touring circus or to be a local preacher. Uncle Herbert was wise enough to understand my first choice—the dream of almost every little boy—a fanciful dream which held little probability of ever coming true. That second choice had him stumped.

"Why a local preacher?" he asked.

"Tired of movin'," was my reply.

And I've remained in Zion, for all practical purposes, throughout the last fifty years—as a permanent resident. And I did, in fact, become a local preacher. But that's not my story this week . . .

I never made it as a circus performer. Nonetheless, the circus has always held a particular fascination for me. One of the grandest days of my life as a young father came off the day Elizabeth and I took our son to Wilmington—when "The Greatest Show on Earth" was still housed in a big tent. I don't know who enjoyed that day the most—our son or his parents. I know that the desire to perform surfaced within my consciousness; for I found myself with tremendous admiration for the entire circus family. They demonstrated then, as they always have and always will if the circus is to exist at all, remarkable teamwork. For precision, dependent upon complete cooperation of everyone concerned, is the name of the circus game.

But isn't that really true of any worthwhile, productive venture in which great (or even small) numbers of people engage? Somehow the circus people seem able to demonstrate the talent for cooperative endeavor with enviable skill . . .

DREAMS HAVE A WAY of coming true. Delayed, yes—even for a couple of generations; but some wonderful dreams do become reality. No, don't get me wrong; I have not turned into a tight-rope specialist, an animal trainer, or a ringmaster. I could never really qualify as a clown. Yet, my dream did come true the evening my grandchildren, Susan Beth and Jeffrey, were given the unexpected and exciting opportunity to be clowns for a night with the Ringling Bros. and Barnum & Bailey Circus during its recent twelve-day stand at the Civic Center in Baltimore.

Under the auspices of Mrs. Gerry Kreml (of Columbia, Maryland), one of the two Public Relations Supervisors for the circus, and with the cooperation of the Hochschild-Kohn Store at the Columbia Mall, fifty youngsters were invited to participate in a "clown-in" with "Buttons," one of the clowns of the big show, acting as Master of Ceremonies. Buttons, whose real name is Leon McBryde, the son of an optician in Fayettville, North Carolina, had once expressed the desire that he might grow up to be a clown, but, as a well-over-six-feet-tall grown-up, he was working in insurance first, then promotional endeavors for a department store, when he made the decision to attend Ringling Bros. and Barnum & Bailey's clown school. Now he's one of the happy young clowns for the big circus—and a mighty delightful individual.

Susan Beth and Jeffrey signed up for the clown-in. The winner, to be chosen by the young contestants themselves, was to become a clown for one real, live performance before the thousands of people assembled at the Civic Center. A promotional event, yes; but a chance for some lucky youngster to have the night of his life.

Susan Beth and Jeffrey carefully rehearsed their two-minute act, under the enthusiastic tutelage of their mother—and father and grandfather gleefully added a few suggestions. The circus folks had generously provided make-up kits and had given directions about the application of the grease paint.

The children's mother followed the directions with considerable success. So much success, in fact, that the family Schnauzers barked their alarm when they first saw the little clowns.

Jeffrey became "Dr. Fuzzy," with Susan Beth, his patient, suffering from apparently severe abdominal distress. Dr. Fuzzy motioned her to the floor, anesthetized her by soundly whacking the floor very close to her head, and proceeded to saw her open, using a carpenter's hand saw. The young doctor expressed amazement as he discovered two bunches of artificial grapes, a whole plastic turtle, a complete banana, an ear of pop corn, a rubber frog, and a whistling hamburger within his patient's stomach. And he displayed both his amazement and his incredible find to the audience.

His prescription, written in large print on a window shade for the audience to read, was, "Eat less. Chew more!"

Despite the fact that, during the performance at the Hochschild-Kohn Store, time ran out, their little act won for both of them the honor of being in "The Greatest Show on Earth," Monday evening, March 5. They were told by Mrs. Kreml to appear at the Civic Center at 2:30 p.m. to listen in on an instructional period during which time persons seventeen years of age or over would have the opportunity to hear about Ringling Bros. and Barnum & Bailey's College of Clowns. Then—they were to report at 6:30 p.m. to be made up for the evening's show.

Of course, Grandfather Prettyman had to get in a word or two with Buttons. I told him of my first picture-puzzle and of my one-time ambition to "run away from home and join a circus."

"Do you know the difference between a little boy and a man?" Buttons asked me.

I had no answer.

"The boys they play with!" he explained, as he patiently gave my arm an understanding squeeze.

Meanwhile, Susan Beth and Jeffrey were happily dazed by the unreality of the reality which was only two days away. They would be experiencing a virtually impossible dream.

MARCH 28, 1973

A Great Night At 'The Greatest Show'

Susan Beth and Jeffrey were excused from school early, Monday, March 5. They had an appointment at the Civic Center in Baltimore. To them, I am sure, that appointment had to rate as the greatest one of their young lives. They were excited. So were we all—their parents and the two of us, Nana and Dad Dad—as we drove them toward that destination which seemed almost like the "end of the rainbow." We were later to meet "Grandma"—Mrs. Roberta Downin—who was to be on hand to see the littlest Prettymans turn into circus clowns for an evening . . .

Mrs. Kreml was soon on hand at the stage entrance to greet the children and put them at ease.

IT WAS A PLEASURE to meet Mr. Bill Ballantine, a once-upon-a-time "citizen of Clown Alley," as the circus program states, and now the headmaster of Ringling Bros. and Barnum & Bailey's College of Clowns. Dead serious, he is, about clowning. He told the group assembled that afternoon—and some of the people were apparently aspiring to become clowns—that the College received about 2,500 applications last year, and from that number, forty were chosen to attend the eight-week session of rigorous training in the art of clowning. Twenty-one made it to "The Greatest Show on Earth." Somehow during his remarks, he stated what I thought to be one of the most important bits of wisdom he could possibly have put into words. While I can't quote him exactly, the essence of that statement was that the "Audience is the greatest teacher!" The response a clown receives from the audience is the measure of his effectiveness.

Susan and Jeff sat spellbound on one of the three rings set up within the Civic Center while Mr. Ballantine explained the arduous training prospective clowns undergo down in Florida during the winter weeks. The children were privileged to see and hear the most famous clown in America today—Lou Jacobs. Mr. Jacobs emphasized that being a clown, being a circus performer, is a round-the-clock job. Obviously the clowns have fun; but, as both Mr. Ballantine and Mr. Jacobs repeatedly told the group, clowning is work—hard work!

Mr. Ballantine told those present that clowning involved two very important words—confidence and cooperation. To perform together effectively, clowns (as well as all other circus performers, I'm sure) must have complete confidence in their co-showmen. And the entire family of 300, making up the circus, must live together in a cooperative manner, as one huge family. Discipline—rigid discipline—is a part of the training to insure that confidence and that cooperation. While people retain their individualities, they must, as Mr. Ballantine explained, accommodate themselves to the circus, not the circus to each individual. The total production is the one and only goal of the circus family.

The children (and, you bet, the adults, too) enjoyed watching the circus clowns instruct several young people in a few aspects of the art of clowning. And an art it truly is—one which involves, among other things, mimicry, a sense of the absurd, talent for sleight of hand, and a kind of explosive, surprising climax to an act . . .

SUSAN BETH AND JEFFREY were welcomed to the circus that evening by the "clown in charge," Frosty Little. Mr. Little was attired as a white-faced or a classic clown. A very pleasant man, Frosty ushered the children to the make-up area.

The make-up was applied by two real-for-sure clowns, Richard, "the human statue," and Richard, "the tall clown," the latter being something over six-foot-seven. These two young men treated the children most kindly, sensing that the whole experience was both delightful and a bit breathtaking for them. By the time the two Richards had completed their artistry, Susan appeared with a charming white-face, a cute red nose and a perfectly charming, perpetual smile. Just as pretty as a little girl clown could ever be! Jeff was made up as an August clown—the clown who is tricked, who bears the butt of the other fellow's joke.

Jeff had ruddy cheeks, exaggerated eyebrows, and an impish grin painted on his face. Each child wore a sparkling clown hat; Jeff, in addition, sported an enormous red bow tie; Susan wore a mass of ruffles for a neck piece.

They simply had to be nervous as Bobby Kay, a veteran performer, took them by the hand and led them around the Civic Center before the several thousands who had come to see the great show. Mr. Kay, it was very evident, has a winning way with little boys and girls, for he soon had Susan and Jeff walking with a not-so-timid bounce and waving, as he was waving, to the crowd. It was easy to see that the children were having the night of their lives!

Three times during the evening Mr. Kay took the children out into the big arena and helped them "clown." Jeff had been instructed briefly in working with magic rings, but before the big crowd, Mr. Kay and one of the other clowns saw that he needed some help—and they aided him. Susan's "magic-flower" burst into view on schedule, thanks to the kindly guidance of a fellow-clown.

When their "acts" were completed, Mr. Kay brought them to the seats nearby their parents. He presented them each with an autographed photograph of himself, chatted with them, and went back into the dressing area to prepare for his next entrance. Never once did he pass the children again that evening without a wave of the hand, a smile, or a pleasant, happy word.

Frosty Little and others who had been in touch with the children behind the scenes made certain that they, too, gave the youngsters a wink and a smile and a cheery wave. They had all taken the little girl and boy in as part of the circus family for the night.

THE FINAL ACT of the evening was over, and the crowd was leaving the Civic Center. Somehow, it had all seemed like a dream to us adults; I can only imagine what it had seemed to be for the grandchildren. This I do know: it was a night they will never forget. Neither will the adults, whose hearts beat a bit faster than usual when Sue Beth and Jeff—one on either side of Bobby Kay—began their first go-'round with the Ringling Bros. and Barnum & Bailey Circus clowns.

"The Greatest Show on Earth" will be in Philadelphia, starting Wednesday, May 30, and will remain there through Tuesday, June 5. The amazing wild animal acts, the daring of the acrobats and the aerialists, the hilarious performances of the chimps, the pageantry, the unbelievable "dancing in the air"—the entire breathtaking spectacle!

But, you know, you just can't afford to miss the antics of those clowns—some of them recent graduates of the College of Clowns and some of them veterans who have made the circus what it is today through their dedication to the art of making people of all ages laugh!

By the way, Mrs. Kreml told me that the ratio of attendance—adults-to-children—stands three-to-one, adults ahead! Who said circuses are for children?

I must add this: they're for grandfathers! Especially when a granddaughter and a grandson are walking right along with Bobby Kay, by George!

MAY 21, 1991

I'm Now A Great-Grandfather

It seems as though we homo sapiens are possessed by a compulsion to complain. The weather, for one thing. The price of groceries . . . or gasoline . . . or fish . . . whatever. And if there's nothing better to fuss about, we gripe about having recorded a number of years on our lifometer. Yes, we complain about getting older when it ought to be obvious that the alternative is pretty grim.

I was feeling some creaks in my joints the other day after having bent over to plant a few flowers. I blamed the twinges of pain on my age. Feeling sorry for myself, I guess. Then something happened.

The telephone rang. I moped my way across the room to lift the receiver. I recognized my grandson Jeffrey's voice immediately and whatever distress was bothering me disappeared.

I could tell by the tone of his voice that something exciting was in the air.

"Is this Grand-Dad-Dad?" he asked.

Then it dawned on me. The little fellow we'd been waiting for must have arrived.

"It's a boy!" Jeffrey exclaimed. "Nine pounds and 12 ounces."

By that time I was catching my breath. "What's his name?" I asked.

"Owen," Jeffrey said.

I inquired about Kathleen—and the first thing I knew I was talking to her. And Owen not more than an hour old! Jeff hadn't left the hospital yet.

Yes, sir! Every ache had left me and I even forgot I'm moving close to becoming an octogenarian. No, that's not right. What I did was to say a prayer of thankfulness for having been permitted to live long enough to have a great-grandchild. Needless to say, I wanted to get to see that boy as soon as possible.

I was so excited when I got Jeffrey's message that I was all but tongue-tied—which is a most unusual circumstance for me. I called later to confirm all that I had heard.

It wasn't until the next day that I learned Owen's middle name. George, by George! After Jeffrey's father and me. Great name!

Now, on Owen's fifth day I learned that Kathleen's parents, John and Marge Lenihan, of Long Island, wanted to stop in Zion on their way to see the baby and take me with them. I told 'em to come right ahead—I'd be ready to go! They came and I went with them.

You can bet that I was mighty careful when Jeffrey handed the baby over for me to hold. It had been some time since I had held an infant. But, as a friend of mine said, it's kind of like bicycling—once you've learned how, you never forget it. Within minutes I felt very comfortable with Owen and he seemed just as comfortable with me. We should get along just fine, thank you! (I've already obtained a couple of baby baseball suits. And his Grandmother Lenihan came up with an Oriole uniform in miniature for him.)

It was a quick trip down to Fredericksburg—down one afternoon and back the next, thanks to Jeff's willingness to get me home in time for the Rising Sun High School Alumni banquet. Funny thing! I haven't had pain one—nor do my joints creak like they did—not since Jeffrey gave me the good news. Wonderful, isn't it, what a bundle of joy can do for an old codger? Yes, a fellow has to learn, though, that he has to have a little age on him to become a great-grandfather.

I'm just sittin' here at this typewriter counting my most recent blessing. Can you blame me?

MAY 11, 1994

Meet Megan, Another 'Great'

She is just one week old, but she has already wound me around her little finger. Megan Elizabeth Lewis was born May 4, out in Seattle, Washington, where her mother and father have lived for the past several years. She weighed 10 pounds at birth and shows little evidence that she has lost any.

She joins her cousin, Owen, the fourth generation of Prettymans; Susan, Megan's mother, is my granddaughter.

Of course, Megan can't talk to me yet, but I did get to hear her when Susan called to tell me the three Lewises had returned home. I am told that she has light brown hair and light eye-lashes and bright blue eyes.

HER MOTHER SET my worst fears aside by telling me right off that the newest sweetheart in my life does not—and I emphasize this—does not have my ears. That is to say, her ears are normal, not outsized and outsticking. Praises be!

Then, on Sunday, I received a telephone call which brought with it a request the likes of which I'd never had put to me before. Kathleen, Owen's mother, wanted me to sing. Yes! Sing over the telephone. Now, for goodness sake, what singing voice I ever had has long since disappeared. The occasion, she said, called for a song—a Happy Birthday song to Owen.

The birthday party was taking place down in Ashland, Virginia—and here I was, sitting in my recliner up in the northeastern corner of Maryland. You could call this a kind of conference call.

SO, I CLEARED my throat and waited for the signal.

"We're lighting the candles on the cake," Kathleen told me. "Now!" she said.

And the folks down in Virginia broke into song and I lent a feeble voice to the celebration. Above all the others assembled, Owen's voice came through the loudest. When the song neared its end, I heard him belt out, "Happy birthday, dear Owen! Happy birthday to you!"—with background harmony from Kathleen, Jeffrey (his daddy), Grandparents Lenihan, of Long Island, N.Y., and Grandparents Prettyman, from near Columbia, Md. If there were other guests, I was not informed of their presence.

As my Elizabeth and I made our journey together in life—53 years, we walked together—we never thought about great-grandchildren. She died before Owen, for example, was even a twinkle in his daddy's eye—his daddy is our grandson, understand. And so it is that I am the great-grandparent representing the Prettyman branch of the family.

I'm making up, I hope, for all the love Elizabeth would be showering on Owen and Megan—plus a whole bunch of love from me, too. It goes without my saying it—even if I am doing just that—that the two youngsters would be shamefully spoiled were they around me day by day.

I'LL BE MAKING my way out to Seattle within the next few weeks and down to Ashland, too. Man, oh, man! There are multiple attractions in my life, you can count 'em, by George!

No wonder that wonderful old song "Blest Be the Tie that Binds" keeps running through my mind here of late. That 3-year-old Owen and newborn Megan, my two "greats," give me reason to travel with a song in my heart all the day long!

DECEMBER 27, 1972

A House To Delight Any Doll

It was a particularly delightful display insofar as I was concerned, for it concerned a subject in which I was not only interested, but also involved at the very moment.

There's a hobby shop down in the Columbia Mall which was featuring doll houses. Now, doll houses come in many shapes, sizes, and at all kinds of prices. Those on exhibition in the mall were not all for sale—not at any price. One which struck my fancy was just that—fancy! It was a replica of a doll house which had been in the Teddy Roosevelt family, probably before the turn of the century. Victorian in architectural design, everything—from appropriate and elaborate furniture to staircases beautifully done. Tiny electric-lighted chandeliers hung from the ceilings of several of the rooms. Oriental rugs had been placed over the floors. The draperies were in keeping with the period. If any detail of design or furnishing—including the placement of knickknacks—was left out, it escaped my attention.

Other doll houses were there to be seen along with the replica of the Roosevelt one. Some meticulous soul had spent hours creating postage-size shingles with which to cover the roof of a cottage-type one. And that, too, was completely furnished with miniature reproductions of tables, chairs, desks, kitchen necessities, stairways, and bathroom facilities.

I don't recall the exact number of the "very special" doll houses which were there. Enough, I remember, to set my imagination swirling—and to give me something of a sense of futility; for, you see, I had been working on a doll house for my granddaughter—as a surprise. And I knew I was not handy enough with tools to duplicate anything like the mansions I saw at the mall.

I am not, however, easily discouraged. I knew that I had something going for Susan Beth and I was determined to pursue the course to which I had set myself. I had already spent countless hours framing little windows and trimming them as neatly as I could. Ten shutters had been put in place. A front door had been carefully paneled, hinged, and made ready for hanging. I was not going to be put down by what I had seen—nor was I foolish enough to think I could measure up to a presidential doll house.

I enlisted some mighty fine help. First of all, my son and his wife—they had the idea in the first place, so I accepted their volunteer assistance in wallpaper selection and the application of same to the walls. Likewise, the floor coverings—some tile, some carpet. A friend, Carl Epstein, of Oxford, together with several relatives, aided in the accumulation of appropriate floor pieces.

Clifton Cook, of the Rising Sun area, (and he's a "real" builder of houses—a builder of "real" houses, I should have said) did the jig-saw work and pre-fab cutting of the large pieces of plywood which Frank Crane had delivered to our house. Mr. Cook carefully followed the "blue print" which my son and I had drawn up—from the bottom floor to the roof-top, including partitions.

My brother-in-law, Dick Touchton, saw that two hands simply couldn't be four places at once when it came to assembling the house, fitting in the molding, and completing the outside trim—so he devoted many hours of manual and mental exertion as my chief assistant. (He says I'm bossy and that he wouldn't relish being under my supervision, day in and day out; but he stuck with me!) And his brother, Howard, came along to lend both advice and a hand; he had already donated paint for the house.

My sister was infinitely more intrigued by finding miniature pictures, mirrors, and the like, to make the interior homey.

My wife was infinitely more interested in getting me off to bed before midnight every night for the past several weeks; she was delighted that I was "creating"—but she kept insisting that she wanted me to be around for Christmas, too—not just a doll house under the tree in recollection of a worn-out granddad!

Talk about "visions of sugar-plums" dancing in one's head! All I have seen these last several weeks has been visions of Susan Beth when she sees the doll house! Yes, I have lain awake "figuring" this and that about the little structure; so has Dick—he confessed that to me. But the primary picture in my mind's eye has been the look on Susan Beth's face when her doll house is presented to her.

This piece is being written before Christmas—in order to meet a deadline. I have to stop, now, to get that doll house absolutely completed before dawn of Christmas morning. That's the major deadline at the moment.

Oh—the dimensions: thirty-six inches across the front, excluding the chimney—which, by the way, was "bricked" by the

Rev. Lloyd Foard, our minister—eighteen inches deep, twenty inches to the attic floor, and about twenty-six inches to the peak of the roof. Color: white—with brick-red shutters. A small porch, of simulated flagstone, two pillars to support a small roof—and that's it! And you can bet Bob Benjamin and those in his warehouse will be glad when I stop dropping in for quarter-round, screen molding, corner molding, etc.

In case you think Jeffrey is being slighted, he isn't! His turn is coming—and will he ever be surprised. As a matter of fact, I'm already surprised—surprised at my own patience working with hand tools and surprised that the only disaster which befell me was that I stapled the palm of my hand one evening instead of the plastic "glass" in one of the front windows!

I'm leaving the furnishing of that seven-room house to grandmothers and parents, by George!

OCTOBER 5, 1966

Real Public Relations

Those who follow the stock market, even casually, have not found the past six months too rewarding, generally. Some particular issues have done well, but they have been the exception. We know some parents who thought they recognized a favorable time during the summer to purchase a small amount of Scott Paper stock for their young daughter's college fund.

After they made their purchase, Scott Paper dropped slightly in price. While the parents are convinced that their investment will be brought to fruition by the time their daughter is ready for higher education, patience is the theme now.

The young lady is old enough to know that she is saving money for college, but naturally it is difficult for the purpose to seem very real or immediate to her. A few weeks ago, Scott's annual report, addressed to her, arrived in the post office. (It had to be picked up since it was considerably larger than the rural mail box size.) Young ladies are always pleased to receive mail addressed personally to them—birthday cards, magazines, toys from cereal companies, etc. You wouldn't think at first that a large box from Scott Paper would be very exciting to her, but nothing could be farther from the fact in this case.

Along with the annual report the carton contained attractive, full-sized packages of about a dozen of the company's newest products—placemats, plastic drinking cups, plastic sandwich bags, paper towels, etc. The emphasis was on the new line and the "color explosion."

For the next several days, our little friend carefully issued HER yellow placemats and HER blue-and-pink drinking cups to the family. Her brother, who at two-and-a-half can be excused for being a sometimes sloppy eater, was told if he messed up one more mat he would be excluded from the next careful rationing!

Our junior stockholder still keeps a watchful eye as her mother uses sandwich bags and volunteers some additional uses.

Obviously, the only tangible evidence of her minority holdings has made a considerable impression on her.

"Some people would say, "a cat is a cat, and that's that!" Not so with Sebastian. He thought he was a people."

—G.B.P.

Pets

MARCH 31, 1971

My Dog

He wasn't a thoroughbred. His canine parents were not champions. He had no pedigree. He was just "my dog." The other day my sister and I were sorting through some old family photographs and we came across a picture of my dog—the only dog I ever had or needed. You see, he came to me as a tiny puppy and remained with us for more than 15 years; he saw me through late childhood, adolescence, and young manhood.

When my preacher-father and my mother lived down in Somerset County, we frequently visited Princess Anne. We came to recognize and casually know a man by the name of Karl Austin—a man who had no use of his legs and who got around by pony cart and a wheel chair. When we moved up to Zion, in Cecil County, in 1923, we were surprised and pleased to find our friend, Mr. Austin, and his wife and daughter and his grandmother residing in our new home village.

Mr. Austin raised Airedales. How productive, financially, his venture was, I cannot say. But I do know that mongrels were of little value to him. The Austins moved over to Spready Oak—west of Rising Sun—and we visited them with some frequency.

One day this little brown and white puppy was at the Austin home when we arrived. He was just about big enough to fit in my jacket pocket. He had a collie-shaped head and a bulldog shaped body—but his tail wagged and his tongue licked—and I loved him! Mr. Austin offered him to me if my parents would O.K. the transfer—no fees attached! (Fees—not fleas, I said.)

He was given no exotic name—simply Rover. He grew to be about the size of a long-legged rabbit dog.

His first night in Zion was disastrous. He was put outside in a box in an out-building; and he let the entire village know how displeased he was not to be with people. Old Doc Gifford let us know how displeased he was that our puppy kept him awake all night! My mother hadn't wanted a house dog; but she eventually had one. Rover became an inhabitant of the parsonage.

HE KNEW HIS BOUNDS. His place was in the kitchen. But, you know, he somehow sensed every illness I ever had while he was with us and whined and fussed to get up into my bedroom whenever I was sick. And Mom was wise enough to know that a boy and his dog belonged together.

Rover would leap upon my bed, snuggle close beside me, give my hand a quick lick, and press his chin against my hand or my knee. Next to Mom and the doctor, he was the greatest!

I think every little boy deserves his very own dog. Dogs sometimes listen to little boys and understand them better than adults do.

MARCH 22, 1995

Sebastian Long Ago Adopted Me As His Own

Carl Sandburg, in one of his famous poems, practically immortalized cats. He was writing about fog, and he likened the creeping of the fog to the stealthy stalking of a cat. Right this minute I cannot correctly quote the lines; but the thing here is, I want you to note that a great poet recognized that a cat was worth inserting into one of his masterpieces.

Now, I don't pretend to compose masterpieces. I just peck away on this instrument called a computer and sort of let what comes out, come out. And when I'm hard up for something to tap out, I more or less day dream, staring blankly at nothing in particular. If George Eliot were to see me staring—of course she can't because she's been long gone—but if she could see me, she probably would say I was having a cataleptic fit, like good old Silas Marner. Not so. Just staring. No pot of gold hidden beneath any of my boards, either.

I AM BROUGHT to my senses by my feline friend, Sebastian. Full name registered down at Davidson College, North Carolina, before he came to live with us: Johann Sebastian Bach Prettyman. Owner: Susan Beth Prettyman, freshman then attending Davidson (now, 15 years later, Mrs. Kenneth B. Lewis Jr., of Seattle). Reason for Sebastian's being in Zion: the top administrator at Davidson decided that cats and dogs did not belong in the dormitories along with homo sapiens—that word includes both regularly recognized sexes—and thus it was that Sebastian, along with numerous felines and canines, was summarily banished from the campus. Within a very short time he was introduced into our household as a college dropout and immediately took command. Cats tend to do that. So much for background . . .

Back to my staring. Sebastian comes tearing into the room, puts on his brakes long enough to set himself for a jarring jump into my lap. I gasp and awaken from my day-dreaming.

"That's it!" I say to myself. I'll write about the cat. If Carl Sandburg can insert a cat into one of his poems, then I can insert my cat into one of my columns (albeit I have inserted him in my pieces myself on several occasions).

SEBASTIAN GROWS more possessive with each passing day. Here of late he has taken to monitoring my perusal of the morning papers. Unless I am quick enough to pick the newspapers from the table after having divested myself of my jacket, the cat sits upon them and dares me to move him. Even harsh words do not shove him aside. I must physically lift him from atop the papers and plunk him rather firmly down on the rug which covers his part of the table. He then sniffs my hands, the papers, and starts worming himself between me and the paper I am attempting to read. He has been known to slap at the paper with sufficient force to knock it out of my hands and then hastily plant himself on it. I have concluded he is jealous of whatever I am paying attention to if it leaves him out. (Not a lot different from people, I'd say.) Sebastian spends his nights in our basement where a hundred or so of my less-frequently-read books are kept. Among them are some of the tales Grandmom Clendaniel gave me when I was a kitten—I mean, a little boy—and I often wonder if he has or has not sneaked a peep about Tum-Tum, the Jolly Elephant, or Jimmy Rabbit, or Muley Cow while I've been sleeping and has come to the conclusion that there ought to be something written about him. Maybe he has the urge to create a piece of literature all by himself. (That's about all he could create, and I think you can understand why. That happens to cute little male cats these days. Better'n having to drown a bunch of kittens.)

Here and now he has done it! He has come racing into our den, slammed himself into my lap, and is staring at the screen of my computer!

Not satisfied to be looking on, he is now putting out his right paw and is about to tap one of the keys. Wham! He really slapped it! Not once, but two or three times. I have no idea what the letters he brought up on the screen mean. Evidently he doesn't either, for he has stopped pawing and has curled up in my lap, tucked his tail around himself, and has started to serenade me with his purring.

FRANKLY, life would be pretty dull without Sebastian. He is a long-haired mix, with Maine Coon Cat the predominant strain: black-brown fur, white vest and apron, and a pinkish nose. Tremendous whiskers, too. And the roughest little red tongue which he occasionally uses to anoint my hand with his blessing.

Hide-and-seek is a game he dearly loves to play. He darts from behind chairs in the living room, hides behind the electric organ or secretary or davenport and peeps out with those bright eyes of his and looks as though he's grinning from ear to ear!

He is one wild romper when he thinks it's playtime. Like the time he disconnected two living room lamps and I foolishly called Mickey McDowell from Bay View to see why the lamps wouldn't light!

Well, it's time for bed. He's knocking at the cellar door. I kid you not! He is rattling the door with his paw and looking at me as if to say, "Get with it, George, old boy! It's bedtime and I have some dreamin' to do." Ah! Life with Sebastian! Purr-fect!

MARCH 13,1996

The Cat Pays A Price To Defend His Turf

He will be 16 his next birthday. I do not know the date. All I know is that he was a kitten 16 years ago. He sometimes behaves a bit kittenish, but most of the time he imitates me. Acts ready for feline social security.

Because the thing we call "territorial imperative" remains a part of his psyche, he becomes feisty whenever another cat or a dog trespasses on our property.

A week or so ago I let him out for a prowl before we settled in for the night. He came to the door when I called him and headed for the basement right away—the regular routine he and I had adopted long ago.

The next morning when I was fixing tuna fish in his bowl, I noticed he had a bloody ear. Upon closer examination, I discovered a cut above his right eye, too. He didn't seem too interested in eating his breakfast and wanted to get to the outside step.

I OPENED THE DOOR to let him out and it was then that I saw matted animal hair scattered on the winterized grass not far from the back walk. It was obvious that fur had really been flying there. As I recall, cat fights are rather noisy affairs.

Since my auditory receptors are grossly impaired, I had failed to hear the rumpus; otherwise I would have attempted to throw in the towel before Sebastian got beaten up around his ear and on the side of his face.

I tried to clean him up, but he resisted. His own efforts had led to increased bleeding. Left to his own resources, he eventually did the job pretty well, however. The bleeding stopped, the hair around his wounds was tidied up, and he curled up in a ball and sacked out for several hours.

While it looks as though he'll be bald where his opponent slashed him, I have the feeling he'll come out of the ordeal well healed. I haven't had any calls from neighbors blaming Sebastian for roughing up a neighborhood cat.

It is entirely possible that Sebastian was unable to inflict punishment upon the intruder. At his age, I doubt that he has the strength to fight with any authority.

About 10 years ago he came in one night missing a bit of one ear. Other than that, he has, indeed, been the monarch of our yard. Until this time, that is. I have seen him out-stare large dogs and cats of all sizes and colors so that they have turned away.

I HAVE HEARD THE HOWLS and yowls and raked up residual fur, all evidence that a war had gone on—and Sebastian has walked in unbloodied. Not this time, though. One fight too many.

I don't know what his injuries have done to his self-esteem. I have an idea it'll be a few days before he raises his bushy tail in the wind as he walks across the lawn on his way to the field where mice are.

SEPTEMBER 13, 1988

Here's To The Ball of Fuzz

I have no right to call Dobbin a fuddy-duddy. I do not even know him. It's that I don't agree with his attitude toward cats. This is what he said in a sort of poetic tirade against feline creatures:

Confound cats! All cats –alway–
Cats of all colors, black, white, gray;
By night a nuisance and by day–
Confound the cats!

I have no idea what touched off Dobbin's outrage. Maybe he stepped on pussy's tail and received a retaliatory bite on the ankle. Whatever, it seems to me that he let out with an unnecessarily all-inclusive and prejudicial condemnation. A thoughtless generalization. And like Dobbin, a great many people are guilty of such thoughtlessness; we tend to become vituperative when discussing members of the human race who happen to be different from ourselves in thought and behavior. Never do we see ourselves more intemperate in our verbal outbursts than during an election year. It is one thing to rail against cats and quite another to engage in character assassination. Most cats could care less about the Dobbins in their lives, but people harbor hurts and hatreds.

But I didn't start out to get into politics. This column was, when I started pushing the keys on my typewriting machine, to be about cats. I do not share Dobbin's dislike for cats. I have considerable affection for our Sebastian. And he for me.

Yes, it's true, Sebastian can become a nuisance at night—now and then, that is. Most of the time he is a model of feline decorum: he comes in from his meanderings at his habitual time, say 10 o'clock, and is ready for his evening snack and goodnight pat before descending the basement steps for the night. But on certain nights, like when the moon is full, he goes a-wandering in search of feline companionship. Or so it sounds. About 11:30 or so, if he hasn't returned, I pick up my flashlight and go in search of him. On occasion I have been known to get into my pajamas before trying to find him. No doubt passersby would think I have lost my senses, for I keep up a running, one-sided conversation in hopes I can persuade him to call it a night and let both of us get some rest. Many a night I have been startled as the cat makes a dash toward me, taps my leg with his paw, and rushes off to hide under some piece of shrubbery. That is the clue to tell me a game of hide-and-seek has begun—he the hider and I the seeker. About three dashes and three bushes later, we wind up on the back doorstep and he is ready and eager to terminate activity for another day.

A nuisance sometimes, yes, as I have indicated. But a fun-creature, to be sure. And don't we all need some sort of variation from the games we human beings try on one another? Sebastian never holds a grudge. He may tease, but for him it's all in fun. The figure-eights he performs around my feet, the rough little licks he gives my hand with his tongue, the purr-fect noises he makes when I scratch his chin, these things let me know he has adopted me as his friend. And he knows I will do his bidding most of the time.

I won't say, "Hurrah for cats! All cats—alway!" I can only speak for Sebastian and a few other cats I have known, such as Mr. Red, Toughie (pronounced Tuffy), Pasha—oh, numerous cats I have known in my time. By the way, the late Milburn Stone was a cat fancier and his widow likes cats just as much as he did and I do. No, I won't make a generalization in praise of all cats. Just those which seem to be people-loving, like our Sebastian. He's a ball of fun, by George!

APRIL 9, 1991

Of Plumbing Leaks And Kittens

One day about two weeks ago, I noticed a wet spot on my kitchen floor. I wiped it up and said to myself, that's that. (When you're all by yourself, you tend to have a conversation with yourself now and then.) A few minutes later, I thought I saw the same wet spot all over again. I did and it got wiped up just as the first one had. Some minutes later, same thing, same place. That prompted me to scratch my head.

For whatever reason, I glanced at the ceiling light and discovered that it was dripping. I hustled upstairs to the bathroom to check faucets, etc. Oh, indeed, yes, there was a leak in the hot water pipe under the cabinet. Not a gushing leak, but a slow, oozing one. Enough to create a problem I didn't want or need. But I had it just the same. There are times in life when there's more of what you don't want than what you do. This was one of those times.

Among the many things I am not, a plumber is high on that list. The last time I tackled a plumbing problem, water flowed from the sink to the ceiling and we had a miniature flood. In remembrance of that soggy event, I hastened to call the plumber; he came and soon had my water situation under total control. No flood.

In due course of time I received the statement from the plumbing people together with an interesting pamphlet entitled "Have a Good Day!"

The lead story in that pamphlet concerned kittens that had been overcome by smoke during a house fire. A hazardous-response specialist administered CPR to the stricken kittens, gave them whiffs of oxygen by turns, and the kittens were given back one of their nine lives.

(There was more to that story but I'm stopping at this point because the rescue of the kittens somewhat paralleled an experience I once had—though I'm in no way setting myself up as a hero. Please understand that.)

About 50 years ago, I arrived home, following the completion of my teaching day, to find a mother cat with a litter of kittens strewn out on the stone-cold floor of the porch. The mother cat was one of our little boy's two pet cats. She had tried in vain to bring her little family into the world in Elizabeth's washing machine that morning, but that wasn't the sort of thing Elizabeth cottoned to, so we had put the cat out, thinking she would find a suitable spot in the woodshed or garage for her little ones. But there they were, lying cold and stiff on that concrete porch floor.

Elizabeth and George B. had gone over to Pleasant Hill for the day and hadn't returned yet, so I hurried to get the dead kittens—I thought they were dead—out of sight before the boy saw them. When I picked one of them up, I felt a slight quiver of life. Whoops! I thought: I can't dispose of these if they're still alive. I scooped 'em up, took 'em into the house, and scratched my head. (I do that when I'm perplexed.)

There were four very tiny inert kittens. What to do with them? I spotted a quart-size strawberry box, got a wad of dust cloths from the closet, put the kittens in the box with the cloths, lit the oven of the kerosene range, and said a prayer as I carefully placed the box full of kittens into the oven.

It wasn't long before I heard faint mewing. I opened the oven door and, bless me, there were four squirming, rather ratty-looking kittens!

A CARDBOARD BOX, lined with more of Elizabeth's cleaning cloths, seemed like a good bed for the feline family. But, no, the mother would have nothing to do with her offspring. I put her in the box, she hopped out.

We repeated that scenario several times. Finally, I grabbed her by the head and rubbed her nose over the kittens—or on them. I was a bit rough, I know. But she got the message; the kittens were alive and wiggling and ready for a meal.

She broke into purring, settled down in the box, and pretty soon there wasn't a sound coming from that bed of warm and furry felines.

That added up to six cats in our household—a circumstance that had to be corrected some weeks later when it became a bit crowded underfoot in our house.

The kittens were cute and we had no trouble wishing them off on other folks. The mother cat and her big brother continued to be our boy's nap mates—one against his stomach and the other at his back . . .

I'm glad I rubbed that nose on those tiny fur balls. I'd do it all over again if I could turn back time, by George!

JULY 17, 1996

Rambling Recollections Of A Boy And Cat

The lady says, "Write some more about the cat!" Well, I appreciated the suggestion and the nice smile that came with it, but I don't want to run Sebastian into the ground, so to speak. Nor literally, either; he's been around this house too long to do that to 'im.

Anyway, there's only so much I can say about that independent rascal, and I'm afraid I've already said it. He's enjoying some summer prowling, though he prowls mighty slowly here of late. (I don't prowl; I've slowed down, too.)

My little next-door neighbor, Macaulay Kinnamon, had several kittens bequeathed to him by Mamma Cat who adopted the Kinnamons a few weeks ago. The baby felines were deposited beneath the front porch of the house. They have grown to, say, a bit past "catinfancy" and may now be seen romping about on the grass most any hour of the day.

NOT A SINGLE ONE of those kittens bears the slightest resemblance to Sebastian and I doubt that he will be the defendant in a paternity suit. As a matter of fact, I don't think he's in any condition to become paternal.

Speaking of Macaulay, he recently had his second-year birthday party. A number of his relatives, friends and pseudo-relatives, including my sister, Julia, and me, attended. He is one precious little fellow.

Macaulay likes my cat and Sebastian seems to like Macaulay. Macaulay doesn't pull Sebastian's tail and Sebastian doesn't bite Macaulay's hand. They have a pretty good relationship going I'd say. As soon as Macaulay enters our house, he searches for the cat which is, invariably, napping. He approaches the napping cat, lightly pats him on the head; the cat opens his eyes, looks sleepily at the boy, then goes back to sleep.

Macaulay hasn't tried to pronounce the cat's name. He simply smiles broadly and says, "Kitt-ee!" If Sebastian happens to be outdoors, lying in the grass or under the shady edge of a bush, Macaulay stoops down and makes an attempt at petting, but the cat, not contained within a room, doesn't lie still; he's inclined to move away—even set out across the back yard. When he's a captive cat, however—fenced in—he's dopedly docile towards his young friend.

MACAULAY IS A FASCINATING NAME, I think. Of course, it takes no great stroke of association to think of another Macaulay—Lord Macaulay. Thomas Babington Macaulay, if you want his fully name. Lord Macaulay was a man of remarkable literary talents, though, insofar as most of us are concerned, his talents have gone relatively unnoticed here of late.

"He was of Scotch descent," so biographer John Lord said in Volume XIII of "Beacon Lights of History," a set of books I reserved for myself from my father's library. He was a precocious youngster, lying on a carpet reading at the age of 3. Lord Macaulay ranks as one of the all-time great English writers of the 19th Century. One of his most famous lines reads, "The Puritans hated bear-baiting, not because it gave pain to the bear, but because it gave pleasure to the spectator."

Oh! I'd better work this in. At about the age of 25, he wrote a piece about John Milton which won him fame. Fame translated itself into a meal ticket, literally. That is to say, he seldom went hungry. He was, from that point on, frequently invited to dinner by the most highly distinguished British families of his time. A gustatorial dividend!

If you want more on Lord Macaulay, I'm sure our county librarians will be glad to lead you to the proper sources of information.

How did I let my train of thought jump tracks today? Well, to tell the truth, I was listening to the news a few minutes ago and there was something on about somebody trying to have conversations with the deceased and I got to thinking of long-gone authors whom I would like to interview if I could only reach 'em somehow. You see, I could use a lot of help. Lord Macaulay—his name, that is—just popped into my head because of my association with my little neighbor next-door who is precocious, too, and who is also of Scottish descent.

TRAVIS, MACAULAY'S FATHER, has admonished me that *Scotch* is an alcoholic drink, a person is a *Scot*, and I forget what he said I was doing wrong with those words. Travis is proud of his ancestry, but neither he nor Wendy, his wife, has shown up here in Zion in kilts.

I looked in the dictionary and learned a lot about one little word and its variations. Without a capital letter, *scotch* has the connotation of thwarting, of stamping out. Like, for instance, "The closer came in from the bull pen and *scotched* my team's rally." Or, to illustrate another meaning, "To keep the piano from rolling off the slanted stage, we *scotched* its likely descent—we blocked it with a chock!"

Next time I go to a restaurant I think I'll order a *Scotch woodcock*. That is, to say, if Webster ain't kidding, "Buttered toast spread with anchovy paste and scrambled egg." How about that?

Oh, boy! This has gone far enough! Just think of little Macaulay Kinnamon as my neighbor, my tiny friend, who is acquiring knowledge at a rapid rate and who likes to pet my cat.

Man! I *have* rambled this week, by George! Could be accumulated summer heat.

MAY 18, 1966

Taking A Walk

I have never been an inveterate taker of walks; usually I think I have so many other things to do that I don't get around to setting out for a stroll. But there are circumstances which alter one's habits. Such a circumstance came up—and I've been walking some here of late.

Our grandchildren have a large dog—black and white, long-haired, and basically of the Springer Spaniel breed, though I suspect some St. Bernard strain became a part of his heritage.

Anyway, he's big and strong, and very affectionate—and can, if he's so minded, upset me, literally, by one big bounce or tug.

Nappie—that's his name—used to visit us when he was a puppy; that was before either of the grandchildren came along. He remained behind in Port Deposit while his folks did their two-year tour of duty in Germany. Susan Beth was all set to meet him upon her return to the States because her parents had made Nappie as much of a reality to her prior to her return as one can possibly do. Nappie fell in love with her—and it was mutual. No matter how rambunctious he might seem to adults, he is as docile as can be with Susan Beth—and immediately took Jeffrey under his huge paw when the little fellow was admitted into the family two years ago. Jeffrey did not—nor does he yet—always enjoy Nappie's affectionate nuzzling; but he does enjoy sitting on Nappie and patting him.

Poor Nappie became sick and required medication. In fact, he was so sick that he couldn't stand the long ride back to Howard County last week, so Nappie has been our house guest for a week—a sort of vacation for him while he undergoes medical treatment.

I have found myself completely absorbed in the business of helping the dog recuperate—and a part of the planned program for him has been a long walk every evening—both on and off the chain. Naturally, he enjoys our outings most of all when I unsnap the chain and let him romp uninhibited across the fields outside of Zion.

Dogs native to Zion look upon Nappie as an interloper—they bark with vigor at him, growl, and generally raise a rumpus. Nappie looks at them with a somewhat unconcerned, haughty air—and goes back to lapping his water or chewing on a bone. (Gnawing would have been a better word choice, I suppose.)

Nappie is not a talking dog. He tries hard, but words won't come out. Each morning he greets me with a long commentary, done in guttural sounds and little yips which seem entirely out of character with his bodily proportions. If I pay him no heed, he breaks into a healthy bark and let's me know he wants some head-rubbing and then begs to have his paw held. I am not accustomed to holding paws, but I am learning. The lick of gratitude on the back of the hand is the only overt reward I receive from Nappie; but that is enough to let me understand he has accepted me as his "granddad," too.

It is going to seem strange when the time comes for Nappie to hop into the Volkswagen, curl up on the back seat along side of Susan Beth, and head for home. I will not have a dog to whom I can give some of Dr. Rigler's get-well pills.

There will be little need for me to hustle into some old clothes and start out across the fields—not without Nappie. But he will be back where his little mistress and master can deluge him with their sincere affection—and he won't have to be tied up all the time, either.

Years ago, when I was just a few years older than Susan Beth, I had a dog—one that lived long enough to see me become a man, marry, and move away from home to start my own family. It would be fun if Nappie could stay just like he is all through the childhood of the little folks who love him so!

Not long ago, Susan Beth and Jeffrey had their "vacation"—a week in Zion with us, unhampered by any other than grandparental restrictions. Now Nappie has had his visit, too.

Boy, this being a grandfather has its dividends!

NOVEMBER 1, 1995

Kids 'N' Cats Can Make One A Prevaricator

Children and domesticated animals can make prevaricators out of unsuspecting and scrupulously truthful adults.

My mother-in-law, the late Mrs. Anna C. Thompson (her real name was Annie), often told of the time their little boy did just that. It runs within my memory that the late Joe Grant—at the time of the incident a house painter, later a mortician down in North East way was eating dinner at the Thompson home near Pleasant Hill.

Grandmom Thompson—as I called her, because that's how our son addressed her—had prepared a chicken dinner, and her chicken dinners were most delectable.

At the start of the meal, Mr. Grant suggested that Leon, then a little pre-school youngster, be served first—so he could have his favorite piece of chicken. Grandmom hastily told him that Leon never ate chicken.

"He doesn't like it," she said, explaining that Leon always shied away from fowl. "You just help yourself, Mr. Grant."

Whereupon Leon suddenly dove in and promptly devoured a couple of pieces of that bird, right then and there! Leon still remembers—says he ate almost all the chicken that day. Joe Grant never forgot it. Neither did Mrs. Thompson; she was mightily embarrassed.

Many years later, when I interviewed him in preparation for a special that ran in *The Cecil Democrat* when the late Clark Samuel was the editor, Mr. Grant recalled that incident. (By the way, that interview had to do with the spread Clark and I put together about veterans of World War I, and Joe Grant was one of the Cecil County veterans featured in the issue.)

Leon, my brother-in-law, still likes chicken! He acquired a taste for it that day when Painter Grant was invited to the Thompson table.

A couple of weeks ago I commented that my cat never jumps on the kitchen table anymore. That he is no longer able to make the leap. I had lamented for several months his having slowed down in so many ways—like no longer chasing wandering cats or dogs from our premises.

And when I call him for supper, he adopts a snail's pace instead of rushing to see how much tuna fish I have laid out for him. That translates into a ripe old age, cat-wise. Going on 16, he is.

Anyway, he's old and I was certain he was past jumping up on the stool and then stepping on to the table where the sun shines through the window pane much of the afternoon. He acquired

Sebastian
Sebastian departed this world on March 5, 1997,
at the ripe old age of 16 years.

that habit when he was a kitten and I've never seriously tried to break him of it.

I have kept a rug on the table just for him to nap on and that table has had more scrubbings than I can count when it comes time for me to eat. (He's a clean cat, so don't turn your nose up.)

The very day I said in my column that he no longer is able to jump, by golly, he jumped! And, by George, he has kept on napping on his corner of the table ever since! He's in a rejuvenation cycle, I guess. I wish I were.

So it is that my cat has made a liar out of me.

"Baseball connects American males with each other, not only through bleacher friendships and neightbor loyalties... but, most importantly, through generations."

—Donald Hall

At The Old Ball Game

MAY 3, 1988

A Great Baseball Trip To Philly In '29, By George!

You'd think I would remember the exact score of the first big-league baseball game I saw. Yes, you'd think I most certainly would. All I remember is that the Philadelphia Athletics beat my Yankees by one run; Lefty Grove came on in relief late in the game and just blew the ball right past my beloved Bronx Bombers. He could do that!

It happened in 1929, the year that Connie Mack's last great team was in its first of three consecutive years of beating up on the seven other American League clubs. Dell Foxx's uncle, James Emory Foxx, was demonstrating his prowess by hitting 33 home runs that year—up from 13, his total in 1928. In batting practice that day in August, he drove several balls over or off of the left field rooftop and his teammate Al Simmons did the same thing. My eyes really popped at the display of power.

Mr. George E. Gifford, my father and I had gone as far as Wilmington by automobile that day; there we boarded a Wilson Line steamer, bound for Philadelphia. Once in the City of Brotherly Love we rode the trolleys here and there, sight-seeing a little. My mind was on getting to Shibe Park in time for the afternoon game. I recall only one incident stemming from our trolley-tour of the city—and that was embarrassing.

We visited the famed Wanamaker Store just around noon in order to hear the organ concert. As we were about to leave, my father and I hustled along, trying to locate the rest rooms. We were not illiterate, but we were mighty careless in our reading. We barged in where wise men pause to get the signs right! We were in the ladies' room before we knew it—and we knew it when we heard a squeal and a couple of shrieks! It's a wonder we didn't knock each other down during our retreat. Mr. Gifford was standing outside the forbidden room laughing at us.

Shortly after we arrived at the ticket window at the ball park, a taxi pulled up and out stepped Babe Ruth. I was no more than five or six feet from the smiling Babe as he made his way to the players' entrance. That made my day! But the Babe didn't play that day. He had scuffed a finger a day or so before and the Yankee management was taking no chances of further damage until that scuff was healed. He did take batting practice and lofted one over the green fence in right field.

Before dawn that eventful day, a thunder storm broke over Philadelphia. I had been told that an early-morning storm usually indicated that another would follow later in the day. It did. And the game was delayed for an hour or so. When play was resumed, Lefty Grove toed the mound and the Yanks went down before his blazing fast ball.

That day I saw more future Hall-of-Fame players in action than I ever dreamed of seeing. Both teams were laden with some of the greatest stars the game has produced. The Athletics and the Yankees had the market just about cornered on talent back then. You could say that those men were truly "the glory of their times." Yes, by George, they were! Jimmy Foxx, Al Simmons, Mose Grove, Mickey Cochrane, Babe Ruth, Lou Gehrig, Lefty Gomez, Bill Dickey—just to name a few. (Well, now, I've got that out of my system.)

SEPTEMBER 21, 1966

Stand Up And Cheer!

When the almost legendary Lou Gehrig was in his prime, my dad and I, in company with a couple of other people, drove up to what was then Shibe Park to see the Athletics and the Yankees play. It was in 1936—two years before the great Gehrig was stricken with his fatal illness; he could still wield a mighty powerful bat—and he demonstrated that ability on the day we were there.

We were seated among hordes of Athletic fans who were extremely vocal in their distaste for the Yankees. Lou Gehrig came to bat at some point in the game with the bases loaded with Yankee runners.

My father was not a retiring sort of person, and he was most enthusiastic in his love for the New Yorkers—an attitude he had picked up from me. (In this case, like son, like father!) Pop stood up and called loudly for Gehrig to "Knock it out of here!" Fans all around us yelled, "Sit down and shut up!" to my father—and I could have crawled right under the seat, I was that embarrassed.

Gehrig didn't wait long to answer my father's plea. He sent a screamer right out over the old rightfield wall—a long, hard drive which rocked the Athletics for four big runs!

The fans who had blasted my dad were pretty silent and glum. Pop stood up, cheered as happily as a school boy, then turned to his tormentors and, making an impish face, said, "Yah, yah, yah!" (Much like the same sound which popularized the Beatles, I'd say.)

He wasn't afraid to stand up and cheer, believe me! No, not much ministerial dignity shown there—but who wants to be dignified at a baseball game? (The Yanks won that day—and DiMaggio moved from right to center for Marse Joe McCarthy during the course of that game—and stayed there for many years.)

OCTOBER 9, 1996

Old Yankee Stadium Revisited

It was 40 years ago. Monday, October 8, 1956. I was in the Aberdeen High School until about 4 in the afternoon, attending my duties as vice-principal.

I knew all along that the World Series was going on up in the Bronx. My beloved Yankees were taking on the Dodgers in the fifth game of that Series. I was more than a little annoyed that duty had prevented me from turning on the radio to listen to even one inning of the game.

As soon as I could leave the school, I headed toward White Hall where I was to speak that evening at a church service. I turned on my car radio, hoping to catch the final innings. Instead of the Gillette jingle that came on between innings back then, I was getting nothing but popular music. Then the news came on.

THE ANNOUNCER began with the comment that Don Larsen could probably be elected president if he chose to run. That's a strange piece of information, I thought. Then he gave the reason: Larsen had pitched a perfect game!

Not a single Brooklyn Dodger had reached first base! Mickey had hit a home run and had also made a great running catch in right-center field to rob Gil Hodges of an extra-base hit. The Yankees had won, 2-0. Larsen was well-known to my son and me since we had seen him pitch for the Orioles in 1954, the first year Baltimore was in the American League.

When I heard that, I pulled over into a vacant church parking lot somewhere north of Jarrettsville, stopped the car, and let out a yell that rivaled anything Tarzan ever managed. I was ecstatic!

You see, my son had been right there! He was my official emissary to New York that day. Both of us had seen our first World Series game in person the Saturday before. Whitey Ford had outpitched Roger Craig and Enos Slaughter had homered for the Yankees.

I'm pretty certain that whatever message I gave that evening at church was somewhat diluted, spiritually, for my thoughts were with my boy. (I understand that confession is good for a fellow's soul, so there you are.) And I knew he would detail each and every play for me, for he was—and still is—a meticulous scorekeeper.

As I opened the kitchen door when I reached home, he was right there, waiting for me. He greeted me with a monstrous hug. I can feel it yet. He lifted me right off the floor! He was one mighty happy 17-year-old young man.

BUT WOULD YOU BELIEVE IT? He had not kept score at all that day! He has often said that was the only game he could remember not having kept score. He had chosen not to stay in his seat in the last row of the lower deck, but had roamed the first base and right field grandstand.

He still recalls a Dodger line drive that curved just foul and that Casey Stengel had a right-hander and left-hander throwing hard in the bullpen the last two innings in case Larsen lost his Midas touch. And that perfect game was, he says, his greatest sports thrill. (The Yankees eventually won in seven games in the last World Series played entirely in one city.)

I often think about all the times George and I went up to New York to attend World Series games. Usually, we'd board the train in Wilmington, arrive at Penn Station, catch the subway to the Bronx, watch the game, then hustle back to the station in time to get a table in the dining car. Our World Series tickets came through the good offices of the Yankees and the Foster Brothers, Elwood and Fred.

When George was a little tot, I tried to emulate my dad by putting my son in my coat pocket, as it were, just as my father had done with me, and taking him to the Civil War battlefield at Gettysburg, or Valley Forge or the Franklin Institute—wherever my school trips would take me.

AS TIME PASSED, we both grew older—he to manhood and I right through middle-age to the graying stage. And the October venue for baseball became Memorial Stadium. We saw some

My son, George, with me in Cleveland
Summer 1989

Oriole victories and a few defeats there together. Plus a cold, damp Phillies night game with Toronto three years ago. Now in the summer, it is he who finds room in his coat pocket for me. He takes me to Veterans' Stadium in Philadelphia, drops me off close to the press entrance, and when the game is over, he drives the car to a place not far from the stadium so I won't have too far to walk. When we go to Oriole Park, he makes certain I'm well fed.

The last time he and I were in Yankee Stadium, he had arranged with the club for me to sit in the press box and to have pre-game access to the Yankee dugout. That was fine. But, to tell the truth, I would rather have sat with him, as we had done back in 1960 when he had planned a three-game visit in June for the two of us to watch Mickey Mantle, Roger Maris, and the other sluggers take over first place.

They would go on to win yet another pennant. He had saved his ROTC money during his junior year at Delaware for that special Father's Day present.

The famous psychologist Erik Erikson called it the "life cycle." Whatever you choose to call it, it means one of us is an old man who needs a bit of caring and receives an abundance of it, by George!

APRIL 17, 1996

More Diamond Lore In The Arizona Sun

Yes, back to elderhosteling out in Arizona . . . Dave Fitzsimmons, the once-upon-a-time catcher and batting practice pitcher for Darmouth, under Coach Bob Shawkey (once-upon-a-time New York Yankee pitching great and successor to Miller Huggins as Yankee manager), kept us leaning forward, as I said last week, as he gave us insights into various aspects of the game. A brilliant raconteur, that man.

He took us through the history of baseball, from its probable beginning as a variation of cricket and rounders in our country's early years to the present day. Skilled in the use of videos, Dave selected excerpts of the Burns tapes to illustrate his five-part course.

He discussed the monetary side of the game—players' salaries from the beginning of what he termed "avowed professional baseball" and management's side of that issue.

HE TOOK US TO THE EARLY DAYS of the famous "reserve clause" and told us how players sought over the years to negate it. He talked about fan loyalty to teams today and to individual players, now that franchise moves and free agency have combined to change team rosters and league divisions.

He told us about some of the heroes of the diamond: Honus Wagner, Pittsburgh's great shortstop, whom many still hail as the greatest player of all time; Ty Cobb, whose troubled character and devious diamond deeds were not always heroic, but whose record as a great player cannot be disputed; Babe Ruth, whose prowess at the plate altered not only the construction of the baseball itself, but also the popularity of the game; Christy Mathewson, who was a class gentleman on and off the mound, certainly one of baseball's greatest pitchers and most deserving heroes.

Also, Walter Johnson, whose fast ball may have been the best of all, then or now, who had to wait until the sunset of his long career before getting to pitch in the World Series (1924 and 1925); Grover Cleveland Alexander, brilliant on the mound but somewhat pathetic in private life, to whom fame made a return visit in 1926 when he saved the seventh game of the World Series for the St. Louis Cardinals by striking out Tony Lazzeri in the seventh inning, with two out and the bases loaded, and protecting a 4–3 lead to the end of the game.

AND LOU GEHRIG, who held the record of having played in the most consecutive games until Cal Ripken Jr. topped that record in 1995, and whom disease struck down, slowly paralyzing him, while he was still young enough to have played the game; Addie Joss, who like Gehrig, died when in his prime; Joe DiMaggio, who, by his consistent all-around excellence helped make Babe Ruth's departure a bit easier for fans to take; Bob Feller, the schoolboy who left his father's Iowa farm to fire the ball past American League batters in a manner reminiscent of the Big Train, Walter Johnson, and then went home to graduate from high school.

Mickey Mantle, who possessed abundant skills and stepped in after DiMaggio retired to help perpetuate Yankee domination of the American League throughout the '50s and the first four years of the '60s. Legitimate heroes, all of them.

Dave pointed out that today's media are not at all reluctant to focus upon character flaws of the players, thereby making them seem less heroic than the great stars of the game from the late 1800s until the mid-1960s.

Radio took some of the mystique from the game, for fans who never made it to a major league park and depended upon newspapers for their baseball thrills were able to hear games being played, to listen to the likes of Graham McNamee, Red Barber and Mel Allen. And then came television and fans finally get to see the men who, somehow, no longer seemed like distant gods.

Dave did not neglect to mention the federal government's role in baseball—the long-standing exemption from the antitrust laws, a legacy from Judge Kennesaw Mountain Landis *before* he was chosen commissioner of the game. And he gave an excellent account of the Negro leagues, their origin, their stars, their demise. He told about Branch Rickey, Abner Doubleday, Alexander J. Cartwright, Harry Wright and his brother George, Al Spalding, Cap Anson—all great names in baseball history . . .

MY PLANE LEFT BEFORE DAVE'S last class; but he told me, as he drove me to the Phoenix airport early that morning, that he envisions many changes occurring in future years: increased numbers of franchises, some of which may well be in foreign countries, such as Mexico, Cuba, even Australia; year-round play, utilizing playing fields according to climate and time of year. He posed the question: What effect will all that have on the average fan?

I probably will not be around to see those possible changes. There've been changes enough for me to date. When I was younger there were two leagues of eight teams each. I knew the lineups of every American League team and some National League teams. Now there are so many new franchises that I no longer feel as though I'm with the total game.

Yes, I saw four spring training games: Giants vs. Angels; Cubs vs. Giants; Angels vs. Giants; and Angels vs. Mariners. Here's a strange one: The Angels play their spring home games in the Diablo Stadium in Tempe. (Diablo is Spanish for Devil.) Some twist, by George!

"We should count time by heart-throbs." —*Bailey*

My Elizabeth

MAY 11, 1982

Remembering Cecil's 'Rally Day'

Along about this time of the year, when I was a youngster (and even after I had started teaching), county school systems used to hold what was termed "Rally Day." Since I was a Cecil Countian, I participated in Rally Day as a student, and later as a softball coach, down in Elkton. But this column isn't going to be about me; it's going to be about my wife's participation in Rally Day and the days following the close of school for the summer.

RALLY DAY was, of course, a day away from the one-room school in Pleasant Hill. (The Pleasant Hill school eventually became a two-room school, but what I'm writing about has little to do with the number of rooms there.) Virtually every boy and girl enrolled in the county schools looked forward to Rally Day. Dodgeball, volleyball, track and field events, baseball, speedball (a version of softball)—all kinds of athletic contests which were in vogue at the time—were highlights of the day. Oh, yes! There was a parade, too. Youngsters and teachers walked what seemed miles in the morning, showing off their school colors—and wearing themselves out at the same time.

My wife's Rally Day schedule wasn't exactly just fun and games. Before she and her twin sister and their brother could go down to Elkton, there was garden to be planted. That meant several hours of back-bending work, dropping seed-beans, corn, etc. in rows. No Rally Day until the garden was planted. Her father took the day off from his regular job to do the work required to cover up the seeds; her mother was busy preparing a packed lunch for the family.

ELIZABETH doesn't like to be the focal point of columns, but she has granted me the right to comment on some of the activities which occupied her time when she was a little girl. First of all, she didn't always like what she was doing; secondly, she never expressed her dislike to her parents since she simply took for granted that what her parents wanted her to do she would do—and no complaining! That garden, for example, was the source of food for the summer and, in part, for the winter, too.

The straw hat and the dusty clothing were exchanged for neatly starched dresses and the family was ready to board the buggy for the big event down in Elkton.

AFTER THE close of school for the summer came one of the biggest tasks of all—that of whitewashing the fence which surrounded the home place. That meant donning that wide-brimmed hat again, old clothes, and work gloves. Now, I never observed the whitewashing rites myself. All I know about it is what she has, from time to time, told me. There was none of the Tom Sawyer-ish monkey business associated with the several days of whitewashing that fence. Just dip-and-swipe, post after post, horizontal pale after pale—getting soaked with whitewash, gloves wet and hands sore. It took, as I have stated, several days to accomplish the task. It wasn't easy. But, there again, it was something which had to be done. It was that simple.

Later in the summer there were cultivated blackberries to be picked, Elizabeth has related to me. Morning after morning, she and her sister braved the prickly bushes and the pesky chiggers to harvest the big, luscious berries, all the while looking forward to the blackberry mush their mother would be making as a special dessert—and, of course, the delicious jelly which would show up on the table the following winter.

ELIZABETH NO LONGER PLANTS gardens. Nor does she whitewash fences. There aren't any Rally Days any longer, either. And "school's out" has little meaning for us; seasons just seem to run together. But I don't think Elizabeth has forgotten those experiences I've touched upon one little bit. There were chores to be done then and there are chores to be done now. Her inclination to tidiness and keeping busy indicates that being a member of a family circle which worked together as a team had carryover. The children loved and respected their parents—and that love and respect was reciprocal.

If there were still oil lamps to be filled, glass chimneys to be cleaned, cream to be skimmed, lanterns to be held while father milked the cow on a cold winter's night, she'd be right there—at home with those tasks.

That's Elizabeth and me in April 1936

I HAVE A hunch, however, that she's pleased enough to be released from bending her back to plant the garden, to have no fence to whitewash and no chiggers to ward off in the blackberry patch. But I know for a fact that she cherishes the recollections of those years when tedious tasks had their reward—the togetherness of a family. Even the ride down to Elkton in those horse-and-buggy days is a treasured memory.

Elizabeth and I have been married for 46 years. We've noted a great many changes in life-styles over those years. And, you know, I don't think she has any real complaints about her life with me—which indicates a high degree of tolerance on her part, by George! I know I'm not complaining!

Elizabeth and me on the occasion of our 50th Wedding Anniversary 1986

SEPTEMBER 23, 1986

Nickel Pickles

Most of us have some little routine from our childhood which stays in our mind as a special thing. Perhaps it was of no particular significance insofar as our growing up was concerned—just a pleasant little recollection now that we're getting to be old folks of sorts. Elizabeth and I frequently exchange anecdotes relating to school days. One of her remembered happenings led me to give her a different birthday gift the other day. A big dill pickle! (That's not all I gave her, but for this column it was the major item.)

When she was in high school in Elkton, pupils were not supposed to venture downtown, so I understand. Now, Elizabeth doesn't strike me as one who would have knowingly or willingly violated a code of behavior unless she was under extreme duress. But she did violate the command given by Principal Guy Johnson—on occasion, that is. When she could no longer resist the temptation, she would join others of her age group or class in a trek to one of the stores during the lunch hour to purchase, of all things, a sour pickle!

Sour pickles, right from the barrel, were a treat to youngsters a generation or so ago. One pickle, slipped into a brown paper bag for holding-on-to, made for a good half-hour of nibbling—and puckering. The pickle prompted a few giggles along the way back to school, too. Innocent fun—and I'm sure Mr. Johnson was able to wink at such a violation.

Thus it was that, having but recently been reminded of those pickle-treks, I thought I'd provide for her a refresher course in pickle-nibbling. I even procured from the Zion Deli a brown paper bag to go with the brine-saturated cucumber.

Times have changed, as everyone knows. Price-wise the present times have little relation to those of a half-century ago: Elizabeth's pickles came at a nickel each—no small sum, back then; the ones today cost more than 12 times the nickel. Be that as it may, it was a bit of sharing of our memories and it was fun. It does us good now and then to take a walk back to yesterday. As that commercial about Colonial Williamsburg suggests, we need to taste the tastes, smell the smells, etc. of the past—our own pasts, especially.

The pickles of today are different from those of long ago, so I'm told. There's a difference between *sour* pickles and *dill* pickles. I'm not sure I can taste the difference, but a connoisseur of pickles has a sharp tongue and can tell you right away what's what with the cucumber.

By the way, the word pickle can set off a chain of meanings if you think about it. Besides being something preserved in brine, it can, in its past participle form, suggest a state of intoxication having no relation whatsoever to a cucumber. It can also mean that state of difficulty synonymous with jam. And if you're visiting in England, you find the word designates a person—a mischievous trouble-maker.

Come to think of it, Elizabeth has it two ways—a pickled cucumber in a brown paper bag and a mischievous character she's lived with for 50 years. And when she reads this, I'll be in a pickle, by George!

AUGUST 17, 1996

Rumble-Seat Offered Hours Of Fun

Someone recently asked the question: "Is George still writing columns?" The answer is, "Yes." Though I must admit to what my Elizabeth said years ago— "George, you're looking into the past again!" She was right, I am, as I once put it, using my rear-view mirror more often than I probably should be using it. But I'm not going to apologize, for recollections are like old coins—they become invaluable. Especially when farewells have been said.

To begin this story—and it's very personal—starting in the spring of 1923, my father became the minister of the old Zion

Circuit which included the Union Methodist Church. He preached there every other Sunday morning and I usually went with him. I attended Mrs. Guiberson's Sunday school class. In that class were two little girls whom I could not tell apart. They were identical and as pretty as little girls could possibly be. They were the Thompson twins. I was right smitten at the tender age of 10, but I didn't know by which one. For reasons I'll never fathom, I took to teasing one of them, but I didn't know whom I was tormenting. I learned later that I seemed always to play my childish pranks on Elizabeth. Snatch her hat and run around the church with it, or pretend to swipe her gloves.

Sometime in June of 1930, after the twins had graduated from the Elkton High School, Children's Day was being held at the Zion Methodist Church and the twins were there with but one young man as escort. I approached them and asked, "Which one of you doesn't have a date?" I don't recall exactly how she answered that question; I do know that Elizabeth and I were soon in my father's Chevrolet. I took her home from church that evening.

There was one hitch. My Dad's car had a flat tire! Evelyn's friend that evening, Mike Guiberson, helped me change the tire, and Elizabeth and I were off on our first date. Our courtship lasted for six years. I was in college for three of those years and even after I had earned my degree, I didn't land a real paying job right away. We were married April 30, 1936, when I was in my second year of teaching.

I didn't often have access to an automobile. But Clarence Griffith, an elementary and high school classmate of mine, did. He started going with Evelyn and we double-dated. Elizabeth and I found that we fit right cozily into the rumble-seat of Clarence's sporty Ford roadster. Even in cold weather, when we would have to cover up, heads and all, with a blanket while Clarence and Evelyn rode up front.

Throughout the years that followed, the four of us continued to have a close and pleasant relationship. Clarence and Evelyn were married in March 1938. While we never lived in the same town, we were together innumerable times. We took a few trips together, like down to Jefferson's Monticello and the Skyline Drive. We spent many an evening at the movies, or in one or the other's home. We four frequently visited Julia and Dick Touchton's big brick house on Sunday evenings and there we had sing-alongs and good fellowship.

Our George and their Ruth Ann, married to Ronnie Bedsaul, are grown. Ruth Ann and Ronnie provided their parents with grandchildren who, in turn, have given them great-grandchildren. Sadly, Elizabeth did not live to see Owen and Neil, Jeffrey and Kathleen's boys; nor Megan, Susan Beth and Kenneth Lewis's little girl. Evelyn and Clarence became great-grandparents of young Ronnie and Michele's boys, Ryan and Dylan, and Matthew and Robin's twins, Cole, a boy, and Callie, a girl.

Our foursome lasted for almost 60 years. Elizabeth left us in February 1989. Then, only last week, August 5, Clarence died. Evelyn and I are both widowed now.

As I said in the beginning of this piece, recollections are invaluable. I think back to the years when Clarence and I were fifth-graders in Miss Lera White's room up at the Calvert Agricultural School and later when we entered high school. Still in knickers, both of us. Just before classes were to start in the fall of 1925, Clarence rode his bicycle down from Lombard Road up above the Brick, and the two of us had an afternoon riding on the dusty gravel roads in the Zion neighborhood. Clarence was the first classmate with whom I exchanged a Christmas gift; I gave him a tie and he gave me a handkerchief.

His father died during the Christmas holidays that year. Clarence, the oldest of three children, more or less made his own way from that point in his life. He cherished his memories of his father. And he treasured his father's carpentry tools. Even today, they are in his basement shop where he had proudly cared for them over many years.

His devotion to his father, mother, brother and sister was evident throughout his lifetime. His brother, Evan, preceded him in death by a few years. His widowed sister, Ruth Hart, lives in a retirement complex up near York, Pennsylvania.

We who are left are going to miss him. We are together here for but a brief time, when you stop to think about it. It's over too, too soon. And I'm still indebted to him for those rumble-seat years, by George! He was, indeed, a good buddy.

MAY 30, 1989

As the Poppies Bloom, So Do Sweet Memories

More than 50 years ago we—Elizabeth and I—fell in love with the Oriental poppies that grew in the flower bed in our yard. That was when we lived up the street in Zion behind the brick house in which Dick and Julia lived. Our apartment had once been a barn and once upon a time the late Murray J. Ewing, a former editor of *The Cecil Whig*, kept his horse in that barn. So he liked to tell me.

Getting back to the poppies: their startlingly brilliant color seemed to give life to the entire collection of flower plants that grew in that bed. We enjoyed them so much that we purchased an inexpensive picture of poppies in a vase and hung it over the buffet in our dining room; that picture is stowed away with other mementos now.

For years, after we had moved down the street into our present home, we talked about getting some poppy plants for our new yard; but until a year or two ago we didn't get around to doing it. I ordered some plants from a company out in Ohio and when they came I was convinced that they wouldn't make it to maturity—they were so scrawny. Just the same, I planted them and did my best to keep them alive and growing. They survived.

Early last summer, while Elizabeth was still home and able to walk some, she and I made a little tour of the back yard, especially to see if—or when—the poppies would be in bloom. There were a couple of buds which looked promising, but they were still very tight. Perhaps two or three weeks away from full bloom.

That was the last time she walked with me on our lawn. And when the poppies were about to break into full color, they bowed their head and turned a sickening brown.

As I write this piece today, I can look through the window and see a burst of flaming red! The poppies are out in all their glory, a dozen or more of them. They are blooming for her—for Memorial Day. They are the stars of the yard, just as those of years ago were when she and I were young.

Someone once said, "I dislike clocks with second hands; they cut life up into too small pieces." Yes, but many of those small pieces become the treasures of memory, the jewels of the clock itself.

Those who are retiring from whatever profession or vocation will find that cherished moments will crop up now and again as flash-backs of their yesterdays and will leave a bitter-sweet taste for them to savor as they ponder their years of service at their tasks. A kind of reward for well-doing, by George!

"Out where the handclasp's a little stronger. . . that's where the West begins." *—Arthur Chapman*

He Was Better Known As "Doc"

AUGUST 7, 1974

It Happened! And It Was Great!

Those of you who have read my columns over the past several years have been aware of my admiration for and friendship with Mr. and Mrs. Milburn Stone. Mr. Stone has, for the past nineteen years, been known to TV viewers as "Doc Adams" in the adult Western program, "Gunsmoke." Not more than a year ago or so, I did a three-part column on the veteran character actor whose portrayal of "Doc" is, in my opinion, in a class all by itself.

In February, 1972, I was scheduled to meet him when he and Ken Curtis— "Festus" in the "Gunsmoke" series—were being honored as the outstanding TV personalities of the year 1971, down in Baltimore. A blizzard got in my way; I couldn't get out of Zion that particular day. Literally snowed in I was.

"Doc" and his wife have corresponded with my wife and me with regularity for about three-and-a-half years now. And we have held several telephone conversations. Yet the distance between Hollywood and Zion has served as a barrier between us in the sense that we had never met face to face.

Thursday, July 25, a plane landed at the Baltimore-Washington International Airport. Elizabeth, our son, and I were waiting at the proper place to observe that landing—and to greet Mr. and Mrs. Stone as they alighted. They had graciously included a visit with us in their scheduled vacation here in the East.

Being greeted by them was like being greeted by old friends. I must admit to having the feeling that I was experiencing the fulfillment of a cherished dream. I will never forget the warmth, the sincerity they exhibited as they immediately "took the Prettymans in"—and throughout the two-day visit that warmth grew so that we felt figuratively embraced by them.

I had expected the Stones to be human beings, certainly; as I have said before, they have not lost the common touch—not at all! I was prepared to find them just as genuine in real life as Mr. Stone appears to be in his characterization of "Doc." But reality far, far exceeded anticipation. He most assuredly is a celebrity by nationwide acclaim; yet he most assuredly gave not the slightest inkling that he regards himself as such. And a more personable, engaging, congenial couple I simply can't imagine.

As for us, there was not a dull moment. It may even be that I appeared a bit starry-eyed, I don't know. All I can say is that the Stones gave us an incomparable "at ease" feeling from the moment of meeting until it came time for us to bid them a reluctant farewell Saturday around lunch time.

We spent our time with Mr. and Mrs. Stone at the Cross Keys Inn at Columbia, in order that Astronaut Bill Anders, his wife, and two of their daughters could meet them at a point not too distant from the Anders home in McLean, Virginia. The Stones were scheduled for a visit there.

The younger Prettymans—Janet, George, Susan Beth, and Jeffrey—were generously included in that get-together. Janet had handled reservations at the inn for us; George had made sure that the visitors from California had a huge bouquet of the Maryland State Flower in their room. Doc and Jane, as they insisted we address them, hosted Elizabeth and me and the four younger Prettymans to dinner at the Olney Inn Friday evening and to breakfast at the Cross Keys on Saturday morning. Mr. and Mrs. Anders and two of their daughters, Gail and Diana, (the youngest is named after the goddess of the moon and is known as the "first moon baby" in astronaut circles) joined us for that breakfast. The Stones had arranged it that way. Doc and Bill Anders are the best of friends. It was exciting to see and talk with a man who has circled the moon in a spacecraft.

Mr. Stone is so easily recognized by people wherever he happens to be that folks walk up to him and call him by name—most often, "Doc." His response to such recognition provides a real lesson in human relations. His ready smile and handshake, his friendly conversations with any and all who greet him, his willingness to oblige with an autograph are indeed heartwarming. It was a joy to observe him as he made everyone who approached him feel welcomed.

We were their guests; their hospitality smacked not the slightest of condescension. Both Mr. and Mrs. Stone gave untiringly of their time to us, recounting innumerable unforgettable incidents concerning his career as an actor and wonderful glimpses into his boyhood years. The long weeks in Birmingham where he underwent open-heart surgery were the subject of much conversation. Of course, being insatiably curious, I asked many questions. I was not once turned off.

Doc knows how to entertain children as well as adults. During a brief visit in Holiday Hills with the younger Prettymans, he sang "Sunbonnet Sue" to Susan Beth. And when it came time to bid the little folks goodnight, he told them the fable of the tortoise and the hare—by way of one of his famous spoonerisms. It was a delightful experience, even for their grandfather, by George!

By what good fortune we came to be included as a part of their trip I shall never quite completely understand. We were privileged, indeed—it was, as I have said, a dream come true for me to be able to meet them, let alone have the pleasure of their company for hours on end.

Doc has made so many "house calls" at our home through "Gunsmoke" that I felt as though I already knew him even before our exchange of letters and calls. His wife, through her letters and telephone conversations, had long been classified as a charming friend. Nonetheless, the "touch of the hand and the sound of the voice" came to be a mountain-peak experience for Elizabeth and for me, as well as for those whom we call our children.

If I seem extraordinarily impressed, truly thrilled by our get-acquainted time together, I am! That such an opportunity came our way—such a real-life bonus!—seems both improbable and impossible. But it happened. And I'm more than ever devoted to the man who has breathed life into that Dodge City character, Doc Adams, and who just has to be the finest man yet to appear on a TV screen—and to his wife, whom he calls Janie—by George!

MAY 5, 1981

Where The West Begins

Arthur Chapman may not be listed among America's top poets, but there's a poem he wrote which provides me with exactly the lead I want for this column (and possibly subsequent ones). Space prohibits my using the poem in its entirety, so I'll settle for a few lines—

Out where the handclasp's a little stronger,
Out where the smile dwells a little longer,
That's where the West begins;
Where there's more of singing and less of sighing,
Where there's more of giving and less of buying,
And a man makes friends without half trying—
That's where the West begins.

And my son and I found Persimmon Hill, Oklahoma City, Oklahoma, to be at least one of the places "where the West begins." The National Cowboy Hall of Fame is situated on Persimmon Hill. What took us there—what event? Well, my good friend, the late Milburn Stone, was among those inducted into the Cowboy Hall of Fame. Saturday evening, April 25; his wife had seen to it that the Prettymans were invited to be on hand.

It was GUNSMOKE night, actually—insofar as awards to performers went. The stage in the huge banquet room was set up to suggest the exterior of The Long Branch Saloon; swinging doors opened and out stepped Miss Kitty (Amanda Blake), Matt Dillon (James Arness), Festus (Ken Curtis), Chester (Dennis Weaver), and Newley O'Brien (Buck Taylor), as well as producers John Mantley and Jim Byrne. "Ol' Doc" was not there in person, but it was evident that everyone among the 1,500-plus audience somehow sensed his presence. Mrs. Stone accepted the membership award for Doc and she and an artist unveiled a portrait of the veteran actor which will hang in the Hall of Fame along with portraits of several other performers. Ken Curtis was given the honor of inducting his late friend, Doc, during the impressive ceremony.

The induction of James Arness, Ken Curtis, Dennis Weaver, and Milburn Stone into the Hall was something unusual since it had been customary that but one living and one deceased performer be so honored in any one year. Their election was unanimous, and the tradition was broken. Buck Taylor was given a Trustees Award for his contribution to GUNSMOKE during the last several years of its twenty-year run on TV.

Lest anyone should think that The National Cowboy Hall of Fame in nothing more than a collection of cowboy hats, ropes, saddles, bows and arrows, etc. may I say here and now that it is one of the most beautiful art museums I have ever seen. True, it focuses upon the "Old West"—but it does so with all the grace and polish of most lavish of museums. Room after room—and the rooms are spacious—contain paintings and sculptures of international fame. In a later column I shall undertake to cite some of the treasures to be seen there.

True, there is space devoted to the artifacts associated with the Great West—the West of the Indians and the West of the men and women who dared brave the dangers of migration to stretch this great nation "from sea to shining sea." The entire exhibit, including the magnificent gardens, the seventeen fountains denoting the seventeen states which make up the West, the colorful state flags, with Old Glory waving with them in the seemingly constant breeze—and I must not forget the three-story high statue of Buffalo Bill Cody with his rifle pointing the way to the Pacific—yes, the entire exhibit is breathtaking!

And it is there for you and me to see—not at the expense of the tax payer, either, for it is financed by the generous contributions of the Westerners and other benefactors who are devoted to the preservation of the heritage of the West.

Friendliness? Well, go back to the lines by Arthur Chapman which I used to start this column. Two Maryland boys could not have been more warmly embraced than were the two Georges—in the lobby of the motel or in The Cowboy Hall of Fame.

Yes, I'll have more to say about our two days in Oklahoma City. Right now, I'm still in a state of amazement and sheer joy over the whole experience, by George! You might say my feet aren't quite on the ground yet!

MAY 12, 1981

Some Of The People

Last week I left both you and myself up in the air, figuratively. That visit to The National Cowboy Hall of Fame held so many surprises and joys for me that I'm still having difficulty sorting out exactly what to comment upon.

Our room in the Lincoln Plaza was but two doors from that of Mrs. Milburn Stone and Mrs. Shirley Gleason, Doc's wife and daughter. We happened to be visiting them when Gary Hawk, an artist whose studio is in Iola, Kansas, arrived with a portrait he is working on which shows Doc Adams at his desk in GUNSMOKE'S Dodge City. Mr. Hawk's as yet unfinished portrait of Doc is to hang in one of the most prominent buildings in Burrton, Kansas, Milburn Stone's birthplace.

IN DECEMBER, 1977, Governor Robert Bennett named Gary Hawk "Governor's Artist for the State of Kansas"—a truly great honor. Mr. Hawk is rapidly making a name for himself as an artist dedicated to the preservation of the heritage of the West. A personable man, he is extremely meticulous in his work. In his pursuit for perfection, for example, he went to Dodge City—where Doc's GUNSMOKE memorabilia is on display at St. Mary of the Plains College—just to feel the texture of the suit Milburn Stone wore as he portrayed his unforgettable role in GUNSMOKE.

Mr. Hawk was eager to get Mrs. Stone's reaction to the portrait—and understandably so. I'm happy to say that Mrs. Stone was pleased with it—and, while I'm not on that jury, I must add that I thought it was just great! I had several conversations with Gary Hawk and his very pretty little wife during our stay in Oklahoma City and have a standing invitation to visit him in the Sunflower State for a tour of the places Milburn Stone made famous just by being who and what he was. Incidentally, Gary Hawk has done some art work in nearby Amish country—Lancaster, Pennsylvania.

DOC'S GRANDCHILDREN—four Gleasons—arrived while we were visiting Mrs. Stone and their mother, Mrs. Gleason. It was as though I were meeting old friends since I had indeed "met" them through conversations with both Mr. and Mrs. Stone. Good old Irish names they have—Ellyn, Kelley (the girls) and Timothy and Casey (the boys). With Doc's portrait right there in the room, I felt as though I were in on a family reunion. One of Doc's closest friends, Paul Savage, a former actor and currently a script writer, was there, too—a fine man whom I was very happy to meet. I'd heard about him through Doc, too, and I have several photographs in which he appears.

Yes, I met and talked with the "regulars" of GUNSMOKE—Amanda Blake, Ken Curtis, James Arness, Buck Taylor, and Dennis Weaver. I'll admit to having enough of the little boy in me to have enjoyed my conversations with them. They were as genuine in person as they had been over the many years during which they were invited into my home by way of TV. Ken

Curtis's first words to me were, "Why, George! It's good to see you. I just wish 'ol' Doc' were here to enjoy all this!"

Standing alongside of James Arness made me feel like a pigmy! Amanda Blake expressed her appreciation of the acclaim which has come her way. She's a very gracious lady—and courageous, too, for she has apparently won a long and tedious battle against cancer. Buck Taylor is an outgoing young man who had the rare privilege of growing up to work in the show that was his favorite when he was a youngster. Dennis Weaver hopes to keep "riding into the sunset" for several more years, so he said.

We Prettyman boys are not celebrities. But the hosts and hostesses at The National Cowboy Hall of Fame seemed not to notice that at all. They treated us royally, by George!

JULY 7, 1993

'Doc Adams' And The Maryland Connection

Alfred Belfield was born in Maryland and he remained in the Free State until he had attained maturity. He followed the waterways of this state until he decided he'd take his chances in the West as a farmer. Heeding the call to the soil, he migrated to Iowa sometime in the 1830s.

Alfred had married and had a family. When word got out that there was gold in California, Alfred became, as his great-grandson told it, "an instant '49er." He left his farm and his family and made his way to the gold fields.

He hunted for gold for five years and found just enough to get him back to Iowa. During all that time, he dutifully and with regularity wrote letters to his wife, Maria—pronounced like what they call the wind in a song which was popular a few years back. Not one of his letters ever got through to her.

IN THE MEANTIME, Maria took to praying with considerable ardor for Alfred's safe return. It was said of her that she was an absolute virtuoso at praying. She held conversations with God like Grandpa Vanderhof in "You Can't Take It With You!"

Her prayers were answered. Alfred returned. But early in the 1870s, when land on the prairie was free for the taking, he got itchy feet again and left his farm in Iowa to stake out a claim in what is now Rush County, Kansas. He and his family were among the first settlers there.

Alfred and Maria helped organize the local government. Helped get the place civilized. They reportedly gave the place some sense of rectitude.

THEY HAD FOUR sons and one of them was named Charles Milton—Belfield, of course. But more about him later. All four of the boys were cowboys—the kind Charles Russell depicted in his paintings and sculptures.

A final word or two about Maria: She never lost her gift of communicating with God, no matter what time of day or night. One morning they found her kneeling by her bed. It was assumed that she was in prayer. She had been; and she had died in that prayerful position. A pretty nice way to go.

Back to Charles. Charles took quite a shine to Ella Merilla Shaw, daughter of a neighboring farmer. They were married. Their eldest daughter was born in their sod house. That was in 1879. They named her Laura.

LAURA GREW UP to be one of the "beautiful Belfields," for she had some sisters. And, as more often than not, there happened to be a young man who wanted to court her. And he did. And they became man and wife: Mr. And Mrs. Herbert Macklin Stone, to be formal about it.

On July 5, 1904—one day after the Fourth of July—their second child was born, this one a boy. They named him Hugh Milburn Stone. He has been often referred to as "a delayed firecracker" because of his quick temper.

With the passage of time, that little fellow became quite a man. When he was just a tiny tot he gave some indication of the career he eventually chose.

On children's day in the Methodist Church, actually the schoolhouse which served a dual purpose, he stole the lines which another youngster was supposed to say and, more or less, was the star of that show.

Yes, Milburn Stone became an actor. He really became known as "Doc Adams" and made housecalls in Dodge City and all across the United States by way of television. "Gunsmoke," remember?

Milburn Stone somehow became interested in Cecil Community College where a scholarship had been established in his name. He became a benefactor of the college, supporting the scholarship and showing more than a passing interest in the drama and public speaking program there.

WHEN IT BECAME evident that there would be a theatre on campus, it was suggested that it could be a memorial to him, since he had taken his final curtain call in mid-June, 1980.

On the evening of August 6 coming up, Mrs. Milburn Stone, his widow, and his daughter, Mrs. Patrick Gleason, both of California, will attend the performance of "The Music Man" on the stage of The Milburn Stone Memorial Covered Bridge Theatre on the campus of Cecil Community College.

Following the lead of her late husband, Mrs. Stone has been a very generous contributor to the Cecil Community College Foundation, Inc.

Going back to Alfred and Maria Belfield, they provided the "Maryland connection" to Milburn Stone's interest in Cecil Community College. It has been a lively one, too, by George!

AUGUST 11, 1993

Praise For Mrs. Stone And 'The Music Man'

It happened! An event dreamed of and planned for over a decade came to fruition last weekend. Mrs. Milburn Stone, widow of the late actor who, for twenty years, played "Doc Adams" in TV's "Gunsmoke," and Mrs. Patrick Gleason, his daughter, came in from California for a gala, celebrating the official opening of The Milburn Stone Memorial Covered Bridge Theatre. Coinciding with their visit, "The Music Man" opened for a seven-performance run, under the direction of Gale Sheaffer. It was planned that way, for Mr. Stone's favorite musical happened to be Meredith Wilson's highly entertaining play.

It was truly a happy occasion, one that will long be remembered by those who attended the succession of celebrations held to welcome Jane Stone and Shirley Gleason. Formalities were soon dropped and friendships founded through mutual interests in the theatre, the college, and the current production. "The Music Man" was hailed by many as the finest production yet performed by the local thespians. There were plaudits for the actors, for their director, for the music, for the sets—for the entire production.

The honored guests were feted during brunches, dinners, and on stage opening night. Cecil Community College Foundation members, trustees, producers of shows, scholarship recipients, actors, season-ticket holders, donors, local and state government officials, and other interested folks were, at varying times, hosts for get-acquainted meetings with Mrs. Stone and Mrs. Gleason. Four successive days were crowded with events scheduled to honor them.

During a ceremony on opening night, Senator Walter Baker presented Mrs. Stone with a framed document, signed by Governor William Donald Schaefer, making her an honorary citizen of the State of Maryland. Both Mrs. Stone and Mrs. Gleason were given honorary Associate in Arts Degrees by Danny Hall and Dr. Robert Gell, president of the Board of Trustees and President of the College, respectively.

Just prior to the opening of the curtain, a ribbon was cut, admitting people to the gallery where an exhibit highlighting Mr. Stone's career in movies and on TV had been set up by Kristi Eisenberg, coordinator of the photography program at the college.

The beautiful red, velvet-like curtain parted shortly after eight o'clock, the orchestra began playing, and "The Music Man" was off to a fine start. It kept the pace throughout the evening. I am too biased—in favor of our troupe—to give a review of the play. I liked every minute of it! And I can say that a good number of people volunteered to say, "This has to be the best! The best play yet on CBT!" (We'll let the professional critics speak their piece, but that won't alter our opinion should they write negatively about the production.)

It would be fun for me to go right down the list of the cast and tell each one how well I think he or she performed. I wouldn't leave a single one out. And I'd like to tell those who fashioned the costumes and the sets how proud I am of them and their contributions to the show. Let's simply say, "Well done! Very well done!" And may I add that Jane Stone and Shirley Gleason join that chorus with me! They were ecstatic. Believe me.

I will mention a name or two—people who orchestrated the four-day celebration. Polly Binns scheduled the events—and such organization I haven't seen in a long, long time—if ever! Kristi Eisenberg and Mrs. Stone made excellent selections from among the many, many photographs and various items of memorabilia available for the exhibit. Dr. Gell lent his support throughout and he and Mrs. Gell opened their home to all of us on two occasions during the weekend.

Those who participated in honoring the guests could not have been more cordial. It was an harmonious journey into remembering those who have been generous to our theatrical venture.

And, by George, it wasn't easy to see the whole thing end! It was so good to have Jane and Shirley with us. They say they'll be coming back someday.

Oh, my gosh! I almost forgot! The eldest of "Doc's" grandchildren flew in Thursday evening to have dinner with several of us and to see the theatre. She is a flight attendant for an airline and, for the first time in more than two years, one of her flights landed in Philadelphia. A monumental coincidence! She was able to squeeze a few hours in to take a look at the building named in memory of her beloved grandfather whom she called "Papa." Her name—Ellyn Gleason Cook.

"Men are made of other things than years."
—Harold Bell Wright

People I Cannot Forget

NOVEMBER 5, 1977

Doctors Are The Greatest

Autumn, 1927, was a memorable one for me. I was approaching my fifteenth birthday which would fall ten days before Christmas—December 15. I had begun my junior year in the Calvert Agricultural High School. Early in that first semester I became ill; I had contracted yellow jaundice which, I believe, is now pretty generally called hepatitis, a disease of the liver. I was confined to my bed or to the couch in the sitting room of the Zion Methodist parsonage for several weeks while my classmates were being introduced to two academic subjects with which I had little or no familiarity—French and geometry.

The teachers up at Calvert, however, kept me posted on my assignments and I managed to keep reasonably abreast of the work though I was not to become proficient in that foreign language nor was my mind in tune with Euclidean thinking. (I memorized theorems; I did not really understand them.) My final grades were sufficient, nonetheless, to permit me to matriculate to the University of Delaware two autumns later, thanks to the patience of Miss Adelle Senft and Miss Marie Parker, both of whom changed names, as women do, when they later married.

But getting back to the autumn of 1927, that enforced vacation from the classroom, while an annoyance, for I truly loved to attend school, gave me the opportunity to follow my beloved

Yankees through a World Series. Years ago I wrote about this—but I have a new generation of readers, so I'm repeating myself. (I am not so senile as to fail to recognize this repetition.)

The late Dr. David L. Gifford, who had started his medical practice in Zion in 1880, lived up the tree-lined street from the parsonage. He was one of my father's stalwart parishioners. He divided his grass-mowing and gardening chores fairly evenly between my buddy, Jimmy Renn, and me. To him I was "Little Man"—and I can hear him yet saying, "Little Man, come over here to the geranium bed next to Miss Georgia's little house. Let's get the weeds out of that." And before I could possibly complete that task, he'd call to me, "Little Man, over here! These onions need weeding." (Could be that I was slow—maybe even lazy; but Doc Gifford never lost patience with me.)

My sister Julia and Dick Touchton were married on October 1 of that year. I was permitted to lie on the couch in the parlor of the parsonage to witness the ceremony. I don't recall the exact dates on which the World Series games were played that year, but it was around the first week in October that the Yankees and the Pirates met in Forbes Field, Pittsburgh, for the first two games. Julia and Dick were away on their honeymoon, I know.

Doc Gifford drove a Model-T, and the afternoon of the first World Series game, he pulled into the parsonage lane. He came into the little sitting room where I was lying, lifted me in his arms, and carried me out to his car. When we reached his home, he lifted me from the car seat and carried me to the couch in the spacious sitting room of the Gifford house—and there I was, resting comfortably close by the radio! He repeated that act of kindness throughout the Series—all four games, for my Yankees, led by Babe Ruth, Lou Gehrig, Tony Lazzeri, Bob Meusel, Earle Combs, and Joe Dugan—the original "Murderers' Row"—swept the Series, four games to zero. Herb Pennock, Waite Hoyt, George Pipgras, Urban Shocker, Wiley Moore, and Bob Shawkey were the main-line New York pitchers. Benny Bengough, later a Phillie coach, Grabowski, and Severeid shared the catching.

I can remember keeping score in a very amateurish manner; I could understand my symbols perfectly well, and that was all that counted. Much to my joy I discovered this past summer—fifty years later—that my grandson, Jeffrey, had latched on to the same symbols—and to the best of my knowledge he had never seen my boyish method of score-keeping.

Mrs. Gifford tuned the game in for me. The radio was equipped with ear-phones and a trumpet-like loud speaker. Part of the time I used the ear-phones. But when Doctor wasn't busy on house calls or with office patients, the loud speaker was used.

The Waner Brothers, Paul and Lloyd (Big Poison and Little Poison) had set the hitting pace for the Pirates that year—and they were great! With them Donie Bush, Pittsburgh's manager, had a line-up which included Pie Traynor, George Grantham, Glenn Wright, Joe Harris, and Clyde Barnhart. (Kiki Cuyler had been relegated to the bench in midseason for failing to slide into second base in an attempt to break up a double play.) Pittsburgh's team batting average was .305—a mere two percentage points below that of the Yankees. But those Yankees were long ball sluggers. Even their manager, Miller Huggins, admitted that they had changed "his game"—he was a mite of a man but a mighty manager who saw raw power and let it explode.

There were stories that when the Pirates saw the Yankees in batting practice the day before the Series opened they were intimidated; that story or those stories, if you will, have been variously affirmed or denied. At any rate, the Yankees did have an assortment of extra-base hits during the four games, including a couple of home runs by the Babe and a pair of triples by Lou Gehrig, with doubles thrown in by Koenig and others. Earle Combs scored the winning run in the fourth game on a wild pitch by reliever John Miljus who was pitching to Push-Em-Up Tony Lazzeri with the bases loaded and two out—an unhappy ending to a game for the unlucky Serb. Miljus had fanned both Gehrig and Meusel before the tension of the game caused him to cut loose with a wild-high pitch that Johnny Gooch, his catcher, couldn't reach. That Yankee team has, you know, been tabbed "the greatest of all"; but there are those who would argue that point and do so heatedly.

Be their greatness what it may, the Yankees of 1927 gave heart to a sick little boy. I really was little! I was under five-seven and tipped the scales at a monstrous 110. The joy of those four autumn afternoons could never have been were it not for the kindness and thoughtfulness of Doctor Gifford, a country physician who befriended the preacher's boy.

Fifty years have gone by, yet time has not lessened the thrill of that act of generosity. Obviously I recovered from that illness. I'm approaching my sixty-fifth birthday—come another December. When, on occasion, I visit the cemetery where my parents are buried, I am aware that right next to their graves are those of Doctor and Mrs. Gifford. There was a closeness there that carried over—even in death.

When the Yankees of 1977 became World Champions a few weeks ago—and I watched five of the six games on color TV—I could not help thinking back to that little boy and his beloved Doctor and a Yankee team which helped ease the discomfort of an illness. In my mind's eye I could see Doc Gifford bending over me, his arms outstretched in readiness to lift me from my couch. I was on my way again up to the Gifford home to hear Graham McNamee describe the play-by-play of a World Series won by my heroes.

That was the greatest, by George!

FEBRUARY 14, 1968

More About Dr. Gifford

In Dr. Gifford's office there was a revolving bookcase. It had been so constructed that each of the four sides would hold books on each of the three shelves. I have seen but one other bookcase like it in all my life—in a Western motion picture on TV, at that.

Well, so long as I am able to discern books in the bookcase, I shall have a vivid reminder of the good Doctor, for, upon his death, his widow called me over to her house and told me that the bookcase was mine! (I was scarcely fifteen then.)

Now that there are two other generations of Prettyman readers, it would appear that Dr. Gifford's bookcase will never cease being useful.

While Dr. Gifford trained as a physician for the body, let it never be said that he did not administer to the "whole person"—he knew how to reach youngsters and grown-ups too through their interests and attitudes and aspirations. Long before I gave serious thought to college, he discussed with my parents my attending the university. And partly because he was interested enough to care that I go, I did just that—even though he was not around to see me there.

The longer I live the more nearly certain I am of the fact that words of encouragement are very often more important than material things. That Dr. Gifford EXPECTED me to go to college was, without question, one of the very reasons I went!

We loosely use the word "immortality" sometimes. So long as I live—and so long as there are those who use his bookcase, too—there will be a part of Dr. Gifford still among men!

You could multiply that idea by almost every soul who has left some bit of hope within some heart and mind—who dropped some word of encouragement which culminated in a step forward.

It just occurred to me, as I re-read the foregoing, that no one could possibly get a clear idea of the bookcase from my scanty description. Well, here's a try:

The bookcase stands about five feet high. It is about two feet deep and two feet wide—you see, it's difficult to tell which is what side, since all four sides are identical. If you look down on it from above, it has a square top. The base has four sprawled out legs and in the center of the base is a gear which serves as a swivel so that the case can turn freely. There are, as I have said, three shelves. About a third of each shelf is covered (vertically) with several strips, each about one inch wide and reaching from the top of the case to the very bottom. The bookcase will hold in the neighborhood of fifty to seventy-five books, depending, of course, upon the thickness of the volumes.

It is finished in what I would assume to be natural oak. The years have been very kind to it, as have the people who have used it. The strips about which I spoke are held in place by brass-headed nails—very decorative.

Many of my father's books have rested within that case over recent years. In fact, the bookcase has become something of a blend of several personalities—for it has served those who have used it as a repository for real literary treasures.

With good fortune, it will last another generation or two! I treasure it greatly.

APRIL 28, 1971

A Cart

Two weeks ago, I made mention of Mr. John Rittenhouse, the blacksmith in Zion back in the days when farm horses needed shodding and wagon wheels had to have new rims. I can't remember how long it has been since Mr. Rittenhouse let the fires die down and the bellows become inactive and the anvil still. But, as I said before, in the quiet of a sleepless night or a thoughtful stroll, I can see and hear him yet. He came up from Virginia, so I have been told, and that quiet, controlled speech of his had a mellow quality that is as distinct a part of my recollection as is my recall of Mr. Wesley Ewing's singing in the church choir. (Mr. Ewing stammered dreadfully in conversation; give him a hymnal or a gospel song book and his voice was as smooth and clear as any song-bird's even after he had turned eighty!)

Mr. Rittenhouse "retired" from his shop. He was placed in charge of the highway—the shoulders and drainage ditches—between Zion and Calvert. He fashioned himself a two-wheeled hand cart for his new job, using wheels from an old pony cart.

He really didn't fit the physical picture we have of a blacksmith at all. He was a short, rather slightly-built man—but strong enough and determined enough to bend steel to his purposes.

He kept the stretch of highway from Zion to Calvert virtually immaculate. His job was accomplished to perfection.

The time came when Johnny Rittenhouse put his little cart, shovel, and rake—and scythe—in the old shop for the last time. There comes an end to a person's ability to keep going. He and his wife completed their life cycles a good many years ago; but their impact on those of us left who remember still remains.

A neighbor of mine purchased Johnny Rittenhouse's two-wheeled hand cart and has used it for years at yard-cleaning time. I should have said, *did* use it for years at yard-cleaning time; for, but a few weeks ago, Leonard C. Wilson—that neighbor—became ill and never recovered. The cart is still in Mr. Wilson's barn—a reminder of two gentlemen whose voices and skills are now a part of yesterday.

That's how it is in a little village. Life keeps going on. Changes happen. There are heartaches—and compensatory joys with each new day. . .

While poetry may not always "communicate," there are a few lines of verse which I have found applicable as a humanistic creed by which to evaluate living. I can't give proper credit to the author—nor to the source from which I became acquainted with the lines—but here they are:

It's the human touch in this world that counts—
The touch of your hand and mine—
That means far more to the fainting heart
Than shelter, or bread, or wine.
For shelter is gone when the night is o'er;
And bread lasts only a day.
But the sound of the voice and the touch of the hand
Live on in the heart always.

That's one lesson that comes from living in a small country village forever.

MARCH 19, 1969

The Fence!

It has been quite some time since she used the gate—but it was placed there particularly for her. Our yards joined and it was convenient for her—when going to the store for groceries—to pass through our back yard. Frequently she and my wife or my mother, when she was living, and our neighbor would carry on a casual, village-style conversation as Mrs. Gambill was either going to or coming from the store.

When we decided to erect the white board fence, specifically to beautify the area, we were, as I recall, greatly concerned that Mrs. Gambill and her family continue to use the short-cut across the back yards to the store. To insure that continued usage, we had a gate placed where the natural pathway had been.

I do know that her failing health permitted her not many walks to Ernie's Store the past several summers. But while the poet Robert Frost suggested that "good fences make good neighbors," it was my contention—and always will be—that a gateway makes for better neighborliness. I wanted that gate-way there—particularly, as I have said, for that little lady who became a neighbor to my parents in the late 1930s, when Mr. and Mrs. Gambill purchased the farm from my father.

The four people who entered into that original exchange which made the Gambills and the Prettymans neighbors have all departed now. Three generations have since that time grown to full manhood and womanhood—in fact, on a summer's day but a year or so ago there could be four generations of Gambills and Prettymans in the adjoining yards at the same time. And yet not too many years have passed since Billy and Dickie helped my dad in his gardening or yard work . . . Dean ploughed my first garden back in 1950 . . . Lorraine occasionally rode out to Rising Sun High School with me during her junior and senior years . . . Bobby grew up to take care of my lawn when I couldn't do the mowing myself . . . Charlotte's pony fascinated our Susan Beth and Jeffrey...“Rocky” helped several of us Prettymans pick cherries from the Gambill black-heart cherry tree... And little Brian discovered he could crawl under the fence and escape into our yard to play.

Scarcely a month ago Mrs. Gambill and I were in the same hospital, and evening after evening members of her family stopped in to say “hello” to me—some of them I hadn’t seen for several years.

I would like to quote a passage from the book to which I referred last week—Theodore Lidz’s “The Person”—because I think it has relevance here:

“Each individual requires many years to find a path through life and therefore becomes aware of the passage of time and his changing position in his life cycle. From an early age he knows that his years of life are numbered; at times he bemoans the fact and at times he is glad of it; but in some way he learns to come to terms with his mortality and the realization that his life is a one-time venture in a very small segment of time and space.”

But let it never be said that this one-time venture has only a small impact upon those whose lives are touched during the “small segment of time and space.” On the contrary, the impact is everlasting—from generation unto generation. That is the story of human life . . .

It has been good being neighbors to Mrs. Amanda Gambill. I am glad that there is that path, that gate, those recollections, and those of us who are yet here to remember. A one-time venture, yet so filled with so many wonderful things.

OCTOBER 21, 1959

The Pot-Bellied Stove

Forty years ago, in the village of Zion, a young merchant opened his till and began the business of providing the basic needs for his community. It was in the month of October. Horse-drawn vehicles were still a bit more plentiful than automobiles. A country store carried just about everything under the sun—from dress goods to patent medicines, from hair pins to plough shares. Of course, the food stuffs were primarily sold in bulk, though packaging was then becoming a recognizable part of the American scene. High-pressure advertising was in its infancy. One of the best sellers in the tobacco department was "Recruits," a little cigarette-size cigar (or a cigar fashioned in cigarette dimensions). "Mule Team" and "Red Apple" were popular chewing brands.

Gasoline pumps were hand operated—by the gallon, at first, then, by the five-gallon lots at one climb up the notched bar at the side of the tank. Frozen foods were not even thought of and out-of-season fruits and vegetables had to be purchased in the dried state, if at all.

Heating the store was accomplished by a huge, pot-bellied, cast-iron stove which glowed rosy red on cold winter evenings. The checker board was kept under the dry goods counter and brought out early in the evening to help pass the time away for those who habituated the social center of the village.

The coal bucket was frequently within range of the professional expectorators—those who were accomplished at the art of chewing.

Ice for the soft drinks came from the ice house behind Mrs. Renn's home. It was always fun to go bring back an express-wagon load of ice. Candy could be had by the piece—and for a penny! Five cents would purchase enough candy for a real treat! Every once in a while, a new gadget would hit the market—a vending gadget, that is. I remember the day the "orange julep apparatus" came! I could hardly wait to get enough pennies to draw some of the pretty orange drink from the huge glass ball which sat atop of the machine.

Came the World War II and ration stamps . . . And then the store was vacated, its contents moved across the road to a new site, where self-service was established—sign of the times . . . And until today, forty years after the beginning, Dick's Store is still in operation and still serving the people of the community in which it was begun.

Oh, I could write a book about it, I suppose—the people whom I have seen there, day after day, year after year. The humorous—and the not-so-humorous—incidents which have occurred there. Dick could write considerably more than I, I'm sure, were he to set himself to the task.

The country store was an American institution. Frankly, it's not exactly what it used to be—it's no longer the social center for the men of the community; it closes early several nights a week. The pot-bellied stove is long gone. The checker board is no more. It's modern. It's where people come, push their carts and load 'em, check out, and go on to some other important phase of living.

The country store keeper has seen America grow in its patterns of purchasing and living.

Congratulations, Dick, on forty years at virtually the same old stand—but with the foresight to keep abreast of the times. Forty more years to you, sir, if you'd like 'em—right at the corner there, in Zion!

JANUARY 26, 1972

A Real-Life Story

Twenty-five years ago, in the village in which I have resided since 1923, my brother-in-law, Dick Touchton, moved out of an old-time country store into a new building—and he opened the first self-service grocery store in our area. He was quite understandably proud of that store—its fresh new look, its shelves neatly arranged and the displays attractive enough to cause people to buy items they hadn't put on their shopping lists. To be very truthful, the whole community was proud of that store. It sort of modernized us, we thought.

Something like four months following the grand opening—and I want you to know that people in the community volunteered to help transfer merchandise from the old store across the street into the new one—everything was fine when Dick locked the doors one October Saturday night. His new venture had caught on, despite what some critics had said about "letting people wait on themselves"—you know, that shop-lifting hazard.

That particular Saturday night was foggy, damp, close; it was a good night for sleeping—and Sunday morning promised to be a good morning for a tired store keeper to sleep in a little longer than usual. But there came a call—his store was on fire!

We lived right behind Dick and my sister; and I can still, to this day, hear Dick's call to us that there was trouble down on the corner—and his bare feet made slapping noises as he literally ran the hundred-plus yards from where we all lived down to the corner. By that time, several of us were out and running, too.

Fire companies from nearby towns responded immediately to the call, and it wasn't too long before the fire was extinguished. But what a sight! The interior of the store was blackened by smoke, some shelves here and there were charred, an area of the floor had just begun to burst into flames when the firemen arrived in time to salvage the main structure.

Investigation soon indicated that the fire hadn't just "happened"—it was an act of arson.

The store had been "fired" many hours prior to dawn. It was discovered that a young boy who had returned home from a motion picture, in which such an event had occurred, had decided to try that adventure out. He had gained entrance into the store, piled dry goods on the tables in the basement, lighted the fire, and left to find a safe place from which he could watch the building burn. He confessed as much. The tight, new construction, the dampness of the night, and the absolute absence of any wind combined to keep the fire from doing much more than smoldering for hours—until smoke was pouring from the windows just at the time of daybreak. The alert had come just in time. Another few minutes and it would have been too late.

The arsonist was apprehended and incarcerated following due trial and sentence.

The people of the community went to work with Dick just as soon as the place had cooled—and the store was back in operation within an unbelievably short time. I have never seen so many people in our village set themselves to the task of lending a helping hand. The display of willingness to serve was truly heart-warming—and effective.

Dick retired from the store business a few years ago. And when he did retire, he simply forgot accounts he had carried on his books. It was over and done with. I am happy to report that some of those on his books didn't forget; they came through, as time passed—many of them. As must surely be the case more often than not, some never remembered that they had owed the little merchant on the corner—and that was that.

Twenty-five years went by—that is, after the day of the fire. Just before Christmas, there came a knock on our door. I answered it—either I or my wife, I don't recall; at any rate, we eventually were both there. A young man, neatly attired, very attractive and genial, inquired of us whether or not Mr. Touchton lived there. We directed him across the street to the Touchton home.

Some hour or so later, my brother-in-law and sister called us on the telephone to tell us what had happened.

"Mr. Touchton?" the young man inquired.

"Yes."

"You don't remember me?" the young man asked, after having given his name.

"No, I don't think I do," Dick responded.

"Well, sir, I am the man who probably caused you the most trouble anyone ever has. I set fire to your store. Now, do you remember?"

Of course Dick remembered! One doesn't forget a thing like that.

They shook hands. Dick invited the young man in.

"Mr. Touchton, I was visiting in Baltimore. Zion is, I know, a scant fifty miles from Baltimore—so I thought I'd come on up to talk with you."

My sister and Dick invited the young man to sit with them, eat a few cookies, and drink some tea. As they sat there, the young man told them that he was now the father of four sons—one of which was working his way through college. The other sons are doing fine, too, he indicated.

"I didn't want them to make the mistakes I made," he said.

You see, after having been apprehended, sentenced, and incarcerated, the young man had been "followed up" by Dick. Dick had learned that his conduct had been good during his time in the juvenile institution and Dick had requested that he be released—placed on parole—given a chance to make something of himself. Authorities had agreed to Dick's persuasion. The youngster had been given that chance.

Dick told me later that the man had no need to say "I'm sorry." Just looking him up, stopping by to wish him well, to tell him of his subsequent life—just taking what must have been a very, very difficult step by returning to face the man upon whom his adolescent act had wrought disappointment and loss—that was enough.

I honestly believe that the visit from a young man who was once what we could call a delinquent boy was one of the best Christmas gifts Dick received.

By the way, Dick had even forgotten the name! It takes a big man to forget a thing like that. Dick is a big man—even though he's about five-foot-seven with his shoes on! Tom Adams, of Churchville, calls him a real "fire cracker"—and for a man in his seventies, he is just that!"

And I must add, he has internalized Christianity as a way of life—not simply as a passport to Heaven. I'm not bragging about my brother-in-law, but I am so proud of him I could almost "bust!"

Some men are just naturally tall, aren't they? I think so, by George!

DECEMBER 2, 1986

Dick, A Country Storekeeper

It was in the spring of 1923 that I met him. I was ten years old. My father drove the old Moon up to the gasoline pump in front of the store and inquired of a lively young man just where the parsonage might be, for the parsonage was to be our home. He directed my father to the house. I'm sure he looked the four of us over—my dad was the new preacher.

With the passage of time, we came to know him well, for he took quite a liking to my sister. So much so that he and she were married right there in the parsonage in October 1927, and they lived happily ever after! That is, until death did them part. On November 20, 1986, Dick died; he and Julia had been husband and wife for 59 years.

He was widely known and loved as "Dick, the Country Storekeeper," as the title of his book indicated. He lived a long and fruitful life—a beloved friend to a host of folks who had known him across the years. While it is not easy to think of him as one gone from our midst, it is comforting to know that he is now beyond the reach of pain or any of the afflictions which could have befallen him at his age. As he quoted in his account of his life as a storekeeper, he was unafraid of death. William Cullen Bryant's words were meaningful to him: "Approach thy grave like one that wraps the drapery of his couch about him, and lies down to pleasant dreams." For Dick had kept the faith!

SEPTEMBER 27, 1995

Another Country Storekeeper

He turned 70 on September 14, and his daughter and I want to celebrate. We have tried to put together something that will let him know how much he meant to the community of Zion. I don't ordinarily do this because I wouldn't know where or when to draw the line, but this man is special.

To the best of my recollection, I first met him in the fall of 1939 when youngsters from one- and two-room elementary schools were being enrolled in Grade 8 at the Rising Sun High School.

He was the speediest softball player I ever coached—stealing a base every time he was on first, which was every time he batted during the games that took our team to the championship of the county in the spring of 1940.

Unless I have filed my math skills where I can't find them, that means I have known Ernest Coulson for 56 years. From one of the smallest and well-behaved pupils I ever taught (weight about 80 pounds), he has grown to be a solid 70-year-old, highly-valued friend.

He came to see me not long ago and we sat for the better part of an hour talking about—well, for one thing, baseball. An old habit we have engaged in for at least 50 years—ever since he became a clerk in Dick Touchton's country store here in Zion in 1943, right after he had graduated from Calvert High School.

He probably didn't have it in mind to become a storekeeper himself when he went to work for Dick, but he eventually bought the business in 1969 when Dick retired.

I said we talked baseball. That wasn't all. We reminisced about life as it was back when he became an important member of the Zion community. Now, Ernie would never admit to that "important" word, but it is entirely appropriate.

He became a presence in the community when Dick's country store was a gathering place for the men who did the major part of the family grocery shopping—quite often in the evening or even late at night.

He remains a presence to this very day because we who knew him remember him with affection when he owned and operated the store on the corner.

Ernie's daughter, Linda, a recent Cecil Community College graduate (1994, I think), once did a term paper titled "Changes in the Old Country Store," in which she detailed an interview with her father about his recollections of years behind the counter—both in the original country store operated by Dick Touchton and the county's first self-service store Dick built right across from his first place of business. Ernie recalled how the men, one at a time, read off their orders—sometimes deleting items they thought their wives didn't really need. He and Dick filled the orders while the men, some of them waiting a turn at the counter, socialized, talking crops, weather, and other interesting topics—and even playing checkers on the dry-goods counter. Ernie recalled that the pot-bellied stove was the target for tobacco chewers with expertise in expectoration.

Ernie's willingness to follow the old custom of carrying customers "on tick," plus the competition from the chain stores, which eventually went self-service too—with extended shopping hours—dictated his decision to sell his store in 1982. It is now Zion Market and Deli, owned by Karl Reichenbach.

It is difficult for me to think that folks would take advantage of a man who was generous, compassionate, and empathetic, as Ernie has always been. But the business world can twist kindness into a liability. Ernie and his late wife, Marge, extended the hand of caring to customers throughout most of his proprietorship years. When Marge died in 1980, some of the spark went out of Ernie's life—and that, too, contributed to his decision to close down his business.

He lives down in Bay View now, in the house he and Marge called home. Linda lives there with him. His son Terry and family reside in North East. One of his pleasures, he says, is seeing his seven great-grandchildren playing in the yard. He also has five grandchildren, all of them grown.

In her paper concerning country storekeepers, Linda correctly characterized her dad as "a warm, sensitive and caring man whom people told their problems to and asked his advice on a variety of subjects." She added, "He helped make the community feel like a family."

She related the following story which her modest father never mentioned when she interviewed him, but which she knew about from observation:

"One Christmas Eve he was late coming home. There was a raging snowstorm outside. After having closed the store, he stopped at the home of a community member and discovered that this family had no food for Christmas Day. He went back to his store to collect groceries so that the unfortunate family could have a nice Christmas meal."

Yes, Linda, as you say, your dad was—and still is—a remarkable person. No wonder you say, "Having a father who was a storekeeper was special."

And yes, Ernie, the hours were long and the work was hard. As you think back, I'm sure you can remember giving credit on occasion to people you knew in your heart could never pay you. You can also remember that you lent money to those who needed it. And you were never too busy to deliver groceries to the sick and elderly.

You see, while baseball was one of the ties that was important to my personal friendship with Ernie, there was much, much more than that. I loved that little boy who caught the screaming line drive to seal victory in that championship game back in 1940.

And I observed him, as he learned from Dick Touchton, the art of pleasing customers and being their friend. I saw him as a man devoted to his family, faithful to his friends, and just plain good. A good man!

He is currently employed at Cecil Community College in the building where there are baseball bats, basketballs, and other items pertinent to sports. I'm sure that if you were to ask the people who teach and coach and play there they would tell you Ernie hasn't really changed, character-wise. He's still the same modest fellow, intent on getting the job done. Friendly still. And a mighty fine person!

A belated happy birthday, Ernie! From your old teacher and friend, and from your daughter, too. We love you, by George!

MAY 4, 1977

Tribute To A Humanitarian

From time to time he furnished me with material for my columns. In fact, I have used his writings verbatim for he was a gifted writer. He was widely known throughout Southern Pennsylvania and in Cecil and Harford Counties as a general practitioner of medicine and as a humanitarian. He was my personal friend.

About a year ago, the Pennsylvania Legislature paid him the honor of issuing a resolution in recognition of his long years of service as a doctor. His office was located in his home on Locust Street in Oxford, Pennsylvania; there his daughter and his son-in-law, both family physicians, maintain their offices.

Prior to his forty-five years of practice in the Oxford area (which, as I have stated, broadened to include a large part of Chester and Lancaster Counties in the Keystone State and portions of Cecil and Harford Counties in Maryland), he had served the people of Briceville, Tennessee, from 1926 to 1930.

He practiced his profession during the years when a doctor was on-call twenty-four hours a day. Until infirmities of aging beset him, he made house-calls with regularity. I know from personal experience that there were times when he visited the same patient—often many miles from his office—as many as three times in one day or night.

Generous, he was—perhaps to a fault insofar as his personal welfare was concerned. It was not unusual for him to treat a patient free of charge and go into his own pocket for prescription money when he sensed the need for helping someone out of a difficulty.

He loved good music. He also shared with his wife an ardent passion for flowers, trees, shrubs—the whole world of nature. Together they turned a wild hillside and the brook adjacent to that rolling land into a beautiful garden where day-lilies of every color bloomed luxuriantly and where other flowers abounded.

"Robindale," they called it; and their acres of beauty served as a camping place for the Girl Scouts of the area.

A deeply religious man, he taught a men's Bible class for a number of years and, there again, shared his teaching talent with neighboring communities. On several Sunday mornings he came down to Zion to teach a men's group which consisted of from fifteen to twenty persons. He never failed to convey his deep faith and to illustrate that faith through his concerns for the human family.

Dr. Fount B. Robinson died on Wednesday, April 27, 1977, at the age of 77. To those who knew him, the recollections of his healing touch, his interesting and compelling insights into human nature, his many acts of kindness will keep Dr. Robinson "alive."

In 1972, Doctor and his wife, Mildred Kimble Robinson, were Oxford's Citizens of the Year. In truth, they were "everybody's citizens of the year," year in and year out.

It was my privilege to speak at a dinner given in Doctor's honor a couple of years ago. At that time I stated that an element of immortality was already evident within that family circle. Dr. Faye Robinson Doyle and her husband, Dr. Russell G. Doyle, continue to practice the profession which endeared Dr. Robinson to thousands of his patients. And his son, Carl W. Robinson, of Newark, Delaware, continues to "practice" Doctor's love of music.

Mrs. Robinson, I know, will devote even more of her love and her time to the garden spot, Robindale; and she will sense that Doctor will be with her when those day-lilies burst into full bloom and raise their many colors toward the summer skies.

JUNE 19, 1963

He Gave Me A Bible

This issue of the paper carries in it the obituary of one who has been very near and dear to us across the years . . . Joseph L. Thompson.

As I look back across the years during which it has been my privilege to know him and to be a member of his family, I find many, many meaningful and pleasant memories. But they are personal and have no place in public print. Those memories I shall treasure, you may be sure—and I am grateful for every moment I ever shared with him.

From him, I received the kind of guidance a younger man needs and hopes for from a father. I looked to him for a pattern and found him to be worthy of emulation. I know I am a better person for having known him—for having felt his influence in my life. It was a good influence.

There is but one incident I would share with you now . . . Back in 1937—on the 30th of April—on the day my wife, his daughter, and I were celebrating our very first wedding anniversary—he presented me with a Bible. And with it was the suggestion—and perhaps unsaid, I do not remember—that I use it—for myself and others. Shortly thereafter, I began using whatever talent I might possess in the local ministry. As long as I live, I shall see him in the congregation, wherever I am; and I shall sense his presence, lending me that kind of support and encouragement born of sincere affection for God's Word—and for me.

A man by the name of Elihu Burritt once said, "No human being can come into this world without increasing or diminishing the sum total of human happiness." May I say of my father-in-law, he put the emphasis upon increasing the sum total of happiness—for those of his family and for all whom he cherished as friends and neighbors.

Now that he has finished his course, may I add—he truly kept the Faith!

AUGUST 23, 1988

Dr. Wid And Seeds Of Friendship

Our daily paper carried a column the other day which reminded me of a most pleasant relationship Elizabeth and I had with a physician and his wife more than 50 years ago. But first, let me go back to that column—one written by a gardener whose advice is worth acting upon. He stated that now is the time to be collecting seeds from this year's flower gardens for next year's planting. And that's what brought Dr. William Marshall Jr. and his wife, Bowdie, to mind. Dr. Wid—that's what almost everyone called him—demonstrated that gardening technique when he was administering advice to us about raising flowers.

The Marshalls lived in Milford, Delaware. My Grandmother Clendaniel, upon visiting us in Zion in the spring of 1937, noticed that I was dreadfully underweight and very lethargic. Since she doubted that I would take kindly to doses of sulphur and molasses, she suggested to Elizabeth and me that we drive down to Milford and let Dr. Wid take a look at me and, hopefully, bring me back to life. We did just that—drove down to Milford—and, yes, he brought me back to life, though it required a dozen or so visits over a period of a couple years to his office. Whatever that tonic was that he mixed for me, it revived my flagging physique to a reasonable degree; at least that's the way I feel, since I'm still around to write my weekly piece.

Dr. Wid came from a doctor family. His father had been my Grandmother Clendaniel's doctor. The Marshalls established their own private hospital in Milford—Dr. Wid and his brother, Dr. Sam, were still operating it back in the '30s. Maybe later than that—I'm not sure. Dr. Wid's home and office were adjacent to the hospital, and he and his nurse-wife had a beautiful flower garden which sloped down to a narrow body of water, the name of which I have forgotten. After he had examined me and given Elizabeth and me directions concerning diet, sleeping habits, exercise, and reading-for-relaxation, he and Bowdie would take us out in the garden to see the array of flowers there—in beds and bordering winding pathways. Dr. Wid would stop every now and then, take a small envelope (pill-size) and collect seeds from a columbine plant or from some old-fashioned pinks, ragged robins, bleeding hearts, daisies—oh, so many different blooming beauties! Seeds from each plant went into an envelope just for that very variety—and he labeled each envelope carefully for us.

We lived next to what was then the Zion Presbyterian Church. Our back yard was not very big, but it was large enough for a good-sized, oblong-shaped flower bed. Dr. Wid's seeds furnished us with a galaxy of color for several years; along the fence separating our yard from the cemetery, we had a mighty pretty row of flowers. The majority of those flowers came from collecting seeds in the late summer and early autumn for the next year's planting. Dr. Wid had found apt pupils.

Dr. Wid and Bowdie (Bowser had been her maiden name) were wonderful people. They had time to spend with a young couple (that's what we were) and they shared many, many ideas with us that we have treasured over the years. When we took our infant son to their home some three years after I had first been Dr. Wid's patient, they gave him a wooly lamb. We still have that stuffed toy in one of the boxes in what we call our attic.

Dr. and Mrs. Marshall had some Cecil County ties; they visited the Constable family in Elkton. If there was any blood relationship, I never knew it. But Doctor often spoke of the Constables with a note of affection in his voice.

Both Dr. Wid and Dr. Sam were graduates of the University of Delaware and were active in alumni affairs. They were regarded as "institutions" by the folks of lower Delaware. Beloved they were. And rightly so.

The last time we visited Dr. Wid and Bowdie, he stopped us as we were about to leave, placed a hand on each of us, and said a prayer. He concluded with a benediction that truly warmed our hearts.

From tiny seeds a lifelong association can grow—right along with the flowers, by George!

OCTOBER 17, 1989

Of A President's Son

Some former presidents' sons and/or daughters are in the news rather frequently and appear, from all accounts, to be very comfortably situated.

Others have a tendency to get into the news because of misadventures of sorts. Perhaps the oldest of the living offspring of once-upon-a-time presidents works very close to the house wherein his dad was sworn in back in the early 1920's. And in that small building up the road a piece from the farm house which is the birthplace of his father, this son of a president makes cheese. A newsworthy tid-bit, don't you think?

Well, now, John Coolidge doesn't actually do the making; he supervises the six people who make up the staff of the cheese factory. But even though he doesn't do the stirring, he's there every day, keeping The Plymouth Cheese Corporation churning.

I can only assume that the factory had its beginnings in the 19th century, but I do not know the actual date. According to a story by Marialisa Calta of *The New York Times* (I think), the wooden curd tub or sink is a part of the factory's original equipment; the stainless-steel vat has to be relatively modern.

The factory closed during the depression and it was not until 1960 that Mr. Coolidge got it started again. He didn't want to see the building destroyed! Plus, it's giving him something to do in his retirement years. He is 82 years old.

I have been to Plymouth Notch, Vermont, twice within fairly recent years. I admit to being partial to Calvin Coolidge, the President who patted me on my head and called me by name during Thanksgiving week, 1925. I recall the sadness I felt as a child when, in the middle-twenties, the news of the death of the other Coolidge son hit the newspapers. I have not talked with

John Coolidge nor have I visited the cheese factory. I have conversed at some length with one of Mr. Coolidge's cousins and found him most affable. You may say that I'm partial to the entire Coolidge family, not just President Coolidge.

I have not yet eaten any of the Plymouth Cheese—but I'm going to eat some. And soon. I'm sending my check for $10 to The Plymouth Cheese Corporation, P.O. Box 1, Plymouth, VT 05056 as soon as I finish this column, by George! And if I can, I'm going back to Plymouth Notch next summer. I hope to meet Mr. John Coolidge and watch the folks in the cheese factory break the curds up into the right texture for that Cheddar-like cheese—caraway, sage, hot pepper, or plain.

(I am indebted to Marialisa Calta for bringing the cheese factory to my attention. And to the Coolidge family for giving me something of New England to feel mighty good about.)

MAY 16, 1962

Oh, The Sand Tarts!

Last week I welcomed a newcomer to our family. This week I am bidding farewell to a very dear friend and neighbor. The point is, life is filled with perplexing contradictions—conflicting emotions of joy and sorrow, gladness and regret.

I first knew her 39 years ago—in May of 1923. I was the preacher's little boy when she first saw me. I liked her at once; she seemed to know what little boys would take a fancy to—such as a doughnut.

When I was old enough to set steel traps with Jimmy Renn, we walked past her house every winter morning. Often she would call us in so that we might have something hot to drink and something pleasing to a sweet tooth.

She was the first person outside my family to surprise me at Christmas time . . . a big package all my own, and inside that package a variety of items which made me very happy.

No one has ever made better sand tarts. They were real Christmas treats.

But she wasn't a personality who existed just because of the kind and nice things she did. She was a neighbor and a friend. She was a part of the church here in Zion. She belonged to us all.

It is going to be mighty strange without her because she has been so long a part of our living—when she was over on the hill near Zion and down in the little hollow just outside the village and then, in later years, right in the village itself.

But there'll always be something of her left among us so long as any who were close to her remain—for she was the kind of woman who left her influence upon people—a good influence, it was, too.

Years ago a little boy called her "NinNin." To this day, she was "Nin" to many who knew her—including me.

We who mourn her leaving us just can't help feeling sorry—for ourselves—yet happy, too, that she has found rest.

JUNE 4, 1991

Ghostly Names On A Stovepipe

I have always heard that an honest confession is good for the soul. Well, if it's good for the soul, it ought to be good for a column. So here goes. . .

Back around the middle-to-late '40s—that's when I was considerably younger than I am now—I was still teaching at the Rising Sun High School. Teachers' rooms had not yet come into vogue, and the men on the faculty who smoked used the furnace room on occasion. At that point in my life I had the bad habit of smoking; I'm not proud of that, but it's a fact and I am herein confessing.

I went into the furnace room one day to sneak a puff or two. I happened to glance up at the big galvanized stove pipe above the furnace. There in white chalk were written two names. High up on that pipe they were. As I read those names I had an eerie feeling. Almost ghostly, in fact.

There, just as bold as could be against the dark gray pipe, were those names: Pepsie McCummings and Charlie Pierce! Two former pupils, both of whom had been killed in the war. No other names on the pipe—no graffiti on the walls. Just those two names, written in each one's own handwriting.

That was probably the quickest smoke I ever took. The coincidence startled me. Why Francis and Charles had inscribed their names there I couldn't figure out at all. Last signatures as it turned out. Neither boy was the sort to commit even the mildest form of vandalism; each was a respectful, friendly youngster. Active in athletics. Each had good classroom deportment.

I thought of them on Memorial Day. They died in battle almost a half-century ago. Their deaths have remained "real" to me over the years because of that strange experience in the furnace room. No, their names didn't mysteriously disappear; they were still there just before the old furnace room was turned into teachers' rooms when the old building underwent considerable growth—the gymnasium, the library wing, and the wing on the east end of the building. And, oh, yes, the cafeteria and the shops. The coal-burning furnace was ripped out. The huge stove pipe, too.

I remember those two boys well. It seems that when I close my eyes I can see them as they were when they attended Rising Sun High School. Charlie had no brothers or sisters. There were other McCummings boys—one older than Francis and two younger, if my memory serves me properly; and their father came on as one of the custodians at the school. Mr. McCummings is a very special person; he is well up into his 90s. Lives up at Sylmar. He is known as Whitey by some and Pop Pop to the grandchildren. He is a much–loved elderly man. I am proud to be numbered among his many friends.

No, Pepsie and Charlie weren't the only boys from my roll book to lose their lives in World War II. I'm not sure I can recall the name of every single one, but I think Joe Hambleton died in that war and Louis Graybeal was killed in an accident on one of the islands in the Pacific after the war was over. Ernie Little, whom I did not have in school—he had graduated before I began teaching—was a Rising Sun casualty, too.

You know, if I hadn't gone into that furnace room to steal a smoke that day, I might never have seen those names in chalk on that stove pipe. Strange how things come to pass, isn't it? Very strange, by George!

JULY 24, 1963

They Were Special

One of the cherished recollections we have of the school days we experienced as parents a few years back concerned a gentleman for whom a great many people have a great affection.

Our youngster was in the first or second grade—I don't remember which, exactly—and he came home from school one evening behaving very much as though he had had a fine day. We engaged him in conversation, and, as parents will do, we tried to get from him something of the goings-on that day.

I cannot recall the details, but the account we received had something to do with an activity outside the classroom—in the halls or on the playground. And he ended his comments with the remark— "And guess who one of my favorite teachers is!"

He didn't wait for an answer from us. Instead, he answered his own stated question. "Mr. Owens!"

Well, Mr. Owens, whom we in Zion and Calvert know better as "Charlie," has been a real favorite with youngsters right through all his years up at the Calvert School—and rightly so. For his kindness to children of all ages is something to behold.

I'm sure he carried in his memory many, many happy and sincere "thank you's"—punctuated with youthful smiles from boys and girls who found in him a friend.

Charlie, may I join with countless others whose youngsters you have befriended in wishing you a most happy and contented retirement—and many years of relaxed living!

Another friend of mine has reached that stage in life when it's time, officially, to hang up the hammer and saw and take it a bit easier.

For a number of years, he performed innumerable maintenance tasks for the Board of Education. I'm particularly aware of what kind of person he is, for I have been a neighbor, now, for exactly forty years and four months, and I've liked being his neighbor, very much.

Several young men whom I have known were fortunate to have been placed under his supervision during months of summer employment—and they found him a fine man with whom to be associated.

As in the case with Charlie Owens, his kindness and patience with young people has been most admirable. And several parents I know have been pleased that their sons worked with him.

It isn't going to be easy for Charlie Owens or Raymond DeMond to break away from the regular routine of their jobs, I know. And somehow it doesn't seem natural to think of either of them as "retired"—they've been so very active in their individual capacities. But maybe a little time to do just as he pleases won't be burdensome to Raymond DeMond nor to Charlie.

So, to Raymond, too, I'd like personally to extend my best wishes for a happy time doing whatever you choose to do, now that you're pretty much on your own insofar as work goes. And many years of happy gardening, sir!

"A laugh is worth one hundred groans in any market."
—Charles Lamb

A Little Nonsense Now and Then

ZION, MD, AUGUST 21, 1991

Fun In A Sidecar—At My Age!

I looked it up in my dictionary and while recently it has come to be used in connection with all sorts of dried flora so mixed as to give off pleasant odors, it traditionally has meant a hodgepodge of things.

That's about what my columns are—a recording of a variety of happenings that have affected me personally. Potpourri is from the French *pot pourri* which literally translated is said to mean *rotten pot*. (Whoops! I certainly hope my columns aren't regarded as rot.)

Languages do take some mighty strange twists in meaning. The mixture of dried flowers, herbs and spices doesn't add up to something rotten. Not at 10 bucks a jar, they don't!

Anyway my columns are my own potpourri—a mixture of happenings that have meaning for me. Let's get on with one.

One morning in July—when it was hot!—Leonard Conrad decided that the time had come for me to be introduced to the excitement and joy of motorcycling.

He rode over to Zion from his home in Colora, told me he was keeping a promise he had made two years ago during the reunion of the Class of 1939 of the Rising Sun High School. That promise had to do with taking me for a ride in the sidecar attached to his beloved two-wheeled vehicle.

Now, I had never been too keen about motorcycles and I was inclined to hesitate, even back out on this deal. But upon seeing the enthusiasm for cycling that Leonard exuded, I just couldn't turn him down. He's a salesman, all right. He convinced me that life on two wheels and a sidecar is fun.

And so it was that, after a cup of coffee and about a good hour of swallowing whatever lingering reluctance I might have been harboring, I followed Leonard out to his motorcycle and surprised both of us by crawling into the cozy little sidecar.

No, I can't say I vaulted into it; I'm not that agile anymore and I'd better not become mendacious. The fact is, I had to use two hands to persuade my cranky right leg to collapse sufficiently to be tucked into the space reserved for it. Then we were off!

My sister Julia, upon seeing the takeoff, waved a handkerchief—as though I were being whisked away into permanent exile.

I have never—and let me emphasize the word never—seen anyone appear to be more pleased to keep his word than Leonard was that day.

He seemed to be as delighted to be giving me this new and thrilling experience as I was to be seeing him and listening to his recounting of his 900,000-mile life-on-wheels, much of which has been shared with his devoted wife, the former Nancy Balderston.

We sped along, in keeping with the posted speed limits, down England Creamery Road and across the country to his home in Colora.

I felt like a youngster, sitting there in that capsule-like seat, the wind in my face and the roadside zipping past me at a right good clip.

Leonard tried to talk to me, but my deafness cut short what conversation we might have had during that ride. He had wanted to get a picture of his old (and elderly, too) school teacher occupying the passenger seat, but, in the absence of both Nancy and a hidden camera, he had to forgo that until later.

We stopped at the Sun Pharmacy in Rising Sun, where I bought a roll of film. A few passers-by and lookers-on who saw me in the sidecar seemed to be astonished. Folks never know what to expect out of me it seems.

We returned to Zion by way of Routes 273 and 272. There we posed for pictures so that Leonard can show us off at the next reunion of the '39ers. Margy Hollowell, an insurance company neighbor, worked the camera for us.

That was a most pleasing happening for me. It was good to renew a classroom acquaintance on a non-classroom basis.

How I do like being with my once-upon-a-time "kids" again! They have no idea how they brighten my life. The reward of having been there with them when they were young and I was, too!

That's me in the sidecar with Leonard Conrad at the handlebars

I really did enjoy that ride! Now, I don't know that I'd opt for that mode of travel for a long journey. Not at my age. I'd have to go through a conditioning program before and a rehabilitation one afterward.

But that's beside the point. What I'm trying to say is simply this: It was worth it, just seeing the look of satisfaction on Leonard's face. He had me right where he had promised I'd be, in that sidecar, taking a spin with him and his beloved motorcycle. He and I were both happy, by George!

Another happening. One I won't soon forget, if ever.

ZION, MD, JANUARY 11, 1983

Insomnia—and Fishing

One thing which amused me very much as I was reading Red Smith's columns was his admitted inability to sleep one wink the night before an up-coming fishing trip. While I know of no blood relationship between Red Smith and George Prettyman, in that one respect there was a kinship. And should you not believe me on that score, you are at liberty to check with Jim Renn.

Several years ago, when the late Samuel Melvin "Trigger" Collyer was taking fishing parties out of Rock Hall, a group of us from the Zion area would engage him for two or three days, at intervals, that is, during the summer. Captain Trigger was the sort of person who took you where the fish were if there were any to be taken to. But the experience of being with him was worth the whole bit—travel time, money, etc.—even though the catch could be limited on occasion to just a few rock and/or blue fish.

I USUALLY called him well in advance to set up the dates he was available and then waited for the time to come when we could take off from Zion very early in the morning and get down to Hubbard's Restaurant for breakfast before it was time to climb aboard the boat for the day's fishing. I would promise to rouse my Zion neighbors early enough so that we could squeeze in a hearty breakfast down on the old wharf. And when I said "early," I meant it! We'd usually agree that 3:30 would be the proper time.

Well, I'd go to bed and make every attempt to fall asleep—having duly set my alarm clock for, say, 2:30, since I am notoriously slow in the morning. Never once during the several summers we engaged Cap'n Trigger was I able to catch a nap which lasted longer than thirty seconds. And never once did the alarm go off. I was up and about long before the clock could sound the "it's time" bell.

TRY AS I would, I could not restrain myself from moving across the street to give Jim a call far in advance of the scheduled hour—or half-hour, as was the appointed time. Jim thought I was crazy, but he didn't come out and say so. He hustled around and was ready by the time I had rounded up Ben Sauselein, Harold Criswell, Howard and Dick Touchton, and whoever else was to be in that particular party. They all thought I was a nut—but since I usually insisted on driving my car down to my native town, they fussed not. I think they were all glad to be sharing the experience which awaited us.

Cap'n Trigger designated Jim Renn as his second mate right off. His son—Cap'n Trigger's, that is—Bucky was the first mate. I wasn't a mate; but I must confess that I had the inside track with Cap'n Trigger. He always saw to it that my line was baited and cast as soon as we were where the fish were calculated to be. If lines became tangled, he was sure to label the fish on one of the hooks as "Mr. George's"—a circumstance which caused Touch one day to raise both his eyebrow and his voice in mock protest. I think it was generally understood that Cap'n Trigger was going to take care of me at all cost. I was native, you see. (My dad had baptized him years ago.)

THE DRIVE HOME was always a hazard. Having had no sleep the night before, I was really in no shape to take the wheel. But I would insist. I had one request: that at least one of my riders would stay awake and keep talking to me to make sure I crossed the canal when we came to it instead of plunging into it. We always made it safely back to Zion where we divided the day's catch, did what cleaning was necessary (the major cleaning job had been done at the wharf and the fish packed in ice), and told our wives extravagant fish stories. There is absolutely no sense in going fishing if a fellow can't lie about the big one that got away!

Cap'n Trigger is now doing his fishing in the serene waters of eternity. Some of our fishing buddies have gone to their reward, too. I won't have the opportunity of calling them up an hour ahead of time because anticipation brings on insomnia in my case. I miss that. But it's fun recalling those summer days when the dates on the calendar were encircled, designating those as ours aboard Cap'n Trigger's fishing boat.

I think what dispelled sleep was the little boy in me who knew we were going home—to the town where I was born—and to be with a very kind old gentleman who not only took us to where the fish were, but also could tell some mighty interesting yarns as he maneuvered his craft through the waters of the Chesapeake Bay.

ONE OF HIS most interesting tales concerned the famous actress, Tallulah Bankhead, and her sister, who would book him and his boat for a day on the Bay—and spend most of the time sunning themselves atop the cabin roof—sipping nectar. One day, I recall, he guided us all for a drive after the fishing was over and some of us visited the grave of Miss Bankhead. She is, you know, buried down near Rock Hall. (Cap'n Trigger had other interesting tales to tell, too; but I won't go into them now.)

Yes, Red Smith's wakefulness the night before a fishing excursion triggered cherished memories of Cap'n Trigger—and my kinship, in spirit, with the famous columnist. It's great to have at least one thing in common with that man, by George!

ZION, MD, NOVEMBER 12, 1978

Self-Images And Other Things

Remembrance, ah, what a sad world 'twould be could we, who write, not lean upon thee! I don't know who said this, but, it is oh, so true!

In conversation with one of my retired neighbors one day this past week, I was reminded of an encounter with a turkey gobbler. We were discussing E.B. White's essays, to which I have alluded from time to time, and his penchant for writing about pigs, raccoons, geese, and the like. And I recalled an experience I once had with a turkey.

We—my father and the family, that is—had a beautiful new automobile. Shiny black, it was, as most cars were in the 'twenties. We were visiting some farm folks in my father's parish, and as we stopped the automobile near the gate leading to the white-fenced lawn, a turkey gobbler put on his strutting act and took on a most menacing demeanor. He approached the car and appeared to be glaring intently at us; a rather threatening look it was.

Suddenly that gobbler went into a frenzy of wing-flapping and strange noises—and came in full-flight at the side of the automobile. He thrashed against the side of the car, using his spurs and his beak with considerable force against the metal.

I don't recall exactly how his owner prevented him from beating himself to death in the struggle which was utterly one-sided. I do recall, however, that my dad's automobile bore the scratch-marks of that tom's assault upon what he evidently thought to be an intruding gobbler, not having, it appears, sense enough to recognize himself when he looked into what passed at that moment for a mirror.

And I was reminded, too, one little Schnauzer in the family was surprised when she first saw herself in a mirror. Maxl put on quite a show in her attempt to get at her own image. The barking, the backing-off, the sudden leap at an imagined invader of her domain were all very amusing, though I must admit that I feared for the safe-keeping of that full-length mirror in which Maxl was seeing herself and not knowing it. She did learn, in due time, not to take herself seriously, apparently discovering just what a mirror is and how it works.

Nothing can be more embarrassing than coming upon a mirror unaware and speaking to the image of oneself. It has happened to me—and I'm neither a turkey nor a dog! I have even carelessly walked right into mirrored walls in museums or restaurants and been startled to find myself running smack into the glass! Such stupid self-encounters can come from woolgathering. Preoccupation, some would prefer to call it. No matter the name, the ego becomes more than a little dented. It's comparable to waving a friendly greeting to a mailbox or a fence post which, out of the corner of the eye, has given the illusion of being a person.

Now, were I as able an essayist as E. B. White, I could really make a good account of this next little episode.

I was asked one Sunday afternoon to accompany a Methodist minister to a creek wherein he would be baptizing a parishioner by immersion. Generally, Methodists are baptized by the dainty process of sprinkling a bit of water on the head, but this about-to-become member of the church requested baptism by immersion—and I was the witness.

I parked my car in the meadow some distance from the creek and duly performed my duty as witness while the minister performed the baptism. It was impressive—and I am being completely sincere in so stating. I was, in fact, pleased and honored to have been chosen to witness that ceremony.

My car was parked several hundred feet from the place of baptism. As I turned to go back to the car, I was astonished to see that it was surrounded by a half-dozen or so cows. I wondered why. I also wondered whether the cows would permit me access to my automobile.

Boldly I approached the cows and the car. I had often heard that goats eat tin cans—and I'm sure that's a myth!—but I wondered what about my assemblage of metal there was to attract cattle. (Happily, I saw no bulls!) I discovered that the cows were giving my car a bath—licking it from bumper to bumper! Since the vehicle had but a few days before been freshly waxed, it had become a most streaked mess! The cows' tongue marks were everywhere!

The feeling of piety which I had but a few minutes before enjoyed suddenly left me, I am ashamed to admit, and what I said to the cows could scarcely be termed to be in the nature of a blessing.

Like the Red Sea, the animals around my car parted and let me through. I opened the door, started the motor, and eased my way out of the pasture, onto the highway, and home.

That was before the days of the automatic carwash. It took considerable scrubbing, accompanied by an equal amount of grumbling on my part, to remove all evidence of that encounter with the cows. I have assiduously avoided leaving my car within tongue-licking proximity of any member of the bovine family from that time on, by George!

ZION, MD, AUGUST 21, 1996

Too Fast And Too Slow Behind The Wheel!

Lest you get the idea that all I do is sit and mull over the past, I'd like you to know that is not the case. For example, I'm already booked to fly to Seattle for Christmas and have been ever since last January.

I plan to spend the holidays with Susan, Ken and Megan. Also, there are dates pending for a visit to Ashland, Virginia, where Jeff and his two boys and Kathy reside. And, I'm committed to Scottsdale, Arizona, in March of 1997, to work out the kinks of winter.

Then, too, there's talk about a little book of my columns, scheduled to be printed within the coming months. Selecting appropriate pieces for that project is taking hours every day. I'm tired of reading something like 2,400 of the things, some of them three times and then some, just to pare the stack down to a reasonable pile. I am looking forward to getting that project completed before I join the majority, if I may use that expression. (Think cemetery.)

ONE OF THE COLUMNS I want seems to have been lost in the shuffle and needs recycling of sorts. It concerns those good old days when I could actually drive my automobile—without "drifting, swerving, or weaving," as Jeffrey accused me of doing when he, his dad, and I were on a baseball tour in the '70s. They put me in the back seat on that trip. This experience I'm about to repeat happened right here at home.

I was coming down Md. 272 from Calvert and was almost ready to turn on England Creamery Road, with my car radio going full blast on selections from the '60s. Pieces I liked. Music, not noise which sadly passes as music these days. (How's that for sounding like a fuddy-duddy?)

I must have been swept into a reverie by "Love Is a Many Splendored Thing" or something like that, for my foot became heavy and I was making time. The siren blew, the trooper came alongside me, and motioned for me to stop. I did.

I handed him the credentials he asked for and waited for his comment. After having scanned my license and registration card, he ducked his head halfway into the car and said, very kindly, "Mr. Prettyman, you don't look like a speeder."

"I'M NOT—USUALLY," I responded.

"You were going 61 and the limit here is 50. What were you thinking about?" he asked.

"I wasn't thinking," I said. "I was listening to the radio. And I'm hurrying home because my wife is ill. I wouldn't have been on this road if there weren't a bridge out on Wheatley Road."

"Well, sir, turn the radio off and slow down." That was all Trooper Phelps said. He handed me back my cards, wrote out a warning, got into his automobile, and drove off. I could have hugged him!

I took a deep breath, placed the license and the registration card where they belonged, went home and told Beth I had been stopped by a cop. I told her what I told him. And, boy! She resented being used as an excuse for my speeding. I apologized.

Evening came. She and I rode down to North East to play cards with Clarence and Evelyn. We four enjoyed a game we call Continental Rummy. Now, don't get fussed up! We don't—or didn't—or haven't ever gambled; we simply played through the six stages of the game two or three times, had refreshments, and enjoyed ourselves. It was close to midnight when Beth and I started back to Zion.

When we crossed U. S. 40 on 272, I noticed some cars behind us, right on my back bumper, so it seemed. The one directly behind was towing a boat. There were also other cars lined up behind me. I pulled over to the paved shoulder, slowed down to a turtle's crawl, and let 'em go past. I don't like having cars rushing me from the rear.

I suppose I was slow getting back to the lane in which I belonged, for there was that siren again. I sighed, pulled back to the shoulder, rolled my window down, and waited.

THE TROOPER FLASHED HIS LIGHT RIGHT IN MY FACE!

"Mr. Prettyman!" he exclaimed. He was right well surprised, I could tell. "Are you all right?" It was Trooper Phelps again.

"Yes, sir," I hastened to say. "I'm not drunk—and this is my wife!" I practically shouted. I was eager to set him straight on all counts.

"Why were you going so slowly, and what were you doing on the shoulder?" That was his question.

"Letting the Pennsylvania Navy go by," I replied.

"You're not supposed to be driving on the shoulder. You let the other drivers take care of themselves. If they want to pass you, they will. And don't drive so slowly." A pause. Then in the most pleasantly concerned manner, almost as if he doubted his wish could come true, he added, "I hope you get home safely." And a final, "Good-night, Mrs. Prettyman."

I would like to see him again one of these days. He's a fine trooper. But I won't be driving, by George! Gosh! Twice in one day! From fast to slow. No wonder the kids say, "Dad Dad! Enough's enough."

ZION, MD, APRIL 10, 1968

The Trumpet Blows

FOR A LONG TIME . . . The first job I ever had after completing my college education was in the "old" *Cecil Whig* building, doing some writing and proofreading for the late Mr. Murray J. Ewing. My first few days in the office and shop were spent sorting copper and zinc cuts which had been stored under the steps which led to the second floor in the *Whig* building—then on North Street in Elkton.

I had had some little acquaintance with the printing trade, but only as a very casual onlooker. My Uncle Joe Prettyman, of Laurel, Delaware, had his own job printing shop, and I used to watch him run his hand-fed press and set his type by hand, little thinking that I would ever be in any way closely associated with the graphic arts.

It was while I worked for Mr. Ewing that I came to know—and like—the men in the shop there—Horace Lilley, Ted Brown, Cliff Pyle. And in the front office I worked with the late Randolph Fields during those first couple of years. I was completely the novice. I scarcely knew lower case type from caps when I first started—and even today I have a terrible time identifying type size by "point," as it is called. I have to rely on my good friends who do the printing for me—those at the Cronin shop and elsewhere—to guide me in the selection of kind, style, and point for the various jobs I have done as part of my work with the Board of Education of Harford County.

Horace, Ted, and Cliff will never, I am sure, forget my proofreading. It left much to be desired in those days—and it's still one of the chores related to the printing process which I would rather someone else do.

This isn't a very sedate, prim little story, but it does illustrate the feeling of utter frustration which comes over me when I am confronted with reading proof. Back in the mid-'thirties, the *Whig* carried theater ads, as it still does. Many of them were hand set—the type, at least—and had to be read for possible errors.

On the particular movie bill which I will never forget—and you will soon see why—there was a movie playing in Elkton called "The Trumpet Blows." The movie starred George Raft. His name was to be set in all caps—RAFT. That much I knew. What I didn't know was that the simple transposition of two of the letters in that name would be—and, so help me, were—catastrophic! Now, I'm not going to spell it out for you—but if you transpose the R and the F in that name you will get the full blast of the embarrassment which came my way when the *Whig* came out that week!

To this day, I shudder when I am presented with galleys to read for errors—for in my present position I had just better be right all of the time! And having once tripped flat on my very red face, I am forever skeptical of my own ability to catch a horrifying mistake before it is too, too late!

I still retain an enthusiastic appreciation for the men and women who are engaged in the printing business. They have multiple opportunity to make laughable and not-so-laughable errors. Writers may get sued, but proofreaders are more likely to simply get a good bawling out—to feel the ever-present flush of embarrassment over the mistakes they make from time to time. The proofreader, I think, has the roughest assignment of them all—he or she can be blamed for goofing up on the whole matter in hand—and so innocently!

A number of the good friends I have are in the printing business. That figures, because my work takes me to the printing shops and newspaper offices—a great many of them—in Harford County, and occasionally I come across the river on some special errands to either the *Whig* or *Democrat* offices.

John Slaten, with whom I worked for several summers when both he and I were with the *Oxford Press* and its affiliates, now has his own printing business in Elkton. Cliff Pyle still does some printing, I understand, in his own shop—now that he's "retired" from punching the time clock in someone else's establishment. Just this very week—Monday, in fact—the Everett Johnsons, of Rising Sun, opened their new printing venture down in North East. (I remember when Everett set type for Mr. Evans Ewing who edited the old *Midland Journal* in Rising Sun.)

I could go on and on naming the people who have made printing fun for me over the years, despite my monumental mistakes now and then and the mistakes others have made in the preparation of work for me.

Suffice to say, if I should be blessed with a life beyond retirement time, I hope I can do a few odd writing jobs and work with printers now and then. I like the people who inhabit printing shops and newspaper offices!

ZION, MD, APRIL 4, 1981

A Wrestling Match

Well, now! Here I am—right back where I started from—in the *Whig*, back in January of 1934 ... But this is 1981, forty-seven years later. . .

I was remembering the other morning, while chatting with Bill Short, an episode which happened while I was a freshman at the University of Delaware in the fall of 1929. At that time, ROTC was mandatory for all who were able to pass the physical. The examining physicians had some misgivings about OK-ing me for the rigors of that course; but I landed in a woolen World War I uniform, wrap-leggin's and all, much to my discomfort. The "piece" which was issued me all but out-weighed me. Nonetheless, I was expected to go through the manual of arms with reasonable facility. Trouble was, I never seemed to be able to control the gun. It was something of a wrestling match whenever the orders were barked— "Present arms! Right shoulder arms!" etc. The gun usually won the match; I simply was not geared to manipulate that piece, as it was called then.

Well, the pay-off came one day when we were ordered to fix our bayonets in place on our pieces. I managed to get that done without losing a finger or slashing a wrist. But what occurred later—that's another part of the story.

Russell Todd—unfortunately for him—was next to me in line for close-order drill. All went well with the marching bit. It was not until the time came for the wrestling match with my piece that real trouble ensued. Somewhere during the drill with the rifle, my hands and arms got tangled with the gun and the gun escaped my grasp. And I whacked Russell Todd soundly on his noggin with the broadside of my bayonet. The blow staggered him—and, I'm sure, brought on a momentary flush of anger, for he was in no way my enemy.

The blustering sergeant immediately took issue with my ineptitude and ordered me two paces forward. I cannot here repeat his sentiments as he expressed them that day. Suffice to say, I was duly humiliated. Had there been any way in which I could have disappeared—crawled into any hole available—I would have done so. Instead, I was handed over to an upperclassman who was directed to take me as far from all other budding soldiers as the space in Frazer Field would permit and there put me through the manual of arms until the drill period was concluded.

Happily for me, someone in the Military Department—could have been that kind man, Lt. E.P. Jolls—came to the decision that I was not likely to help win any wars, with or without a gun. A drum and bugle outfit was organized and I was assigned to a snare drum. At least I outweighed the drum sticks! And I could manage to be harnessed to a drum.

You know, that drum and bugle corps—other fellows found their way into it—evolved into a band before the year was out. I became one of the drummers—oh, I beat a mean drum, let me tell you! The next year found us playing at football games—at home and on the road occasionally. We were eventually decked out in beautiful blue and gold capes and the entire ROTC Corps had comfortable new uniforms.

That little band was the forerunner of what has become a fine musical organization which entertains fans during half-time at football games every fall. Our band was the first to play George Kelley's "Fight Song," I'll have you know. What we lacked in numbers, we made up for in spirit.

While I was found to be an unlikely prospect for advanced ROTC, I was retained in the band—played in it all four years as an undergraduate and one fall as a graduate student. I loved every minute of it!

Strangely enough, my grades in ROTC were very good—all A's except for one B. I was even made an "honorary sergeant" somewhere along the way. The only demerits I ever received

I was in the band!
University of Delaware

were for my failure to shave early in my freshman year. It didn't seem to matter that I had nothing on my face to shave except a bit of fuzz. So I began to shave—at least once every six weeks; then the stubble began to form and shaving became a daily part of my routine.

When the Class of 1933 held its 45th anniversary of graduation a couple of years ago, I saw Russell Todd and we reviewed that embarrassing moment on the drill field. Russ assured me that the blow on the head had in no way figured in his life since that day. In fact, he had to scratch his head a minute or two to recall the incident.

Since he suffered no permanent damage and since my bruised ego healed in due course of time, I'm kind of glad it happened. Out of it came that fledgling drum and bugle corps out of which came the band. Oh, the good times we had in the East Wing of Old College on cold winter days, practicing indoors while our classmates were on the drill field listening to the barked orders of the drill masters!

And I never had to wrestle with a rifle—not one other time, by George!

ZION, MD, JANUARY 10, 1989

Never Wear Your Best Trousers When . . . .

In one of Henrik Ibsen's plays there's a line I'm going to appropriate for my own purposes, though, in all honesty, I'm sure Ibsen didn't have anything like my purposes in mind when he wrote the line. In fact, only a part of the line is appropriate for my purposes. Now that I've confused even my own self, I'd better give you the line—

"You should never wear your best trousers when you go out to fight for freedom and truth."

(If I remember correctly and can still read with any acuity at all—you see, I am actually reading at this very moment—the line is from Ibsen's *An Enemy of the People*. Ibsen is one of my favorite playwrights, but that is beside the point right now.)

The part of the line that I am appropriating is this: "You should never wear your best trousers when you. . . " Let me explain.

It was back in the early winter of 1926 that my parents took me to Wilmington where, on the corner of Sixth and Market, The Jas. T. Mullin Store offered all kinds of haberdashery. I was still a boy, all thirteen years of me. It was there and then that I was fitted for my first pair of long trousers. And I was delighted! It meant a happy farewell to knickerbockers. (The dictionary says that knickerbockers are, and I quote, "loose-fitting short pants gathered at the knee.")

Now, a-way back in 1926, boys of my age wore long underwear lined with a soft fleece-like material which, in due course of time, got balled-up and was no longer fleecy. But the worst part of ankle-length underpants was the necessity of tucking them under the brown-or-black, whichever, lisle stockings.

Lumps formed in the folds and showed through. Utterly unattractive! Kid stuff! I felt as though I looked like a scarecrow. (You see, I was beginning to take notice of the girls in our class and wanted one of them to take notice of me—but not the legs deformed by the stuffed-in longjohns.)

I was proud of myself the morning I walked up the concrete steps of the old Calvert Agricultural High School. I was suddenly grown-up, so I thought. And it went to my head—the excitement of wearing my new long trousers. In Miss Bassford's English class, I behaved like a grown-up; but in Civics class, the sheer joy of the new-trousers experience overflowed and I turned my tongue loose to the annoyance of that same Miss Bassford. Since nothing she said nor did shushed me, she sent me to the acting-principal. My first visit to the office that was!

Following some harsh words of remonstrance, Mr. Gifford pronounced the sentence: "Go to the senior room and stand on one foot in the corner until I tell you to sit down!" It wasn't the standing on one foot that crushed me; it was that my sister was a senior and was in that very room where I was one-footing-it in the corner. I knew that I would probably *want* to stand after my father heard of my misbehavior; it was, I knew, my sister's duty to report any and all of my failures to reflect righteously upon my father's place in the community. *Papa Was A Preacher*, that's the title of a book and a play and that's what my father was.

When school was out and the punishment meted out by Mr. Gifford was over, I had only the dread of the storm which would soon break upon me. Before that happened, however, I wanted Mrs. Renn and Jimmy to see my new trousers—so, instead of going directly home, I veered to the east when I came to the crossroads in Zion and ran as fast as I could for the Renn house. As I was making a turn by the lilac bush, I encountered a very muddy puddle and most unintentionally executed the most nearly perfect fall-away slide you'd ever want to see . . .

And now you know why I appropriated a portion of the line from Ibsen's play. Indeed, yes, by George— "You should never wear your best trousers when you . . . ."

The epilogue: My parents, having learned of my misbehavior in school, were in no mood to take lightly the sight of my mud-laden trousers. The physical punishment was nothing compared with the anguish occasioned by the removal from my wardrobe of the new long trousers—for two whole weeks, confound it!

ZION, MD, MAY 26, 1981

The Bovine Brigade

I was alone. My spotting shift was from 1 a.m. until 4 a.m., up on the Charles Morris farm about a quarter of a mile from the village. It was cold outside, but the little cast-iron stove warmed the tiny spotting station quite well. This was—to give you a time-frame—during World War II.

To be truthful, I wasn't exactly ecstatic about manning that station all by myself. Since it was one way I could assist in the war effort, I felt obligated—even eager—to do my part, though it was a relatively insignificant contribution at best. "After all," I kept thinking, "a good number of my former students and very close friends were scattered all over the various theatres of combat, facing death, and the least I could do was to scan the night skies for airplanes and report flights over our area to the spotting headquarters."

The telephone in our station was an old crank model; it worked well enough and that was all that was necessary. I was afraid to read a magazine or a book lest I lose myself in something all-absorbing and neglect the defense of our great land. I simply sat and listened for the droning of a single plane or the roar of several planes, then rushed outside, determined the number of planes and their direction as best I could, and gave the phone a crank in order to report my observation.

One night when the moon was down and a leaden sky hid every star, I heard what sounded like a multitude of planes approaching. I stepped outside to get the necessary information to relay by code to the spotting center. As I stood there shivering and doing my best to put together an accurate report, I was startled by a strange sound—a clearly audible rustle, it was at first—an unusual sound I had not heard there before.

ALL KINDS OF WEIRD THOUGHTS crossed my mind. "An enemy intruder bent on doing me in? A prankster out to give me a scare?"

Before I could gather my wits, the rustle became a thumping of hoofs on the frozen turf—and I was almost immediately surrounded by a whole herd of cattle making its way toward the barn several hundred feet distant from the spot where I was prisoner. I almost went into a dead faint when one of the cows roughly brushed my shoulder and let out a long, mournful, "Moo!"

The planes were, by that time, roaring overhead while the cattle began collectively to join in a chorus of mooing. Cows to the right of me, cows to the left of me, cows in front of me, and more cows bearing down upon me, their pace increasing all the while. "The charge of the bovine brigade," I muttered to myself.

"Suppose there is a bull among them to take exception to my standing in his path," I thought. "Or suppose they quicken their pace and start a stampede?" I panicked!

The planes had long since cleared the area—unreported. "Suppose the Germans have penetrated our warning barrier and Washington will be bombed? And here I stand, praying that the cattle pass me by, leaving me unbutted and untrampled!"

I envisioned my relief—I forget who that would have been—arriving to find a bloodied body lying outside the spotting station. "What an inglorious way to lay down my life for my country," I said to myself. "Done in by cows!"

That old time-worn expression, "This too shall pass away!" was indeed true. The cows made it to the barn. I made it back into the spotting station, trembling from fright and shivering from the cold.

My relief arrived in due course of time and did not find a coward's corpse after all. And I continued to take my shift, though I thereafter kept on the look-out for both planes and cows.

By the way, Washington did not get bombed that night. You know, to the best of my knowledge, no enemy plane ever flew over Zion during the entire war. And the bovine brigade never again bore down upon me. Just an occasional "moo" from the somewhat distant pasture.

What puzzles me to this day is why those cows were out on a cold winter's night in the first place!

ZION, MD, SEPTEMBER 25, 1996

Ready Whipped!

What I'm about to write essentially involved two of my very favorite people: the late Raymond M. Shingler and my son, George. (Elizabeth and I were what you might call innocent bystanders.) Mr. Shingler had come down from Altoona during the late autumn of 1936 or 1937, I'm uncertain which. But I do know that he and I soon became friends. He was single—boarded at Miss Mary Brumfield's for the first year or so until he and Marie, also from Altoona, were married. Elizabeth and I invited him for dinner now and then—even overnight on occasion. After Sandy and Ramie had joined the Shingler family, the Shinglers and the Prettymans shared many good times together. We even vacationed several summers at the Touchton cottage down at Fenwick Island.

THE INCIDENT I HAVE IN MIND occurred one evening when Ray had come to our home in Zion to help me work out an income tax problem. He visited us frequently. Used to help George construct model airplanes out of balsam wood. And almost every time he came, he managed some kind of prank: hiding our pillows under Elizabeth's vanity skirt to surprise us when bedtime came, or putting a roll of cartoon-printed toilet paper in our bathroom. (As a matter of fact, I still have that roll stashed away in the linen closet.) It was his way of letting us know there was a real bond between the two families. Nothing offensive. Just mischief.

This one time, however, George got there first, as the prankster. We had been eating some dessert Elizabeth had prepared and were still at the kitchen table, chatting. Ray's back was to the refrigerator. Without the slightest hint as to what was about to happen, George, who was not more than 10 or 11 at the time, quietly reached into the refrigerator, walked right up to Raymond, and squirted a glob of Ready Whip squarely in his ear and all over the side of his face. Even into his hair. We adults were aghast! He was a sight!

I SHALL NEVER FORGET the look of astonishment on Shingler's face. Nor the embarrassment Elizabeth and I felt as Ray undertook to wipe the white fluff from his face, ear, and hair. All the while, George was doing a poor job of stifling a laugh and, at the same time, looking a bit apprehensive as to what our reaction and Ray's would be.

Being the great sport that he was, Ray didn't get the least bit indignant. He laughed, too. He seemed to take the incident as assurance that he had become a favored visitor insofar as George was concerned.

Elizabeth helped him clean his face and ear and wipe the white foam from his hair. It was a happening she never forgot.

Several years later, after George had completed his nine years at the Calvert School, he was enrolled in Ray's algebra class at Rising Sun. While Mr. Shingler and he had a teacher-pupil relationship during school hours, the friendship between the two families was such that their rapport was quite comfortable. Not that George received any overt favoritism from Ray; it was just the opposite. Mr. Shingler demanded excellence from George. It was understood between them, though, that they were on the same friendly beam, so to speak.

That Ray had not forgotten the Ready Whip episode was made clear to George the very first day of algebra class. Without warning, there came a loud whistling, foaming sound —a minor explosion of sorts—in the classroom near where George was seated. A very patient Mr. Shingler had waited several years to even the score with his young tormentor. He had stealthily activated a commercial-grade fire extinguisher directly behind George. And he had achieved what he set out to do—startle George almost out of his seat. The two of them had many a good laugh over that. They both understood.

I DON'T SUPPOSE I'LL EVER THINK of Raymond Shingler without linking my thought to that evening when he, Elizabeth, George and I experienced a time of wholesome friendship in our kitchen around the table of long ago. That table has long since been discarded, and day in and day out, I sit at its replacement alone. Except for my cat. Two of the principal characters of that episode, Elizabeth and Ray, are gone. George is home frequently; he's a grown man now, and has his own home with his wife down in Howard county. Even so, it's like old times when he and I get together and recall that genial visitor whose friendship—and pranks—we both will always cherish.

Ready Whip and a commercial-grade fire extinguisher combined to make certain we will never forget a real friend, by George! There are recollections which the passage of time cannot erode.

ZION, MD, OCTOBER 9, 1974

Let's Go Fishing

A few days ago a group of my friends were getting ready to join me in an afternoon-evening fishing party out on the Chesapeake. Yes, we had as our guide our favorite waterman, Captain "Trigger" Collyer. This was our first venture for rock fish and blues during the after-lunch and twilight hours.

Some of the conversations and behavior prior to our expedition seemed interesting to me—for, as we all have heard said so often, anticipation is supposedly just about as much fun as the real experience, if not more fun. Now, this is particularly true of a fishing trip; the planning and the joshing sometimes make up for the disappointing catch.

First of all, I received a telephone call from Milburn "Doc" Stone on Sunday afternoon, wishing me well and also wishing that he could be out on the Bay with us. He is eager to meet Cap'n Trigger, though he thinks with that name the Captain ought to be a character in "Gunsmoke," not a fishing guide. The good Captain has taken us out so often that he has come to know how to needle certain members of the group. Howard "Touch" Touchton, whom Cap'n Trigger refers to as "Pop," keeps trying to figure some way of getting even with the owner of the "Lydia May"—and some of their banter is hilarious. Cap'n Trigger berates Touch's fishing skill and Touch retaliates by accusing the Captain of taking us where the fish "ain't."

Dick Touchton hasn't stopped bragging about his catches of last year and unabashedly lets the rest of us know he's the champ—which, in fact, he was, pound-wise the only time he accompanied us. Jim Renn goes off his diet by the time we reach Hubbards Restaurant on the wharf and orders enough pancakes, usually, to serve as ballast for the whole crew. The Captain, recognizing Jim's expertise at fishing, calls Jim his "Second Mate"—Buckie Collyer is No.1 in that category. Jim very quietly goes about whatever tricks he's likely to pull on the rest of us. Touch, though, is the real prankster; he'll lean over the side of the boat and give a tug on anybody's line just to see that startled character come alert and think for a minute he has a fish.

Clarence Griffith spends an entire year dreaming about Rock Hall and that next fishing outing. Last year when he went he caught the first fish and tied for top honors in total catch. He is a dead serious fisherman, taking time out only to light his beloved pipe. Ordinarily, Clarence is not partial to hotcakes; but at Hubbards he forgets his dietary dislikes and eats with gusto right with the others. He has visions of landing the biggest fish one of these trips.

Touch and I ought to know better by now not to converse during a church service, but we squeezed in a few words before the opening hymn last Sunday.

"Should I take the tub?" I whispered.

"We always take that tub!" Touch answered.

Dick, who was sitting by me, added, "Better take two—I'm going along, you know."

"What about lunch?" Touch asked. The organist had already struck the first several chords of the opening hymn.

"Let's stuff hotcakes at Hubbards," I said.

"And eat a bite when we come in," Dick sang, in lieu of the words printed in the hymnal. "Crab soup!" he added.

Then we behaved right well throughout the remainder of the service.

"What time do we leave?" Jim asked when I saw him later.

"Two-thirty in the morning," I replied.

"For an afternoon trip?" Jim, who seldom raises his voice, almost yelled at me.

"Why not?" I teased.

"You're a nut!" Jim told me. "So we'll have time to eat and listen to Cap'n Trigger and Touch go at it before we get on the boat," I added.

Ben Sauselein and Harold Criswell couldn't make this one. Nor could Donnie Thomas nor Harold DeMond nor Gene Shorter. And Kevin's in school. With a little bit of persuasion, could be that the fish will come right into the boat. This wasn't to be the last time for this season, you know.

"Happiness in life comes in minute fractions— the little charities: a kiss or a smile or a gentle word or that healing touch. . ." —adapted from Samuel Taylor Coleridge

Marching To Zion

MARCH 2, 1980

Marching To Zion!

William Bryant's few lines are indeed apropos:

The stormy March is come at last,
With wind, and cloud, and changing skies;
I hear the rushing of the blast,
That through the snowy valley flies.

Helen Hunt Jackson, however, looked beyond the "ugly looks and threats" of March and turned her thoughts and words to "April's violets." (Which, I cannot resist adding, is difficult to do when the thermometer is hovering close to ten degrees Fahrenheit and even I, semi-deaf though I am, can catch the whining of the wind in spite of storm windows.)

I can't remember exactly what the weather was like in March, 1923, when the Prettyman family roared into Zion in my father's old Moon, almost immediately following the session of the old Wilmington Conference. Our wooden packing boxes, trunks, etc. had to be shipped from Deal's Island over to Baltimore and thence to North East, I recall. It took preachers a bit longer to pack up and get moving after the bishop had read the appointments than it does today.

I also recall that we stopped over in Lincoln, Delaware, at my Grandmother Clendaniel's home for at least one night, for it was while we were in Lincoln that one of my two pet cats escaped and was nowhere to be found when it came time for us to start the drive to Zion. I was very sad; but at least I still had one cat left as a security pet pending our arrival in our new environment.

My dad had been forewarned that Zion was located among the hills of Cecil County and that driving on the narrow roads north of the Canal was going to be a bit of a challenge to him. So he engaged a chauffeur, "Punk" Parker, who was a resident of Lincoln; his expertise at the wheel had been proven since he was in the employ of the Clendaniels who were in the fruit brokerage business. Punk was just what we needed, for he guided that old automobile around the hair-pin bends from Middletown, Delaware, across to Chesapeake City and on up the road to where the hills really began to roll.

From North East to Leslie on up to Zion, the road was a graveled one—a far cry from the oyster-shell roads we had been used to seeing and riding over. And that covered bridge north of Bay View was something new and exciting to me—and, I think, to my sister Julia and my mother. I'm sure my dad had seen covered bridges before, since he had studied up at Drew Seminary and had served as a student pastor up in that part of the country where covered bridges were not unusual.

The Moon was a fine, classy automobile—bucket seats and leather upholstery and a motor that gave off noises befitting an airplane! It was a sports roadster, but it was equipped with isinglass-and-leatherette side curtains which had to be fastened in place to shut out rain and wind on stormy days. Often whoever undertook the task of getting those curtains in place when a storm came up got a good soaking for his efforts.

Fortunately, we didn't need those side curtains the day the Moon nosed its way into the village of Zion. Punk, on orders from my father, brought the car to a halt in front of the corner store at the crossroads. A pleasant young man with a quick step

The Prettyman family at Tolchester Amusement Park
Circa 1916

and a rapid-fire response to the questions my father directed to him pointed the way to what was to become our home for the next ten years—the Zion M.E. Parsonage! The young man, the proprietor of the store, took note of my mother, Julia, and me sitting somewhat travel-worn on the back seat. Obviously he took most note of my sister, for he addressed her thusly: "How are you, sister?" Little did he know he was going to be calling her something other than "sister" within a couple of years and would be standing in the parlor of the parsonage "gettin' hitched" to her four-and-a-half years after the initial greeting.

We unloaded and were met at the door of our new home by two ladies from the Ebenezer Church, one of four churches my father was to serve. Mrs. Mabel Logan and Mrs. Eva Kirk—sisters they were—had prepared a sumptuous meal for the new minister and his family. It was a most gracious way of welcoming us. I remember the hot rusks with a sugar icing; they were great!

Our own household goods hadn't arrived yet. Bedding was furnished us by kind people in the village, and I began my years of sleeping in the little room next to the tin roof, upon which rain, hail, sleet, and occasional falling apples combined to play a special kind of music for me throughout our years of residence there.

The Moon may have roared into Zion, but I was as meek as a lamb—lonely, homesick, and with only one of my two cats! It wasn't long before I found playmates and life-long friends, however—Jimmy Renn, the Kennedy children, the Rogers boys. Zion was more of an old-folks village fifty-seven years ago. Just a few of us kids. Jimmy lives now right where he did when we first became buddies. Oh, he migrated down to Essex for a few years, he and Ann, his wife; and Guy Rogers left Zion for a time, but he's back in the village now, he and Mildred. We three—Jimmy, Guy, and I—are the only "youngsters" who still make Zion their home—youngsters from the 1923 era, that is.

No. I'm wrong. Julia lives right across the street from us—and that peppery little man, the first person we met in the village when we got here, still calls me his "outlaw."

Fifty-seven years ago . . . We sang "We're Marching to Zion" as Punk Parker gave the gas to Pop's Moon along the way, by George!

MARCH 13, 1977

Just Like Tom and Huck

We have, as I have said many, many times before, been buddies since the spring of 1923. If I remember correctly at all, he was the first person of my own age to visit the Zion parsonage and welcome me. I was not very kind to him that day; for, as soon as I discovered that he was not of my father's congregation—but was a Presbyterian, indeed!—I hit him with such force as to knock him from the tree-stump upon which he was standing. Slow to anger he was then—and still is. I have related this before in previous columns, but it bears repetition: he picked himself up from the ground, made no effort to fight back but suggested that we play at something. I do not recall the kind of play we engaged in that day, but throughout our boyhood years we were almost inseparable.

Whatever the season, we found something to do to cement our companionship. During the winter months, we hunted steel traps together early in the morning before going to school. In the evenings—after supper—we often worked on electrifying a wooden box which we had fashioned into a miniature house, using dry-cell batteries—sometimes discards from the homes of those more affluent neighbors who had that wonderful new invention, the radio. You see, Zion was not electrified as yet and radios operated on A and B batteries—and even after they were no longer of any use for the radio, the B batteries still had enough juice in them to light up tiny flashlight bulbs.

When we were tired of conducting our experiments with electricity, we might turn to setting up a little theater, also fashioned from a wooden box which Dick Touchton, the town merchant, provided us. We had our magic lanterns, our crank-style movie projectors; but we also had our imaginations—and we held shadow-shows of our own by placing a lighted candle behind a white muslin screen and operating characters we had created out of cardboard so that the action resembled motion pictures without detailed features—just simply shadows.

We were also avid readers. Since in neither of our homes were Sunday games looked upon with approval, we got together in either his house or mine and read books—not aloud, but each with his own book. Our folks used to comment about the fact that we seemed not to need to talk at all—just to be at the same place at the same time—to be satisfied. Now, we did not read the classics, but The Rover Boys, Frank and Dick Merriwell, Buffalo Bill, Baseball Joe, Tom Swift, Roy Blakeley, Pee Wee Harris and, later, Zane Grey's heroes and those of other Western writers—those were the fictitious persons after which we began to pattern our lives. To the best of my knowledge, neither of us ever mastered the "double-shoot" that the Merriwell boys and Burt L. Standish gave life to and were able to throw at opposing batsmen; but we tried just about everything in our power to emulate the characters about whom we read.

One Sunday, I distinctly recall, we spent the entire afternoon and evening devouring first one volume then another. Four books apiece we read that day—after which I was so sick I was unable to go to school the next day. Too much of a good thing, I guess you'd call it.

I mentioned not too many weeks back the snow houses we dug out of deep drifts and our other winter-time activities on snow and ice. Years ago I wrote about the time my parents decided that, since we hadn't had any ice skating up to that point in time that particular winter, they would see to it that we did have some. So, after I had gone to bed, my mother and father, noting that the thermometer registered well below freezing, carried buckets of water from the kitchen pump and poured that water over the cement walk leading from the parsonage to the church. Sure enough, the next morning there was a thin coating of ice—and they had me up just about daylight and alerted Jim's mother to send him over. Jim and I skated up to the last minute before time for us to start off to school.

Oh, we were just as mischievous as any other pair of boys, I'm sure. Like Tom Sawyer and Huckleberry Finn, we wandered from the path of righteousness from time to time. Our initial venture at smoking—that happened one morning while we were hunting traps—was made possible because we had surreptitiously "borrowed" some Camels from the jar in which Dick kept his supply in his home up the street aways. The results were agonizing—for me, at least. We'd never heard of chlorophyll, I'm sure, but we chewed some grass to try to subdue the probable odor which would have given our naughtiness away; no one suspected what we had done—but when I arrived at school I was so woefully ill that I thought I was being punished from above and would soon be cast into eternal flames for my sins. I shall never forget the undeserved compassion shown me that morning by teachers and fellow pupils—while Jim stood by in utter silence, bless him! Someone arranged that I be driven home where my parents could stem the nausea or, if necessary, take me to Dr. Gifford for healing.

My home at 161 Old Zion Road in the village of Zion

Fifty-four years have gone by since we first met on the parsonage lawn in Zion. We are still neighbors. In fact, we live nearer, distance wise, than we did fifty-four springs ago. Jim lives right where he did then; in 1950, my wife and I and our son moved into our present home directly across from the Renn property. We are within hog-calling distance, day and night. Now that Jim and Ann's boys are grown and live elsewhere—and the same goes for our son—Jim and Ann and Elizabeth and I frequently make a foursome, though we by no means monopolize that relationship for there are others in the community with whom we all relate very well.

Just the other day, Jim handed me something which I had admired whenever we were in their home—a 1912 calendar issued by Goldey College, Wilmington, Delaware. (The picture on the calendar is entitled "Ring! Ring for Liberty!"—by Henry Mosler.) Now, Jim gave me that calendar because that's the year I was born—1912. And the first thing I did was to check December 15! Sure enough, that was the Sunday—the Sunday night I broke up the meetin' and my father was called from the pulpit to hasten home in order to summon Dr. Selby to the parsonage in Rock Hall to administer the breath-giving smack that started it all—in a sense—for me.

The calendar—bearing the date 1912—in excellent condition—was a most appreciated gift. But the real gift has been simply friendship. That's what counts, by George!

FEBRUARY 28, 1979

I Wanted An Express Wagon

Dr. Simpson termed it "inflammatory rheumatism." To me, it was simply a series of intermittent pains. I was not old enough to know or to care what the name of the disease was. I only knew I hurt.

My parents set up a World War I army-surplus bed in the dining room of the parsonage, close by the coal-burning stove. I was blissfully unaware of any possible involvement of the pericardium and the heart valves in relation to the illness I was undergoing. (I am still relatively ignorant concerning the pericardium since I have had no training in medicine, and I have learned to leave such anatomical niceties up to those who are professionally qualified to talk about them.)

Getting back to my bout with inflammatory rheumatism: the bed was set up near a window and I could see the old, gray, weather-beaten schoolhouse and watch my schoolmates at play when the winter weather permitted them to be out-of-doors. The iron pump in the school yard became a focal point of my attention, for it was from that clanking pump that the children obtained the water—in large buckets—for the several classrooms in the school. The parsonage family used that pump, too, for the water from the pump on our back porch was unfit for human consumption, having, so I was told, an unbearable odor.

Mother was kept rather busy heating woolen cloths in which to wrap my aching joints: one day, my wrists or elbows; another, my ankles or hips. I do not, I have been informed, possess a high degree of tolerance of pain. Personally, I think when a fellow hurts, he hurts; and no one, not even a doctor, can measure the degree of pain one is suffering. Dr. Simpson, I recall, never once scolded me for hurting; he was patient, sympathetic, and kind throughout the long ordeal, for I was bedridden many weeks.

Sometimes at night when I couldn't sleep, Mom would sit by my bed with needle and thread in her hands and work on a new flannel nightshirt for me. (Pajamas were not yet in vogue, you see.) I remember that during that winter she tufted a new quilt for my bed—a very lovely quilt dotted with bright red tufts. She literally burnt the midnight oil, making certain that I be as comfortable as possible and that I knew she was by my side. She read to me by the hour— "The Tale of Jimmy Rabbit," "The Tale of Sandy Chipmunk," "The Tale of Muley Cow," "Tum Tum, the Jolly Elephant"—books which I still have in a packing box as keepsakes.

Dr. Simpson's major concern was that there be no permanent danger to my heart—just as, years later when my wife was down with the same disease, Dr. Robinson expressed concern that her heart suffer no damage. Unfortunately, I came out of that illness with what is termed a "leaky valve"—a heart murmur which remained discernible for years thereafter whenever a doctor applied his stethoscope to my chest.

When we moved to Zion in 1923, Dr. David L. Gifford became our family physician. The Kennedy boys, Frank and Abbie, and Jimmy Renn all had express wagons. There was a concrete walk between the Zion parsonage and the church and that was a wonderful place on which to propel an express wagon: one knee in the wagon and one foot for propulsion; the handle, a tiller or steering device.

I envied Frank, Abbie, and Jimmy of their ability to zip along in their express wagons. I wanted one myself, but Doc Gifford, cognizant of that heart murmur, advised my parents against allowing me any vigorous exertion. I begged him to give in, but he was adamant on that score. Eventually, however, he did relent and my dad took me up to Oxford, Pennsylvania, and bought me a splendid rubber-tired wagon. I could finally join the crowd!

Later, when Jimmy and the Kennedy boys acquired bicycles, I was again eager to be one of the little gang. Doc Gifford said, "No!" That old heart murmur was apparently a threat to my physical well being—and it certainly was keeping me from enjoying the same kind of activities my playmates enjoyed. The old doctor used to take me with him as he made house calls miles away from Zion, and I was forever wedging in a word now and then to express my desire to have a bike.

"Little man," he would say, "we'll have to wait and see."

I waited. Doc was sensitive to my feelings, I knew, and one day he OK'd my repeated requests that I be allowed to have a bike and ride it. I was ecstatic!

We ordered my first and only new bicycle (I had a secondhand one which I bought from Virginia England, now Mrs. Herbert Smith) from a mail-order catalog and directed that it be shipped down to Lincoln, Delaware, where I was to spend several weeks of my summer vacation. I remember how excited I was when the bike was discovered on the platform of the freight station almost directly across the wide, clay street from my grandmother's house.

My father and Uncle Howard Postles uncrated the red bike and did what assembling was necessary. I was then able to join my Clendaniel cousins and ride from Grandmom's to Uncle Harry's or to Uncle Frank's—all over Lincoln! Despite warnings that I not ride too much the first day and become sore in the saddle, I rode and rode and rode. I was so sore the following day that I could scarcely straddle my beloved Elgin.

That old heart murmur stayed with me until the modern miracle drugs came along—until the middle-to-late 'sixties, it was, in my case. Successive illnesses and/or injuries called for dosages of antibiotics, and there came a day when the doctors attending me found no audible trace of that murmur. I wish that Dr. Simpson and Dr. Gifford could have been around to realize that the thing they feared would curtail my activities and possibly shorten my life-cycle became little more than a bad memory—and that I have lived long enough to have more gray hair than they ever calculated I'd have, by George!

JUNE 6, 1989

There Was 'Big Money' In Thinning Corn

About this time of year when I was a youngster, farmers in the Zion area could use extra hands in the corn fields. Time to thin the corn!

The corn had been planted so that the field resembled a checker board—sort of, that is: each hill, I'll call it, was equidistant from the one ahead of it, the one behind it, and the ones on either side of it. And each hill had been allotted three or four seeds. If more than two of the seeds sprouted, those in excess of that number had to be uprooted and tossed aside. The uprooting was done by hand. By men and boys, usually, though I'm sure there are some women who can recall taking part in that special rite of springtime.

Since the corn had, at that point in time, attained a growth of, say, ten-to-twelve inches—about as high as a rabbit's ears—the persons doing the uprooting had to bend low to accomplish the given task. It was stoop, step, step, stoop, step, step, stoop—and that was back breaking, believe me!

The long, straight rows presented a challenge. There'd be as many as six or seven of us, adults and boys, each with his own row to hoe—I mean, to thin. No hoe! A short cane, fashioned from a broomhandle or the like, with a cross-stick atop it to serve as a hand-hold; the end of the stick pointed so that should it become necessary to replant an accidentally pulled-out young plant the stick would serve to make a neat hole for that purpose.

That little cane supported the thinner—kept him from falling on his face as he stooped to yank out the unwanted stalks. Technological advances had not yet come to the fields. Not around Zion. And so it was, across the field and back, across the field and back—many times.

It was not easy for us youngsters to keep pace with the grown-ups, but we tried. Once in a while, one of the adults would notice that a boy was lagging behind a bit and would reach over and help the youngster catch up.

The thinning started around seven in the morning. After, say, the first hour, the farmer would often call a halt—a sort of coffee break except there wasn't any coffee. There was, sometimes, a bucket of cold water and a dipper out of which we all drank.

During the brief respite from the endeavor, we could lie on our backs in the shade and feel the cool green grasses cushion our tired muscles and bones. Then it was up and at it again. Step, step, stoop—step, step, and stoop, pull, toss aside, pull, and toss aside.

There wasn't very much conversation until we'd come to the end of a row. Oh, there were a few jokes now and then—and some adult talk that served to "educate" us kids about the birds and bees, maybe. (We needed that.) But it was mostly just work.

And was that dinner bell ever the most welcomed musical instrument stationed close by the farmhouse! That bell gave off an appetizing sound!

The farmer's wife—and daughters, too—knew how to satisfy the hunger of a growing boy—and that of their menfolk, too. Meat and potatoes and hot biscuits and jelly! Or chicken-pot-pie and canned beans! Plenty of milk and some fruit pie or a pudding!

Then some rest under the shade trees before going back to the corn field to tackle the task again until late afternoon.

Jim Renn shared that experience with me. So did the Kennedy boys, Frank and Albert. And Johnny Peterson, too. And before we knew it, we were young men—no longer the little boys with aching backs and sore muscles. And corn-thinning seemed suddenly to become a thing of the past. New farming techniques made that chore obsolete.

They're gone, now, those farmers who gave some of us an introduction to the world of work; they tolerated our short-comings and paid us well for our aches and pains. Well for that era: $1.50 or $2 a day. That was big money, by George!

The good old days? Well, yes and no. I'm not hankering to start thinning corn tomorrow morning, but, you know, it wasn't really so bad at that. Those men were mighty kind to us kids. And the food was, as we say, something else!

JULY 25, 1989

Farm Jobs Helped Raise Funds For PK

About this time of year, give or take a couple of weeks, I was in the straw mow on the business end of the blower—that was six decades ago before progress in harvesting had hit us. I got plenty hot up there in the mow. Dirty, too. And my respiratory system was pretty well choked up from the dust and chaff. I think sometimes I'm still wheezing from that experience—which I repeated several times during my 'teen years. Right this minute I'd like to blow my nose to clear out the irritants which recollection seems to recreate.

I was not a farm boy. I was a PK—preacher's kid, in case those letters are meaningless to you—and, in retrospect, I think you could say I was more or less puny and pampered. Pampered because there really wasn't much in the way of chores for me to do around the parsonage. Oh, pushing the old-type lawn mower, pulling weeds in my father's garden, or helping with the small flock of chickens at feeding time. Therefore, I was glad to have some paying jobs to do when near-by farmers could use a boy.

The farmers never assigned me a task too difficult for me to handle. I tended the bagger on the threshing machine now and then, but most often I was sentenced to the mow to guide the nozzle of the blower. When I was up there, I wasn't underfoot, nor was I likely to hear language unsuited to a PK's ears. The farmers and the operators of the threshing rig were careful about that; they didn't want me going home adept in the use of expletives. Little did they realize that Jimmy Renn and I held practice sessions in backyard language when we were hunting frogs along the creek which twisted its way across what is now Underwood's meadow. You see, I always have had over-sized ears and an inclination to imitate my elders. (At 76, I find elders a bit difficult to find.)

Of course, wheat had to be cut and bundled—the horse-drawn binder spat out the sheaves. (The combine wasn't in use in these parts yet.) And the sheaves had to be built into shocks—sort of stacked into little hut-like creations—and capped so as to shed the rain and keep as much moisture from the kernels as possible. I remember well that, when Jimmy Renn and I were learning to shock wheat down at the J. Lawson Crothers farm, Mr. Jake Benjamin was our teacher. Very patient he was, especially with me, for I was not the most apt pupil. (A few years ago I met Mr. Benjamin on the street in North East, and he remembered giving Jimmy and me our lessons in shocking wheat.)

The whole process of getting the grain separated from the straw has changed. There is no blower for a boy to guide and the straw is baled, not tramped. It's called progress and it eliminates the boy and the blower. (How's that for saying the same thing twice?)

Well, I have managed to do the threshing in this column before the wheat was even cut; but that figures. I wasn't a farm boy, as I said, and not very sharp in the field. And it's easier to put things through this mechanical quill as they pop into mind than to arrange them in an orderly manner.

By the way, if the date-line on this column looks different from my usual one, it's because I am in Cleveland with my son visiting Ruth and Bill Hart. George B. and I are, along with the Harts, taking in a couple of baseball games in cavernous Municipal Stadium on Lake Erie. The Indians hosting the Yankees.

But I'll be right back in Zion almost by the time you get to read this, by George!

SEPTEMBER 18, 1990

The Squeaking Seat

It no longer worked. Not really. Not even in "make-believe." The time comes when all our medicines and human tricks are to no avail and death steps in to claim someone whose life we had cherished.

Many years ago—sometime during the summer of 1925 or there about—Dr. Gifford of Zion, and Dr. Richards, of Port Deposit, kept watch all day while a boy lay in his bed struggling to stay alive, for he had developed a reaction to anti-tetanus serum and his jaws were all but locked and his neck was pulled back in an almost-rigid position. It appeared that he wasn't going to make it.

The two physicians kept their vigil while the boy's mother waited anxiously for a word of hope.

It was a warm summer day and the windows of the bedroom were open, and he could hear the sounds of traffic on the gravel road which went past his house. And, intermittently, he heard a sound which told him his buddy had joined the day-long vigil. A bicycle seat squeaked every time the bike bumped over a root by the lilac bush just below one of the bedroom windows.

Toward evening, the severe pain lessened and the boy was able to open his mouth wide enough to drink some milk through a straw and the rigid hold on his neck eased. The doctors agreed that he had passed the crisis. The next morning he was able to eat the breakfast his mother prepared for him and within a day or so he was back to his normal, lively self.

EVER AFTER THAT DREADFUL DAY, he declared that the squeaks from the bicycle seat had helped him battle against his illness. He said that he had listened for that sound throughout the day. And throughout his adult life he remembered the sound, crediting it to be a psychological boost during the traumatic hours.

I know the foregoing to be true for I rode the bicycle with the squeaking seat. It was my way of letting Jimmy know I was anxious, too. I did not count the times I circled the house and passed over the root by the lilac tree. I didn't want him to die. I was praying that Dr. Gifford and Dr. Richards could find some way to pull him through.

Not many weeks ago—when Jimmy was up in Rochester, Minn., at the Mayo Clinic—I wrote to him to let him know that the old bicycle seat was still squeaking—figuratively, of course. He knew exactly what I meant. Some sounds never fade away.

But life does. And I have lost a dear and devoted friend. A life-long friend! We were little boys in knickers in 1923 when we first met. I'm not sure we ever entirely grew up; there's a lot of "little boy" in most men, so I've been told.

During our last conversation about two weeks before he died, we decided we'd get out our old pup tent and go camping again one day—down in Mr. J. E. Crothers's meadow, like we did years ago before we ostensibly grew up. We both grinned; it beat crying.

GEE WHIZ, JIMMY! It's not going to be easy, waiting for that camping trip. We'll make it, though, by George!

(In memory of my life-long friend and neighbor, James M. Renn whose death on Sept. 8, 1990, left a void in our town and in our hearts.)

As Bacon wrote, "A man dies as often as he loses his friends."

NOVEMBER 12, 1985

Remember The Old Country Icehouse?

I can't name the exact year the icehouse on the Renn property here in Zion fell into disuse. It was more than just a few years ago, of that I am certain. Of course, it wasn't the only icehouse in our vicinity, though it is the one with which I had the closest association. Icehouses became unnecessary when rural electrification brought to most homes the electric refrigerator with its novel capacity for keeping things cold and for making ice cubes on its own. No longer did farmers or villagers need to brave the winter's chill to saw the ice on ponds into chunks and bed them down in straw, ten-to-fifteen feet underground. All that took place in the very dead of winter when the ice was laid by for summer usage.

Commercial ice was available by the pound before icehouses lost out as a kind of necessity hereabout. But folks who had become accustomed to filling their icehouses continued to do so until, as I have already stated, refrigeration by electricity came into general usage. And the old zinc-lined kitchen ice boxes, upright or chest model, became instant victims of progress along with the icehouses.

It took a good many years for the roofs of the icehouses to deteriorate and either collapse or be torn down. Then there remained the task of filling in the gaping hole which had once been the repository of a winter's harvest of ice. I have noticed in my travels that some few people living in so-called historic regions have preserved the icehouses as mementos of a once-upon-a-time. But, for the most part, icehouses in our area, a luxury of sorts three-quarters of a century ago, have long since had their day.

I frequented the Renn icehouse several summers when Jim and I were youngsters. We often descended the ladder, tongs in hand, in order to fork aside the straw and lift out a few chunks of ice for loading into an express wagon and delivering to Dick's store. The rectangular metal tub which held bottles of sarsaparilla, cherry smash, orange crush, and other soft drinks of that era was not self-cooling and the ice we conveyed to the store was placed in that tub. And ice cream cans had to be packed down in ice, if I'm not mistaken.

Once in a while Jim and I would tease our mothers into making ice cream. That process, of course, required ice from the icehouse. We would crack up a chunk or so, take turns cranking the freezer, and then enjoy that special moment when the paddle was extracted and we were permitted to spoon off the ice cream which had clung to the wooden blades.

No, I was never a party to an ice harvest. I recall the little pond up on the Morris Farm which provided ice for the houses in the Zion vicinity—not all of the ice, certainly, but a portion of that which was required to fill the icehouses. That pond also provided a natural ice rink where the Rogers boys (Guy, Howard, and Lee), the Kennedy boys (Frank and Albert), and Jimmy and I played our variety of hockey. Our sticks were, indeed, crude, and not all of us could be called skillful skaters. I for one, could not have been classified as more than a poor imitation of that character, Hans—with his silver skates. (What was his name? Oh, yes, Hans Brinker!) My head still aches when I think of the hard knocks it received during my many tumbles!

To the best of my knowledge, the little pond has dried up. And I don't know of any icehouses still intact within miles of Zion. No need for 'em. They were once a part of the rural scene, like the wind mills and the wooden water tanks. They are just a part of the remembered past.

You know, I'm afraid I'd have a bit of difficulty, now, going down that ladder, using those tongs, and climbing backup to daylight with a chunk of ice. But I'd give it a try by George! Just for old times' sake.

MARCH 10, 1993

Time Tells On Both The Walk And The Boy

I'm about to re-tell something I wrote, say, 25 years ago. That's recycling, isn't it? Here goes. It recycles me back seven decades.

Back in the early '20s, when winters were rougher than they seem to be today, Jimmy Renn and I were eager to do some skating on ice. Mr. Charlie Morris had a small pond just beyond the northern end of the village, but we couldn't do any skating there before school.

MY PARENTS THOUGHT up an alternative to the Morris pond. It wasn't easy for them, but they worked it out—and had a work-out doing it.

There's a cement walk running from the house which was once the Methodist parsonage over to the church. At the time about which I am writing, the walk was relatively smooth—smooth enough for roller-skating, let's say. (Now it is pretty bumpy and cracked, not at all level as it was years ago.)

One night, when it was very cold, my parents glazed that walk—by dousing it with bucket after bucket of water from the hand-pump in the kitchen.

The water froze, so they told me, as soon as it hit the pavement. And in the morning when I awakened there was a glassy sheet of ice all ready for two little boys to skate on!

I HAVE NEVER forgotten that surprise. I probably gave no thought to the trouble Mother and Daddy went to to provide a half-hour of ice skating for us. But over the years, I have treasured the knowledge that their love for two youngsters couldn't be chilled by the blasts of a winter's winds.

Jimmy and I often talked about the things my parents and Mrs. Renn did to provide exciting and valuable experiences for us: trips to Tolchester, where we could ride on an assortment of the park's amusements; trips to Wilmington, where we could see a movie in a somewhat palatial theater; access to good reading in "The Book of Knowledge" 20-volume set; daily visits to the Chautauqua when it was in its one-week stand up at Rising Sun. All that and much more!

MY PARENTS AND Jimmy's mother needed no blueprint from Washington to know about child care—and they didn't feel enslaved by what they did for us, by George!

No, they didn't have television for us—no electronic games, either. They managed to get wooden boxes for us, out of which we fashioned make-believe threshing machines. And they lent a hand when we hit an obstacle we didn't know how to overcome. Maybe they spoiled us; I'm sure some folks thought they did. At any rate, they found parenting a pleasure. They put it high on their priority list.

WHEN WE WANTED something expensive, such as an express wagon, they encouraged us to do chores to earn the money to pay for it. And we did. Dr. Gifford kept us busy weeding his flower beds and mowing his lawn—or similar tasks.

When we were old enough to help farmers thin corn or tramp hay, we did that too. And helped with threshing. When our banks contained enough money to purchase the wagon we were allowed to do so.

I think you have had enough of this until some other time. By the way, Dodie took a picture of me standing on that walk after church a Sunday or so ago. Both the walk and the "boy" show the effects of time—its passage and what it has left of what once was.

The Big Comic Book

When I was a very little boy, my comic books were home-made affairs. In our immediate family we did not take a Sunday paper. There were various reasons why we did not, but the primary reason was that we were a preacher's family and preachers' families just didn't, as a general thing, subscribe to Sunday papers. Therefore, my comic books were home-made.

My grandmother (and I do not feel she was aiding and abetting my moral downfall) kept the Sunday funnies for me. Since it was often many months between our getting to see each other, there would usually be quite an accumulation of funnies by the time she visited us or vice versa. I sometimes wonder whether I was ever cordial or devoted in my greeting her when we met or whether I hastily disposed of greeting in my eagerness to get my hands and eyes on the precious funny papers I knew she had for me. I do not remember that she as much as once disappointed me by forgetting the papers or by having carelessly destroyed them.

My mother was always an ingenious person at guiding her two off-spring in paths of care—care, that is, for the possessions that came our way. With her help, my sister and I sewed the comic sections together until we had a huge book, five or six inches thick, of the funny papers. You know, those big books—just stacks of funny papers sewn together—lasted us for years and years, and when we disposed of them finally, they were still pretty much intact, though torn and frayed about the edges.

We used to keep the funny books up in the attic. And on rainy days, we'd either haul them down into the living room or settle ourselves in the attic for a day's reading. Jim Renn and I must have read those books through often enough to have memorized every prank Hans and Fritz, the famous Katzenjammer Kids, performed.

HAPPY HOOLIGAN, Barney Google, Maggie and Jiggs, Gasoline Alley—they were the standard fare in the Sunday papers—seldom disillusioned their readers by failing to come up with a comic situation, real enough to be funny and unreal enough to leave little likelihood of imitation.

The stories were not of a continued nature—I believe Gasoline Alley was one of the first to adopt the continuing angle in that Uncle Walt's little ones grew older as days wore on, just as they might have done in real life.

Basically, the funnies were good—and just plain amusing. They weren't exciting, tense, emotional episodes from adventure plots. They didn't stress any moral such as "crime does not pay" and, by so doing, depict dramatically and glamorously the role of the criminal and his methods of crime. They merely satirized and caricatured life's amusing aspects—and let it go at that. I can't remember ever getting any devilish suggestions from my reading the comic books that I treasured so very highly.

There's something about me I can't quite understand myself—but, you know, there are times when I most certainly do wish I could mount the attic stairs and sprawl out in front of that homemade collection of just plain fun and forget the problems that seem a bit too oppressive now and then. A psychologist would suggest that I am trying to escape reality by re-living the past, I suppose. Maybe that's it. But, fundamentally, I am crying out against the common trash we permit our youngsters to possess and read—we call them comic books. The real name is frequently "horror books."

Don't blame the kids for wanting to read them. They're geared to attract any youngster. But they're dangerous and damaging, many of them. You and I permit them to be published. We have, thereby, given our approval. So let's just blame ourselves, if that's as far as we care to press the case. Guilty by assent, that's what it amounts to—you and I are just that.

NOVEMBER 14, 1989

Sorting Through Filing Cabinet Of Memories

I make no apology for my penchant for remembering. I know that I am not alone when it comes to thinking—and talking—about the yesteryears, especially the people and the events which touched my childhood and youth. And those years when my Elizabeth and I were setting up housekeeping and, later, waiting for that blessed event which came about 50 years ago, almost to this very day.

No, I know that I am not alone in treasuring my recollections. Jim and John and Bill and Bob, all of whom are septuagenarians like me, enjoy their bygone years. Or so it seems from their conversations with me.

If the inclination to reminisce suggests aging, so be it; I'm not exactly a youngster, you know. Unless you measure my years against Mr. Robert Baker's. That man is giving us all a lesson in longevity. Well, anyway, now I've let it be known that I'm leading a double life of sorts—trying hard to keep pace with this ever-so-aghasting present time while at the same time sorting through my mental filing folders in order to relive, in a sense, the less hectic past. (Aghast is really an adjective, I know; but why can't it be the present participle of the verb, aghast, and have an *—ing* ending? After all, some folks have been tampering with the wording of the Bible. And our hymns. Seems as if what was ain't good enough for now.)

Yes, I know I strayed from the subject. But that's what parenthetical comments are for. To deviate a little from the main line of thought so as to confuse the reader. Wake him up!

As I was saying, I like to sort through that filing cabinet in which are stored more recollections than I could ever relate even if I'd like to and you were patient enough to read 'em. Right now, though, I'm going to focus on a mailman. (I'm not being chauvinistic. It was mail*man* when I was a child, not mail*person.*)

The first rural delivery mailman I remember was Mr. Abrams. I don't know his first name and I don't know anybody who does. He was our mailman back in 1923 when my family moved to Zion. Rock Hall, Sharptown, and Chance—towns in which our father had been assigned by the bishops to preach—all had post offices. Zion had one once but lost it some years before we arrived in the village.

MR. ABRAMS DELIVERED the mail to the people in Zion from the post office down in North East. He was a horse-and-buggy mailman. He must have been an early riser, for he was usually putting the mail in our box by 8:30 a.m. Remember, now, he had delivered the mail to the folks in Leslie, Marysville, Bay View, and fringe areas before he got to Zion.

In all kinds of weather, too. When winter set in, Mr. Abrams fastened the curtains on his buggy. The curtains had isinglass windows so that he could see where the horse was taking him. I don't know how he kept warm when the thermometer dipped well below the freezing mark. As I look back, it seems as though the winters were colder and snowier then than they are now. I know that kind folks along his route often placed warm rolls or crullers and some hot coffee in their mail boxes, gauging the time Mr. Abrams would be along to be thawed out by the act of mercy. Mrs. Lila Touchton, over on Rock Hill, was one of his caring patrons. (She also baked Christmas cookies for the preacher's youngest kid and I wasn't even a mailman. Some youngsters are lucky, eh?)

As Christmas neared, Mr. Abrams made two deliveries daily. You see, there were extended families then and many gifts came by mail from relatives who lived many train-miles away. Mr. Abrams saw to it that packages for people on his route arrived at their destination before Christmas morning.

I thought Mr. Abrams was truly special. He always had a kind word to say to me. He was something like another grandfather since both of mine were deceased. His smile was the sort that would warm a little boy's heart.

You might say that I have a warm spot in my heart for mailmen. I had two uncles who carried the mail—Uncle Joe, like Mr. Abrams, was a horse-and-buggy mailman; Uncle Harry ran his route in a Ford.

That's it for this week, by George!

DECEMBER 7, 1983

Mumps Almost Ruined Christmas Time

It was not what I wanted for my twelfth birthday. In fact, I had never wanted it and had hoped I would never get it. But when I awakened on the morning of my birthday, I was dismayed to discover it had come my way, despite my inhospitality toward it. Christmas was coming and I wanted no untoward distractions. As had been my custom, I was already hyped for Christmas surprises and didn't care to have my enthusiasm diminished.

MY FATHER, who, as I have stated many times in my columns over the years, was inclined to put me in his pocket, figuratively speaking, and take me wherever he went. He had, a few days prior to my becoming twelve, stuffed me into his overcoat recesses and treated me to a train ride from North East to Philadelphia, solely for the purpose of letting me feast my eyes on the fantasy-world of the Wanamaker store adorned in all the sparkle of the Yuletide season. He also knew that I enjoyed listening to the great organ music played there, for it had often been relayed to Zion over Station WOO. (Again, it was through the kindness of Dr. and Mrs. Gifford that I had had the opportunity to be on the receiving end of a radio broadcast.)

THERE WAS, I must admit, a pecuniary reason behind his excursion with son in tow: since I was about to turn twelve, I would no longer be able to ride the rails at half-fare. In retrospect, I admire his thrift. And I have never forgotten that he showered upon me so many delights. I have put that down as the result of my having been the final twinkle in his eye which eventuated in the enlargement of the family circle. In short, I was the last begotten son and was the recipient of all the fatted calves he had at his disposal.

GETTING BACK to my sad plight the dawn of December 15, 1924—I couldn't swallow. My throat hurt and there were swollen places in the region of my ears and neck. In short, the "it" I had not wanted was the mumps! To be sure, my mother went to our sour pickle jar and said, "Take a bite." I did and I wished I hadn't! I am ashamed to admit that I wailed. My mother went to great pains to stop my caterwauling, but the pains from the mumps outdid her best mothering. In due course of time, I shut up and ruefully accepted my plight.

DR. GIFFORD was summoned and duly pronounced that I be kept off my feet. I couldn't quite understand that order, since it was my ears and throat that hurt and not my feet. However, it was not mine to reason why. Thus it was that I spent the ten days before Christmas having iodex applied to my swollen neck and lying on the couch in the sitting room of the old Zion parsonage.

Jim Renn and the Kennedy children—Frank, Abbie, and Ruth (Leora, whom I have always called "Sweetie," was too young to get in on this caper)—frequently came to the window and peered through the glass to alternately console me and/or to demonstrate their freedom to play in the snow. Not one of them came down with the mumps; I had taken unto myself all of the mumps germs in the village and there were no more to go around.

THE EVENING of the Christmas program in the Zion Methodist Church came along while I was still restricted. I had watched some of the men take the tall cedar tree into the church by way of the side door. I knew how beautiful it must have been after it had been trimmed. The stained-glass windows cast multi-colored shadows on the snow that night. I watched for Santa, for I knew he would enter the church by the side door and I would get a glimpse of him. How I envied those who could be inside the church as he handed out the little box of candy and one orange to each member of the Sunday School!

THE LIGHTS went out in the church and my dad came home. I heard him stomp his feet on the back porch to rid his over-shoes of snow. Pretty soon, he came into the sitting room and handed me the Christmas treat Santa had designated for me. Good old Touch (he was Santa—he really wasn't old then). He hadn't forgotten me!

I was ecumenical, by the way. I not only attended the Methodist Sunday School and church, but also the Zion Presbyterian services. I was a member of Mrs. Charles Morris' Sunday School class because Jim Renn was and I didn't want him to have a head start to heaven on me. That very year, Mrs. Morris sent me a Christmas booklet which I came across while clearing out my files a few weeks ago. I did not dispose of that little treasure from the past.

MUMPS CAME AND WENT. So did Christmas. And though I would have chosen to escape what seemed to be a tribulation, I'm sure I was one of the happiest kids on earth on Christmas morning. Looking back fifty-nine years, I'd have to say things could have been a lot worse, by George!

APRIL 30, 1975

Scouting Days

In what has been for the last fifty-two years my home county, Cecil, during the month of March, 1913, Scout Commissioner H. Lawton Eddy visited Elkton for the purpose of setting forth the advantages of establishing a Boy Scout troop in the county seat. About that same time, down in Kent County—in the community of Rock Hall—my father, the Rev. J.W. Prettyman, and Professor Walter H. Davis, Principal of the Rock Hall School, were among a group of interested men who helped form a troop in that watermen's town. I was not old enough to be included in that Rock Hall scouting venture, but my dad kept his Scout Handbook. As I grew in years and acquired a sense of adventure, I frequently turned to that manual and longed for the day when I would be old enough to become a Boy Scout. I knew the Scout Law, the Scout Oath, and could pass the Tenderfoot tests several years before I had attained the magic age of twelve which was necessary then for eligibility for membership. Likewise Jim Renn.

By that time we had moved to Zion—where there was no troop. Jim Renn and I pestered my father to help us form a troop in the Zion-Calvert area. Though he was in his sixties at the time, he agreed to find a sponsoring group, and enlist some committeemen. He talked George E. Gifford, Sr., Principal of the Calvert Agricultural High School, into becoming our Scoutmaster.

I don't suppose there were ever more than a dozen-to-fifteen boys in our troop; but we were an enthusiastic bunch! Few of us had the money at hand to purchase regulation uniforms right off, but it wasn't long before every youngster in the troop was completely outfitted. Mullin's Store, in Wilmington, was the official outlet for Scout clothing, and a group of us went up to Wilmington and came back with the essential uniforms, patrol flags, arm badges, etc.

Our troop was fortunate to have the leadership Mr. Gifford and my father gave it. Our meetings were well-ordered and we boys made reasonable progress—from the Tenderfoot rank up through the First Class—and several of us earned quite a number of merit badges. To the best of my knowledge, that early troop did not produce an Eagle Scout. Nonetheless, the program was a boon to us rural kids—and we took our oath and our law seriously.

WHILE CAMP RODNEY was in existence and readily available to us for camping purposes, we chose to select our own camping sites—the first, Slaughter Beach, Delaware, on the Delaware Bay, and for the next two summers, Tolchester, on the Chesapeake. The mosquitoes almost decimated our troop during our ten days down at Slaughter Beach. We had failed to equip our pup tents with netting. After a couple of nights of fighting the stinging pests, we were ready and willing to move on to another site. However, the proprietor of a dance hall at the beach granted us the privilege of sleeping in the enclosed porch of his establishment—which was fine except on Saturday nights when the dance went on until midnight. Sleepy little Boy Scouts could hardly wait for the last blare of the dance band and the chance to crawl into blankets and dream about the activities planned for the following day.

We did our semaphore signaling, passed swimming tests and cooking tests, hiked—and swatted mosquitoes. My father, having once served churches in that area, knew the proper persons to contact in order to take us out in the Delaware Bay for a fishing trip. He and Mr. Gifford planned a day-long excursion to Rehoboth Beach—some of the kids had never yet seen the ocean! While we might not have followed a strict Scout Camp routine, we had a whale of a time—and, I think, were better for having had the association with the two men who were in charge of us and one another.

The following two summers—1929 and '30, I think they were—we traveled to a rather isolated spot a couple of miles south of Tolchester Beach. There we were relatively unmolested by mosquitoes—and had we been bothered, we had the netting and the repellents to provide us some protection. Too, we had acquired one large tent which would hold almost all of us and we still had a couple of pup tents for the overflow. Who decided the sleeping quarter assignments I cannot recall, but there was no quarreling among us—we accepted the decisions of the group and of our leaders.

Again, we had the opportunity to pass all sorts of tests, for we were situated right beside the Bay, had open fields and woodland, too, in which to do our hiking, flag-waving for our signal tests, cooking—everything in the handbook we could attempt at our own camp. Most important, the leadership was great! Well into his sixties, my father thoroughly enjoyed being with us boys, and I know that I can honestly say that the boys respected him. Mr. Gifford, as befitted his age, was considerably more active in outlining our test programs—and we thought he was the greatest!

Together they planned extra-curricular excursions for us—a day at Tolchester Beach, where we were granted special prices on all the rides, and a cruise across the Bay to Baltimore on a steamer. The return trip to Tolchester was the first half of a moonlight excursion for Baltimoreans—and we boys found the romantic behavior of the couples aboard the steamer extremely amusing. Our primary interest at that stage in life was to eat bananas, swill soda pop, and demonstrate our amusement as lovers waltzed or did the two-step.

At our Tolchester site, we inherited two "buddies"—Cap'n Will and Cap'n Frank. They observed our scouting activities with considerable interest. And they accompanied us both years on our "moonlight" trip to Baltimore—Cap'n Will finding a commodity in Baltimore which rendered him excessively generous with talk and treats on the journey back across the Bay. He also stuffed us with bananas until we must have each added a couple of pounds to our weight.

Jim Renn, Earl Lucas, and I often talk about our scouting days. I wish I could accurately remember every name of every boy who belonged to our troop. My memory is somewhat unclear on that score, so I'll just say we were a lively gang—and being Boy Scouts was a highlight of our youngster years.

Next week, I'm going back into Scouting—this time with my grandson, Jeffrey, over at Broad Creek. Jeff's a Cub Scout. Whether I will be able to emulate my own dad and be as lively and helpful to Jeff as my father was to us boys, I'll have to wait and see. At any rate, I'll give it a try, by George!

JANUARY 21, 1980

After I Grew Up

It was forty-five years ago, almost to the day. It had rained rather steadily for about two days. The temperature began to fall rapidly, and before we knew it, snow began coming down in blinding, dazzling sheets.

I was in my first year of teaching at the Rising Sun High School. Except for what clothing I had on, my wardrobe was divided between Zion, where my sister and her husband lived, and Lewisville, Pennsylvania, where my parents were living. I drove over to Lewisville and gathered what I thought would be enough shirts, underwear, socks, etc. to last a few days should the snow continue, stopped by Zion on my way back to Rising Sun, and took up temporary residence with Ruth and Harvey Ewing on Walnut Street. By the time I arrived back at Rising Sun, the snow had reached such depth as to cause "Buck" and Charlie Crothers, Ruth's brother, to suggest that my automobile be parked in the Ford Garage which Buck operated. It was a good suggestion, for the storm raged on throughout the night and well into the next day. Travel by automobile was utterly impossible.

School was not called off, however, and I walked from the Ewing home up to the high school. Temperatures had dropped close to the zero mark and the wind kept the snow swirling and piling up into huge drifts. By the time I reached the high school, my hands were all but frozen. Warren Warren, a fellow-teacher, spent what seemed like hours to me running cool water over my hands and rubbing them to get them back to near normal.

School buses were not running, naturally, but the youngsters who lived in the town and within walking distance of the school were right there—perhaps thirty to thirty-eight of them. Marlin U. Zimmerman, who was principal at that time, herded all students into one classroom, under the supervision of one teacher for one period at a time, freeing others for preparation of mid-year examinations which were to take place within a few days.

Ruth Ewing came in as substitute teacher in home economics since Selena Mackie was snow-bound in Elkton. Ruth's primary job was to prepare lunch for those of us who were in the building; and she did an excellent job—hot soup, biscuits, and sandwiches.

Those of us who were teachers and who were able to get to the school and the pupils who managed to trudge through the snow enjoyed two days of rather irregular schedules. We teachers did not have the equipment for duplicating our exams as do teachers today. There was no school secretary and no mimeograph machine. But there was a box of gelatin-like material we could use to "ditto" the material we had written or typed on a master copy. There was one catch: after one teacher had used the "box," another had to wait until the purple ink on the gelatin had faded before another master copy could be laid upon the gelatin and clean copies obtained from that magic box.

Fortunately, we were not a temperamental faculty. We took turns with admirable patience. And eventually every one of us was able to duplicate a sufficient number of exam sheets for his class.

HIGHWAYS WERE CLEARED in those days by hand. Teams of men shoveled one-way lanes on the major roads throughout the days and nights, adding cut-outs here and there in order to permit backing-up or pulling-in so that should two vehicles meet there would be a way to work out passing.

The snow had ended by late Friday, but the winds kept driving the white stuff into higher and higher drifts. And sub-zero thermometer readings lasted for several days. My supply of clean clothing ran out, and it became necessary for me to purchase some shirts and other necessities at Mr. Johnson's clothing store. And, having nothing better to do, I went into Cliff Marker's barber shop for a hair cut, a shave, and a shampoo. Ashby's was, back in those days, a great place to get a coke and to pass the time chatting, too.

By Sunday of that week, there was a one-lane highway open from Rising Sun to Bel Air, while the roads out toward Calvert and Zion were still pretty well clogged with snow. Charlie and

Buck decided that it would be fun to drive down to Baltimore to the auto show at the armory. Mr. Zimmerman was in agreement with that thought, too. When the decision to do that was made, I was soaking in the bath tub. I hustled out of there as fast as I could, put on the warmest clothing I had, and the four of us started out in my 1934 Chevrolet. We stopped by the Haines Hardware Store to get a temperature reading, and, believe me, it was a low one—something like five-below.

CHARLIE DID THE DRIVING. We arrived in Baltimore without any trouble, visited the auto show, had dinner at Miller's, and took in the movie, "David Copperfield." I had some guilt feelings about attending a theater on Sunday, but I also thought that the Lord would take the circumstances into account and absolve me of my sin. After all, I was in good company and "David Copperfield" was wholesome entertainment.

But the next morning I was unable to go to my work. I had caught one of the nastiest colds I had ever had—or have since had. Dr. Dodson came around to the Ewing residence, prescribed medication, and Ruth put me in a bedroom all by myself where my coughing was less likely to keep the household awake all hours of the night. I missed a few days of school—two or three, I'd guess.

Obviously, I survived. And I decided to take room and board with the Ewing family for the remainder of the winter. That Ruth and Harvey were willing to take me in was a God-send. And for five dollars a week, at that! What a bargain! The best of meals and just the nicest people!

Right after Christmas the next winter, I moved in with the Ewings again. The winters of '35 and '36 were winters to remember, too. Seems as though we don't get winters like 'em very often anymore—and that's fine with me, what with the OPEC nations putting the bite on us who need oil for heat.

But, then, I am told, we who are past middle-age tend to think back; and the more we think, the deeper the snows were and the lower the thermometer readings. I'd like to say that I haven't exaggerated one little bit in this column, by George!.

"Nothing that was worthy in the past departs..."
—Thomas Carlyle

There Are Days When We Stop To Think

APRIL 10, 1990

Greatest Story Ever Told

I don't know about you, but I would have a hard time getting through a single day if it weren't for the promise Jesus made when He said, "Because I live, ye shall live also." I am thinking right now of the one who is on the immortal side of eternity and with whom, one day, I shall be reunited. And not only her, but also those others who were near and very dear to me throughout my years on the mortal side of time—I shall be once again with them. I believe this!

When, on that first Easter morning, the tomb in which He had been laid following His death upon the cross was found empty—the stone rolled away and the burial cloths laid aside—the resurrection became a fact. That is why now, on Easter mornings, we who believe in Him sing those hymns which proclaim that He lives! Jesus lives!

I am not a theologian, and I certainly do not know—nor understand—all the intricacies of the rituals and stated beliefs of the many and varied denominations marching beneath the Christian flag. But that one fact should serve to cause us to shout in unison, "He lives!" And through His life and death and resurrection He has given us the keys to the kingdom if we will but accept them.

The teachings of Jesus tell us to trust Him, to put our faith in Him, to imitate Him as best we can in our daily living, to carry our crosses in the spirit He displayed. There are obligations and responsibilities, yes; they are means of expressing our faith in Him. They are requisites if we are to be beneficiaries of that wonderful promise He gave us. They are found in the parables and in the sermon which gave us the beatitudes. They are expressed in everything He did or said of which we have any record.

When we have allowed the Easter story to fade from our thinking, perhaps we need a refreshing reminder from the gospels, a review of that miraculous event, "the first day of the week" and the events which followed. We could go with the women to the empty tomb and run with Simon Peter to see for ourselves that the tomb was indeed empty. We could walk with Cleopas and his companion on the road to Emmaus and find Jesus there too. We could put our hands into His wounds as Thomas did. And we could join the multitude who saw Him alive again.

No wonder the records which tell us of His birth, His life, His death, His resurrection have, collectively, been called "The Greatest Story Ever Told." Not a fable, but a fact!

With that beautiful benediction— "Because I live, ye shall live also."

MAY 17, 1995

Remembrance Of Veterans Was Memorable

One of the year's finest local events took place Tuesday evening, May 9, at the Cultural Center on the campus of Cecil Community College, when Cecil County's veterans were featured guests at a photography exhibit and a band concert booked in their honor.

It was an occasion that caused me to say, "This is what the center is all about! Our own people, to whom we are all indebted for what they did for all of us when our country needed them. They are our very own heroes!"

I could not help thinking of those who would also have been there to be honored but who, in the cause for which they were enlisted, died on the beaches and in the foxholes, particularly during World War II which ended 50 years ago in victory for the United States and its allies. It's trite, I know, but I viewed the evening as a "lest we forget" occasion, an emotional interlude in a world that seems somehow to have its deeper feelings dry up at times.

A PHOTOGRAPHY EXHIBIT honoring the veterans opened that evening in the lobby of the Milburn Stone Memorial Theatre. The exhibit recognizes the veterans' organizations within the county for their generous contribution to the Cecil County Veterans Memorial Library which is housed in the Cultural Center.

An estimated 500 people, including many veterans, were present during the evening—viewing the exhibit, attending the band concert, and touring the photography laboratory in the recently rededicated Arts and Science Building. And seeing work the students in that department have accomplished.

Dr. Robert Gell, as he spoke briefly to the veterans, along with guests gathered in the lobby, told them, "This is yours—this center, this library to which you made such generous contributions."

But the real thrust of the evening was that of appreciation, as expressed by Dr. Gell; by Kristi Eisenberg, coordinator of the event, and Pat Crowe, distinguished photojournalist, for the service to our country performed by the veterans of World War II and subsequent military engagements.

The exhibit was prepared by the instructors and students of the Visual Communications Program at the college. Kristi Eisenberg coordinates that program.

THE PHOTOGRAPHS of 43 veterans displayed in the lobby of the theatre were created under the direction of Pat Crowe, the photojournalism instructor and a former National

Photographer of the Year whose work appears regularly in national publications. For the exhibit, he worked with Ed Coburn, Fran de Rushi, Todd Zook and Jeff Swinger of the *Cecil Whig*, advanced students in the program. Along with the portraits of veterans (a few in color), American uniforms from World Wars I and II, the Korean War, and the Vietnam War are displayed. They are from the Cpl. Theodore Gorzkowski Sr. Memorial American Uniform Collection.

Kristi Eisenberg announced that recognition for ex-service persons will be expanded to include women who have served our country. It will be an annual event. The current exhibit will remain on display in the lobby of the theatre for several weeks. The public is invited to visit.

Following the time set aside for folks to view the exhibit and to chat with the many veterans in attendance, a stirring band concert was given in the theatre by the 389th Army Band, under the direction of CW3 John S. Fraser, commander/bandmaster, Aberdeen Proving Ground and U.S. Ordnance Center and School.

CW3 Fraser at one time served as bandmaster/commander of the 79th Army Band stationed in the Republic of Panama. He has served in the Army since 1972. A graduate of the Warrant Officer Bandmaster Course, he also earned his B.S. from the State University of New York. Honors accorded him include the Meritorious Service Medal, the Army Commendation Medal, and the Humanitarian Service Medal.

Immediately prior to the playing of the national anthem, master of ceremonies Matt Mangano, Community Cultural Center manager, asked the veterans in the audience to stand. The applause was loud and long!

The concert included favorite marches plus selections from popular patriotic music, such as George M. Cohan hits from "Yankee Doodle Dandy" and Irving Berlin's "God Bless America," the latter popularized by the late Kate Smith.

DURING THE PLAYING of the Armed Forces medley, veterans of the various branches of the military were requested to stand as the selection representing their particular branch of service was played. It was impressive to see the men rise with evident pride—those who had been in the Army, the Navy, the Marine Corps, the Air Force and the Coast Guard.

The audience enthusiastically called for two encores, the concluding one, "The Stars and Stripes Forever," a favorite from among the marches composed by John Philip Sousa.

Two young Cecil Countians, Adam Williamson, a junior at North East High School who is enrolled in the Cecil County School of Technology, and Rhonda Anderson, a senior at North East High, read award-winning essays they had written on the subject, "The Voice of Democracy."

The contest in which they entered is one which has been sponsored over many years by Veterans of Foreign Wars all across America, but specifically by the North East post in this instance. By the way, Adam won for the second consecutive year. Both students received a $1,000 scholarship for their essays.

It was, indeed, a night to remember, by George!

JUNE 12, 1996

Ponder The Meaning Of Freedom

Every morning when I wake up I expected to! After all, back in the early spring I went through a series of health tests. It was discovered, among other things, that I am still alive and breathing, in spite of my inability to score high on a blow-as-hard-as-you-can test. The little lady who administered that exercise actually succumbed to the giggles as, time after time, I failed to puff above the very bottom line, no matter how hard I exhaled.

The only advice the doctors gave me may be summarized thusly: "I'd keep on doing what you've been doing, but we wouldn't advise skydiving or bungee jumping." Boy, what latitude! Suffice to say I'll limit myself to an elderhostel or two, some visits to Seattle and Ashland, and my usual routine right around my own home, my church, and the village of Zion. Of course, I'll take care of my cat.

SPEAKING OF THE CAT, all he seems to want from me is to be fed tuna fish, to be petted at his command, and to sleep in my chair if he can get there first, which he just did.

Back track with me, please: The doctors did ask me to lose 20 pounds. Not an easy assignment, especially since I've been introduced to Tim Fitzpatrick's Sunday brunch at Chantilly Manor Country Club. An occasional splurge there should brighten my spirits. (Yours, too).

To change the subject, let's talk about Flag Day. It's no longer identified on all calendars. There don't even seem to be many sales pitches related to it. In fact, I had begun to think that Flag Day is almost a secret. Then I discovered that there will be a Flag Retirement ceremony at the American Legion Post 194 in Rising Sun, June 14, at 7 p.m.

Worn and tattered flags of all sizes and types will be disposed of in the proper and official way that evening—by burning. The notice from the Legion invites persons having flags that should be properly retired to take them to the pavilion where the ceremony will be held.

There's been a lot of talk about safeguarding our flag—our national symbol—from flagrant acts of abuse, such as burning it in protest or otherwise defacing it. Untoward disrespect to the flag has wrongfully, I think, been classified as an expression of freedom of speech. Which leads me to quote a statement I ran across recently.

IT GOES LIKE THIS: "Civilizations commonly die from the excessive development of certain characteristics which had at first contributed to their success." (Those are the words of Rene Dubos, an agronomist-philosopher, about whom I know little save for the quotation I've just given you but promise to search him out.)

There's no debating but that the word freedom has been the basic ingredient in the evolution of this nation from Colonial days down to the present. Our wars have been fought for freedom, ours or that of oppressed peoples.

Our founders pluralized the word and bequeathed to us a number of freedoms—freedom to worship as we please, freedom to bear arms, along with freedom of speech, etc. We have pushed some of them so far as to have degraded the word and its essential meaning as stated in our Constitution—and, if I may fashion a concept, commonly accepted common sense.

By our far out excesses relative to freedom, we have loosened our hold on significant moral and ethical values, even accorded ourselves lethal choices, and such excesses can only dilute the character of our nation. We have allowed extremists to ride herd on such societal attitudes and behaviors which once were believed to stabilize responsible individual conduct and, by so doing, stabilize the American family and thus the nation. We give the appearance of having adopted the title of an old Broadway play as our national motto—*Anything Goes!* instead of *In God We Trust.*

SEVERAL YEARS AGO I USED A STATEMENT from the words of Robert C. Winthrop which seems to me to put it in absolute terms: "If the people are indeed to be sovereigns, they must exercise their sovereignty over themselves individually, as well as over themselves in the aggregate—regulating their own lives, resisting their own temptations, subduing their own passions, and voluntarily imposing upon themselves some measure of that restraint and discipline which, under other systems, is supplied from the armories of arbitrary power ..."

A confession: Whenever I read the papers or watch the news on TV, I feel absolutely anachronistic. Chronologically out of place and time. I don't like that feeling. It's an uncomfortable one, by George! But it's there. I try hard to have a positive, an optimistic outlook on our future, but I so often become saddened by the turns taken by our political, judicial, academic and church leadership to elasticize freedom beyond all bounds.

Flag Day, June 14. A day to pay proper homage to our flag and to contemplate our freedoms and what we're doing with them. Quo vadis, America? Quo vadis?

JUNE 19, 1996

Declamation Contests Part Of Life

What with Flag Day having been with us last week and the Fourth of July coming up, I am still in the mood to think about why we celebrate our historic moments. Certainly not just for the sake of fireworks. Those moments had to do with freedom—with being independent from our mother country!

We far too often say that we wanted independence from England because of "taxation without representation" and let it go at that. Well that's oversimplification. But I'm going to take a detour before I get into that, however.

Declamation contests were once a part of high school life up at Calvert. I'm talking about the '20s. Youngsters were given famous orations to memorize and recite. Like Spartacus' speech to the Roman gladiators which was assigned to Charlie Crothers. Or Marcus Antonius's speech over the dead body of Julius Caesar. I think Bennett McPhatter took care of that one. The most popular selection for budding orators, however, contained the following words:

"Is life so dear, or peace so sweet, as to be purchased at the price of chains and slavery? Forbid it, Almighty Powers! I know not what course others may take; but as for me, give me liberty or give me death!"

Those were the words of a reportedly hot-tempered Southern gentleman, Patrick Henry. He spoke them during a session of the Virginia Convention in 1775 that met in place of the legislature which had been dissolved by order of the King. It may or may not have been the most inflammatory speech of that time, but it has come down to us as a masterpiece of vocal firebrand. It seems to have encapsulated the emotional pitch which swept through the Colonies at that time.

I remember so well when Estelle Nickle, a student at Calvert High School, was on the stage down at Washington College during a declamation contest there, and won deserved applause for her rendition of Patrick Henry's plea for freedom.

And I, not yet in high school, under the spell of Estelle's dramatic recital, memorized that speech and practiced my juvenile oratorical skill on Rover, my dog. A symptom of youthful patriotism—which Rover ignored. End of the detour.

So now, something about the Declaration of Independence: after the introductory statements, including the familiar " . . . We hold these Truths to be self-evident, that all Men are created equal, that they are endowed by their Creator with certain unalienable Rights, that among these are Life, Liberty, and the Pursuit of Happiness . . . ." We find that there were 18 stated accusations against King George III, each one beginning with "He has..." The author of the Declaration, Thomas Jefferson, made it very personal, putting the onus squarely upon the Head that wore the Crown!

THE 13TH ACCUSATION contains nine separate sub-accusations, you might call them, including the line about taxes and non-representation which reads like this in the text: " . . . imposing Taxes on us without our Consent . . . ."

Those 18 accusations, plus the nine sub-accusations, include items other than taxes. It's good to get out a copy of the Declaration and read it. The grievances contained therein led 54 (55, counting Thomas McKean of Delaware who didn't sign until 1781) patriots figuratively to place their necks on King George's chopping block or, if you prefer, to slip their necks into his noose, by ratifying Jefferson's masterpiece, on July 4, 1776.

Actually, only two signed it that very day—John Hancock, President of the Continental Congress, was one, and I'm ashamed to say I forgot the name of the other delegate. It was right on the tips of my fingers, and it skipped away before I got them tapping on the keyboard. I called Mrs. Ruth Ann Johnson in the Reference Department down at the County Library and she helped me out. The other signer that day was Charles Thomson, Secretary. The other delegates signed it later—the next day, I think. I do know that, of the Thirteen Colonies, 12 delegations went along with it right away; the New York delegation waited until July 9 to endorse it. July 4th is, however, the official date of our break with England. (The news of that event didn't crack the Liberty Bell; the big crack we see today came while the bell was tolling for the funeral of Chief Justice John Marshall, July 8, 1835.)

There was still a war to be fought to bring the Declaration to full fruition. General George Washington, who, by the way, was not one of the signers of the Declaration, led the Continental Army to victory over England. He had admirable assistance from France's Marquis de Lafayette, Count de Grasse's fleet and the heckling skirmishes by General Pulaski's Legion. Cornwallis's surrender at Yorktown, September 14, 1781, made independence real. (If you ever have the opportunity to do so, take a long walk over the battle field at Yorktown. It'll do more for you than burning up a few calories—if you have a yen for history.)

Later on, a Constitution was framed. It was signed by all but three of the 55 delegates to the Convention in Philadelphia, September 17, 1787. Those three never signed it. It was later ratified by all the original states and became the law of the land. Still is, by George!

JUNE 26, 1996

Another Fourth: Time For Flag-Waving

When I was a little boy, the Fourth of July meant a variety of things to me. First of all, it meant decorating our big parsonage porch down in Sharptown (Wicomico County) with bunting, red, white, and blue. And with flags, the Stars and Stripes!

Now, during my early childhood years, we were engaged in World War I and patriotism was running at fever pitch. People tried to make their towns beautifully American.

I was not old enough to discern more than the superficial gloss of patriotic fervor. All I remember is that people seemed to care about demonstrating their love for America, "the land of the free and the home of the brave." It was an exciting time.

GEORGE M. COHAN'S musical salute to our involvement in the war—that great old song, "Over There!"—was clearly a calculated rouser. Bands and choruses almost wore that song out during war bond rallies. Parades were staged at the proverbial drop of a hat. Sousa's marches were standard favorites in the band stands everywhere and I still love 'em!

Sharptown was a ship-building town during the war. I can recall being with my parents at the launching of a submarine chaser. The presence of that endeavor may have given the people there an intense surge of patriotism and a feeling of direct participation in the conflict.

One of the things that has stuck with me over the years was my personal reaction to the poster featuring J. Montgomery Flagg's stern Uncle Sam pointing his finger at and fixing his eyes directly on me, with the plea—pretty close to a command, really— "I want you for the U.S. Army!" That poster made even a little boy feel guilty for not being in the trenches.

By the time I had grown older, the Fourth of July had become a day of frolicsome activities, quite apart from parades and bunting: outings at the beach; picnics in the park, barefoot or shod; baseball double-headers; races on land and sea; carousing on the part of those who took any and every excuse to carouse. And fireworks—until it became illegal to light one's own firecrackers, Roman candles, etc. because of the hazards involved.

A MORE MATURE AMERICA celebrated the Fourth more sedately during WWII. Bunting and flag-waving seemed less in evidence than during the First World War. There was a grimness in the '40s that I hadn't been old enough to discern when we were fighting the Kaiser, though it may well have been there.

People of the '40s were not, however, loathe to exhibit their devotion to their country. In short, patriotism was more restrained, more business-like. But it was there, nonetheless, in full stride, as evidenced by the way in which men and women went to war along with the fighting men as they worked in war-related industries all across the country. The flag still flew over the cities and villages as the concerted effort to defeat the Axis powers crystallized.

Since the mid-'40s there has been much discontent with the old established patterns of social, economic, political and religious attitudes and behavior here in our land. Some of that discontent was unquestionably justified. Some of it has been discontent for discontent's sake. Some of it has been close to being un-American.

There have been three major armed conflicts since WWII. Two of them found our fighting forces stalled by executive policies which denied them conclusive military victory. The no-win policies were unpopular with the fighting men and the general public, thereby limiting significantly demonstrations of patriotism except for the natural concern for the safety of the combat personnel.

Operation Desert Storm perked patriotic zeal for its duration, but the nation seemed to forget rather quickly about Saddam Hussein. The lavishly staged Fourth of July extravaganzas of recent years have momentarily brought on patriotism's goose-pimples; but as the fireworks have faded and the music has ceased, we have settled back into the routine of everyday living.

IT IS DOUBTFUL, so it has been said, that we could now be as collectively aroused as we were when the Japanese bombed Pearl Harbor—or when Kaiser Bill ordered unrestricted submarine warfare—or when Hitler's war machines swept over Europe and North Africa and his planes bombed Britain without mercy. We have become considerably more diverse population-wise, engendering increasingly diverse dreams. And we seem to be considerably more cynical.

We appear to have condoned—even rewarded—anti-military protest, even in wartime, something that once would have brought the wrath of the entire nation upon the heads of those who dared participate in such goings-on.

We desperately need a turnabout in so many areas of American life. Serious prayer and serious flag-waving—and maybe a bit of bunting.

The Fourth of July, 1996, is coming up next week. I plan to fly the flag, for by so doing I will be proclaiming my love for this nation of ours, despite its flaws and imperfections. I'm but one small voice, but other voices will be joined with mine, I know. And for that reason I believe there can be a turnabout, by George! There will be one!

AUGUST 21, 1960

A Piece of String

I'd like mightily to be able to call upon Mark Twain, America's greatest humorist, to do this little stint for me. In the absence of that great genius, I'll have to tackle the thing myself, so here goes.

His mother had told him that he'd have to get himself up in the morning if he really wanted to go fishing with Beau and Steve; that he was old enough to rely upon himself, now, for an early start on the trip to the creek. So he went to bed, giving every indication that he'd know how to go it on his own the next morning.

But the next morning came and his mother heard the soft, half-whispered voices of Beau and Steve—and she wondered if Michael had begun to stir. She really didn't want him to spoil his day by sleeping through the fun of fishing, so she went softly into Michael's room to rouse him.

As she entered his room she noted that the screen on his window was pushed ajar, and she wondered what on earth Michael had done! There'd be flies and mosquitoes in the room! She hurried over toward the window—and stopped! There was a string hanging out the window and the string was moving. Her eyes followed the heavy white string into the room, across the floor, and into the bed.

Michael had begun to stir and he pushed back the covers and called out the window to his companions, "Coming!"

His mother then noticed that the string was fastened tightly around Michael's waist and Beau and Steve, below in the yard, were pulling vigorously on it.

Mike had been his own alarm clock, with able assistance from his buddies, Beau and Steve. With scarcely a word, Mike was into his clothes, down the stairs, and out into the yard and the three fishermen were on their way in the gray light of early morining.

Mrs. Owens went back to her room and considered that age-old saying: "Where there's a will, there's a way!" Quite true, as her son and the other two youngsters had shown her.

NOVEMBER 22, 1982

The Pathway Of Time

The yesterdays I speak of are so often those of more than a half-century ago. I suppose that may be attributed in part to my age; but when Thanksgiving comes 'round, I think it only natural and fitting that my thoughts turn to those who taught me the meaning of the season, both in the religious sense and as a member of the family.

AS ON EVERY other day, our Thanksgiving morning began around the breakfast table when I was a tot of four or five and we were still living in Rock Hall, my birth-town. My mother's buckwheat-cake batter was "started" with the first hint of approaching winter. I am not good at recipes; I only know that each night Mother added something to the batter in the tall pitcher, carefully wrapped the pitcher and placed it close by the stove which had been stoked to keep the fire alive all night. And when morning came, the batter was ready for the iron griddle and the buckwheat cakes were baked and placed before us. The family circle, as I first recall it, consisted of our parents, three of my sisters and my brother. (Before long there were to be only Ruth, Julia, and me left, as children: Lank had moved on to attend the old Wilmington Conference Academy in Dover and Marguerite had married Harrison Jones.)

BUCKWHEAT CAKES, homemade sausage or scrapple, essence from the frying pan, syrup, for those who had a sweet tooth, and coffee, though mine was mostly milk—that was our breakfast. Then came the morning worship.

My father read a special Thanksgiving scripture, after which we all knelt at our chairs for his time of prayer. In all honesty, I spent that latter period peeping through my fingers to see if Ruth and Julia had their eyes closed.

As for dinner, I don't recall that turkey was on the menu. My dad seemed always to have a big red rooster saved for a special day; and my mother made delicious oyster fritters. Along with the stuffing in the fowl, there was always that big dish of baked sweet potatoes. Mother's own rolls, of course. Her mince-meat and pumpkin pies couldn't be matched!

Thanksgiving Day was a holy day, a festive day, a family day.

THIRTY YEARS or so later, we had two Thanksgiving feasts: my wife's parents had their family for a turkey dinner one day and my parents provided dinner the next day. At both boards, we were provided with "elegant sufficiency," as my father-in-law used to say. The only complaints came when those of us who had eaten too much suffered from a stomach ache.

My parents were by that time in their very own home, the little white house just across the lane from where we eventually built. Long after my father died, Mother kept on having us around her table for holiday meals. Elizabeth's parents, too, maintained their family tradition. Even yet, on Thanksgiving Day, I think back to those years when family circles, though broken by the passage of time, seemed especially meaningful.

WE ARE NOW the older generation. We have tried to keep tradition alive. But there are so many distractions that it seems almost impossible to keep even one little family circle intact.

Our Thanksgiving will take place, you may be sure. We'll have family around the table—maybe in shifts—but we'll be thankful for having them.

The grandchildren are grown-up, now. And that little boy who used to take his pillow across the lane to spend the night with Mom Mom is well along in manhood.

Don't get the idea that I'm about to fold my hands and sit and wait for time to swallow me—not at all! I'm so thankful we'll keep on having days to look forward to, by George!

MAY I ADD a few lines from Will Carleton's poem:

We thank Thee, O Father, for all that is bright —
The gleam of the day and the stars of the night,
The flowers of our youth and the fruits of our prime,
And the blessings that march down the pathway of time.

Have a good Thanksgiving Day, you and yours!

DECEMBER 18, 1990

Recollecting Those Christmases Gone By

One upon a Christmas there came a house gift from a little boy, a gift of his own choosing. A celluloid Santa Claus straight from his Uncle Dick's store! It was a beautiful Santa—red suit, white hair and beard, and holding a sparkling bubble-light candle.

Now, I know that there are folks who take a mighty dim view of Santa, but, so far as I know, this particular Santa did no harm to anyone. He simply took his place on a stand—or on the corner of the TV—and lit up his little space in our world. And he delighted one generation after another; his bubbling candle has never gone out. Somehow, I feel, our home wouldn't seem at all Christmasified if that celluloid Santa wasn't aglow in our tiny family room. He is a bright reminder of those Christmases when that little boy—and, later, his own little girl and boy—made Christmas seem like a day when wishes come true.

There's a ceramic tree, about 20 inches tall, that has a host of multi-colored tiny candles that light up when the electric switch is turned on. Dick fired that tree in the kiln he had in his basement. It claims a special place, too, at this time of year and helps to remind those who see it of a jolly gentleman who had the Christmas spirit right up to the end.

Not an entire set, no—but a few pieces of Christmas china which Susan and Jeffrey selected just for their grandmother. Without them, cookies don't taste just right, though the cookies no longer bear Nana's inimitable stamp. Those dishes belong on the buffet during the Christmas season.

Dick's kiln fired some remarkable ceramic figures which, over the years, made up the Nativity scene. Not garishly colored, but done in a light brown with umberish shadings—exactly what we had wanted for the crèche in the niche in our front hallway. Without that scene, there would have been nothing of the spirit of Christmas for us.

They're all here yet—and many more items for which there are certain emotional attachments. They will, so long as I am able, continue to be a part of our house at Christmas time. The excitement of Christmas has been lessened by the passage of time; no bright red bicycle standing beside the tree; no electric train purring around a curve and into a tunnel and out; no doll house to evoke a cry of ecstasy from a little girl.

The Christmas tree has long since lost its all-blue look—bulbs and glass ornaments creating a rich sapphire glow on Christmas morning. That changed when little eyes sparkled as multi-colored bubble lights replaced the blue ones. And later, the crystal-clear midgets seemed the appropriate ones. But in each stage of our family life, the tree held a fascination of its very own. It's remarkable that a symbol of a season can create something of a stir in one's inner being.

We all know full well that we have, as a people, bundled a great many knickknacks, customs, and rituals and made them into Christmas of a secular sort. I am not prepared to defend such goings-on, for, like the majority of you who will read this, I have been a party to much of it. But I also know—and I would hope you know, too—that Christmas is really a birthday celebration. The birthday of the King! Above and beyond all the extraneous business we put into our celebration, the real joy lies in our remembering that very first Christmas in Bethlehem when Jesus was born and began His life as our Savior.

And so, in the words of the translator, Frederick Oakley, sung to the tune of Wade's Cantus Diversi—

O come, let us adore Him,
O come, let us adore Him,
O come, let us adore Him,
Christ, the Lord.

DECEMBER 6, 1995

Conjuring Up Images Of A Christmas Past

Goodness gracious, here we are in December and Christmas chores are bearing down on us! Now, I've never been one to buy Christmas presents in the middle of the summer because I can't work myself up to the Christmas spirit then. I have to revert a bit to childhood in order to feel Christmas. (There are those who would say I'm in my second childhood, that I don't need any reverting at all. Well, that's a matter of opinion.)

I do know that when my Beth was here with me, we did the cards, baked cakes and cookies and made candy, and shopped for and wrapped Christmas gifts together. Sometimes it became rather hectic, but we did it all in the spirit of letting other people know we were thinking of them with real, sincere affection. I still feel that way about the people with whom I communicate during this season.

IT'S JUST THAT IT ALL comes at once, so it seems, and I feel a bit overwhelmed by preparation. As I think back, I wonder where we found the energy to do all that we did—including participating in the Christmas cantata for our church and helping to decorate our church for the season.

Let's see, there were several different kinds of cakes—some from recipes handed down by mothers and grandmothers and favorite aunts. Like my mother's mahogany cake, which called for coffee, vinegar, glazed citron rind, and plenty of nuts. Or the Minnie-Ha-Ha cake which was nothing more than a yellow cake with gussied-up frosting that contained raisins and nuts and got a little crusty.

And the cookies! I think we used to make a dozen different kinds (and had them on hand for weeks, so it seemed). I remember that the late Lawson Crothers thought Beth's chocolate sparkles were absolutely the best! I was particularly partial to her fruit cake—the one she put together from Bob McCauley's wife's recipe. It was a white fruit cake, as opposed to the dark kind. (I have no trouble eating fruit cake, be it white or dark.)

WHEN WE WERE first married and in our first home, we couldn't afford a refrigerator right away. A school teacher's salary wouldn't stretch that far. We bought a galvanized window box, fastened it to the outside sill, and kept milk, butter and other perishable edibles out in the cold.

Our first Christmas turkey weighed 20 pounds. My mother had raised it, along with a dozen or so others, in a wire pen elevated a foot or so off the ground. Beth roasted it and we had family members in for a Christmas dinner a couple or more days after the fact. (We ate Christmas dinner with her folks and a second one with my parents. I would be so full I felt like a blimp, so we didn't have our dinner until the other dinners had been thoroughly digested and our belts were back to normal). We parked the partially mutilated bird in the window box and served it cold to guests who came in for the evening.

We had a neat group of young couples in Zion then. We'd all be at one house, say, this evening, and all at another the next, and so on. Seems like we didn't feel that Christmas had happened if we didn't get all our visiting in before the holiday season was over. Of course, all that stopped when we started having families of our own and our social circles increased in number.

I can still see Touch eating a turkey sandwich, nibbling on a sweet pickle, and topping that off with a piece of Beth's fresh coconut cake. See what I mean? Neighborliness. Hospitality. Friendship.

The cast of characters has changed and the past seems like a dream from which I would never want to awaken. But that's not the way it is at all. And I must get with it, put up my little tree which I decorate with mementos that I gave Beth, collectibles in annual series, so to speak. I have kept the series going despite her physical absence, and the tree gets one new decoration each year.

AND OWEN and Megan and Neil must have something special from "Dad Dad," as they are being taught to call me. That's because our son called my father by that name, and his children called me by that name, too, and now, another generation is picking up where the others have left off. I am Dad Dad to—let's see—six youngsters now, some of them in their 30s. Yeah, the old man! But not in derision.

Yep, I'll make it. The cards will get addressed, the gifts wrapped, and I may even put a turkey in the oven, by George! I won't have to use a window box for a refrigerator, either. But what was wrong with that? The winters were cold back then!

DECEMBER 24, 1995

Let's Not Forget Whose Birth We Celebrate

For the purpose of reminding myself that Christmas is a religious celebration, I turned to the two gospels which tell of Jesus' birth—The Gospel According to Matthew and The Gospel According to Luke.

The two narratives are not identical; in fact, they are different in several aspects. Luke's account tells of shepherds in the field who were startled when they saw a great light and heard an angel proclaiming the birth of Christ the Lord; Matthew's report tells of wise men going to Jerusalem to inquire where they might find the newborn King of the Jews.

And they are not the only differences. It could be fruitful were each of us to restudy the accounts and see for ourselves wherein they differ. Not to suggest that either is more accurate than the other, but to see how two "reporters," if you will allow me to call them that, have vastly different news stories for their readers.

READING WHAT MATTHEW and Luke have to say would certainly cause us to focus upon the reason that we celebrate Christmas in the first place.

In our celebration of Christ's birth, we have tended to mix the two accounts—in songs, in pictures, and in pageants. We have also borrowed from pagan sources some traditions which we have added to our Christmas scenario. We have created a holiday season that sometimes gets out of focus.

There are many children who have never heard much more about Christmas than, "What do you want Santa to bring you?" Now, I personally have no quarrel with Santa Claus; I love the old codger. He was always mighty good to me—even when he was called St. Nick, Old Kriss or whatever.

He is (or should be) the embodiment of parental love, and that is good. Let him come down the chimney and fill the stockings. But he is not the reason we celebrate Christmas, and we all need to remember and accent the real reason.

MAKE SURE THE CHILDREN know that Christmas is not Santa's birthday. That we adults do, too. That it is Christ's Birthday!

And there are many adults who give scant thought to the scriptural accounts of Christmas. Christmas has been turned into one huge sale, so it seems. (Especially when we sort out the so-called "junk mail.")

If I'm sounding like a cranky old man, I'm really not. You see, when the focus is upon Christ, we're talking Christmas love. Christmas love is not a toy. It can't be wrapped up in fancy paper. Nor put in a box. It is an attitude which translates into warm acceptance of and caring for others. More than self! It is best expressed in the so-called golden rule Christ gave us: "Do unto others as you would have others do unto you." That's a fairly accurate version.

When Christmas comes 'round, we tend to be friendlier than we sometimes are. That's Christmas love coming through. We also tend to be forgiving. We sometimes surprise ourselves and reach out to folks we haven't been close to all year long. Maybe we haven't even liked them.

We forget our snits and smile again. Think about it. We even say the prayer He taught us to say with deeper feeling—as though we honestly mean it.

And because of—and out of—all that, we love to give! He was God's gift to us; because of that Gift, we have the promise of eternal life; we emulate Him when we give our love and our gifts to those about us.

I'M NOT A THEOLOGIAN. Nor am I a biblical historian. I cannot tell you why Matthew and Luke have different versions of Christ's birth.

I can put the two accounts together on the mantel, piece by piece, with evergreen and holly, and somehow feel that I am there at Bethlehem. I can even let that dear little drummer boy in, too.

Would you turn with me for a few moments and read: From Matthew, Chapter 2— "Now when Jesus was born in Bethlehem of Judaea in the days of Herod the king, behold there came . . ." And then we'll turn to Luke, Chapter 2—"And it came to pass in those days, that there went out a decree from Caesar Augustus that all the world should be taxed . . . ."

I think you understand what I'm trying to say. I hope so, by George!

JANUARY 5, 1994

Remembrances Of Christmas Past

As I was walking up my lane, on my way home after having eaten dinner with my sister, I noticed that there were a couple of boxes up against the side door of my house, within the screened-in porch. I recognized one of them immediately as something I had ordered for Christmas; but I couldn't imagine what the smaller box could contain.

When I got into the kitchen, I opened the smaller of the two boxes and found a mass of plastic foam peanuts hiding whatever was in that box. I found, first, a letter which I read with interest, discovering that the parcel was from a gentleman who started off his note with a compliment to me, which is always pleasing. (I am human, you see.) I appreciated the words: "Have enjoyed your *Whig* articles for years—also all the stories, etc., about Milburn Stone and [the] Covered Bridge Theatre."

AS I READ further, the gentleman told me he sends my articles "to all [his] family and they enjoy them too."

Sure! I liked that. But that's the lesser part of the story. For Mr. George Wilson, the writer of that letter, had sent me something special. Something that showed me that he, like me, looks back into his yesteryears for something to hold on to in remembrance of his boyhood and events which helped shape his life.

There, semi-buried beneath the peanuts, were a red apple, a plump orange, a box of animal crackers, and 10 brilliant, shining 1993 pennies. I wondered, at first, how come I was sent such a package. I read the letter again. I guess I had been so taken by the introduction that I hadn't caught on to the remaining lines.

"THIS YEAR," I read, "I finally got this little Christmas trivia done and sent out and thought you might enjoy it, too."

Then I discovered a certificate-like piece of paper with some drawings and writing on it. There were the drawings of an apple, an orange, and a cracker box, and beneath them, very neatly placed, 10 coins—the shiny new pennies, I figured, and I was right. (The real cracker box had bars and was painted like a circus wagon.)

The written words told the story: "Our Christmas treat!" The time frame for the explanation was probably 1938, or thereabouts. (An aside stated that "Hitler was still on the small continent of Europe.")

I LEARNED THAT the Mill invited all the kids—and each child got a gift—the fruit, the crackers, and the 10 pennies. "We thought it was great," Mr. Wilson wrote. And he went on to say, "The Mill had a cedar tree, probably 30 feet high with lights on it. Mill people had made the lights up. It was the first lighted tree we had ever seen. People came from miles around to see the lighted tree."

The youngsters, of which George Wilson was one, were just finishing the seventh grade and would be going into high school, Kenmore High School, the next fall. Kenmore High was a three-room school at that time, with two teachers. There were folding doors between the rooms which, when opened, made an auditorium for plays and the like.

THAT CERTIFICATE-LIKE paper had more information inscribed upon it. "The men of the Mill, Providence Paper Mill, got either 1 cigar or 3 cigarettes which were loose in a cigar box. These were factory-wrapped cigarettes and something to see as most people rolled their own. The non-smokers got nothing unless they swapped the cigar, etc., for what they could get."

Side notes told me that the Rock Church people led in singing a few songs (no musical instruments, as Mr. Wilson remembers). And along with all the kids in the area assembled for the occasion were some men who "didn't pass too good" and were still in school.

YOU KNOW, Mr. Wilson, I really did appreciate getting that UPS package from you. I told you so over the telephone, and I meant it. You have given us all a bit of history that just might have been forgotten had you not brought it to mind. I hope others who received the gift you had been thinking about for the past year or so enjoyed it as much as I have.

The next time you come up with something like this, let me know. I think it was great, by George!

DECEMBER 1, 1993

Mom's Christmas Spirit

Regular readers of my personal essays—if I may call them that—know by now that I very often reach back into my childhood for an episode that may be of interest to someone. My parents were prone to reminiscing, and it is entirely possible I picked up the habit from them.

Particularly at this time of the year, Mother would relate something of her childhood years spent in the house by the side of the Clendaniel Pond, a few miles south of Milford, Delaware. Her father operated a mill there.

Mother and two of her brothers (Herbert had already gone away and Edna was not yet born) looked forward to Christmas in much the same manner as do youngsters today—in eager anticipation of a visit from St. Nicholas.

IT WAS TIME for a new pair of skates for Harry or Frank and a new doll for her; she already had skates.

She enjoyed telling us of the winter Uncle Frank spent learning to skate. There was a pole set in the pond a very few feet from the bank and there Uncle Frank went round and round, one hand clinging desperately to that pole lest he fall. I never found out just when he became adept enough to let go and strike out with Harry and Grace. Yes, Grace was my mother.

One of the first non-religious carols I learned was one my mother sang to me when I was little more than a toddler. She had a beautiful singing voice, soft and very expressive. And her facial expression indicated that she was feeling what she was singing—if you know what I mean.

SHE COULD "SELL" a song, so to speak. That was especially true whenever she gave a solo in church. Singing was religion and religion was singing.

But getting back to that carol. It isn't often heard these days, though once every now and then some popular songster will dig it out of the past. Perhaps you have heard it. It goes like this:

Jolly Old Saint Nicholas, lend you ear this way;
Don't you tell a single soul what I'm going to say.

It is—well, how should I say it?—a sort of "unselfish" little song. Yes, that pretty much says it. For after the singer gets St. Nick's ear and tells him what the other children in the family need, she says:

As for me, my little brain isn't very bright;
Bring to me, dear Santa Claus, what you think is right.

CHRISTMAS MEANT MORE to mother than a visit from St. Nicholas. There was the Christmas program at the church, Union Church, a bit north of Ellendale, not far across the fields from the Clendaniel Pond.

It was there, in that church at the edge of the woods, that my mother and Uncle Harry learned to sing—by note. Grandmom was the organist at Union, Grandpop was an active layman. I can't remember the name of the music teacher.

Mother cherished the experiences she had in Union Church, and throughout the remainder of her years singing was something special to her. It was a warm and loving part of her motherhood. And her grandmotherhood, too.

GRANDPOP EVENTUALLY moved his family from beside the mill pond up to the town of Lincoln—just a few miles up the road. Mother continued singing in the church there, and when my preacher-father was assigned there, mother's voice must have charmed him. A widower, with five children, he asked Grandpop for her hand. That's how come she became my mother.

Let's see, I strayed a bit from what I had in mind. Oh, yes. Mother never lost the spirit of Christmas, not even during that final week in 1967 when she was bedridden and not always entirely lucid because of the intense pain she suffered whenever medication wore thin.

SHE WAS SITTING in her bedroom chair Christmas morning when Dr. Robinson came to check on her condition. He asked her to sing for him. And she did!

Silent night! Holy night!
All is calm, all is bright
'Round yon virgin mother and Child!
Holy Infant, so tender and mild,
Sleep in heavenly peace,
Sleep in heavenly peace.

It was beautiful! And it isn't hard at all to recall those brief moments during which she sang in an angelic voice. That last sweet Christmas carol which, over more than eight decades, had been one she dearly loved. Perhaps right then and there she felt herself back in that woodland church, singing as her mother played the organ and her brother and her father joined with her, in perfect harmony.

OH, YES, INDEED, I'm beginning to catch again that spirit of Christmas and it is causing me to reach back a good many years—even to that Christmas when all I wanted was not two front teeth but a pair of red-top boots like Mr. Ira Webster's.

But that's for another time, by George!

ZION, MD, NOVEMBER 16, 1994

It Gets Complicated

I knew we weren't too many minutes from the Sea-Tac Airport because the flight attendants were walking the aisle checking seatbelts.

I looked out the window to see if I could get a glimpse of Mt. Ranier. And there it was, standing stark and white and awesome. I recalled the day when the pilot announced that he was flying directly over Mt. St. Helens so that we on board could see the blackened crater; and I thought how chilling—almost frightening—that sight had been.

I was lost in my thoughts for a moment or so when I suddenly became aware that the scene had changed with a tilt of the wing and there was a broader view below. I could see not just one mammoth mountain, but yet another, far distant to our left, and barely visible, but there, nonetheless. And then another — and still one more.

Four great peaks in sight at the same time! Yes, Mt. Hood, Mt. St. Helens, Mt. Ranier, and Mt. Baker, standing like sentinels over a vast white field of nothingness. (I think I have all four names correct, though I am not infallible.)

THE SCENE didn't last long. In seconds, so it seemed, Mt. Hood was lost to my sight, and soon the remaining three had disappeared, and I was conscious of the fact that the plane was completing its descent, for my ears were feeling strange and I wanted to remove my hearing aid and scratch deep down inside my ear. Of course, I didn't and I was soon bracing myself for the seemingly inevitable jolt that comes when the wheels of the plane hit the tarmac. We landed.

I'll admit that I let out a pretty good breath when I knew we were safely down. That probably comes with being a relatively unseasoned flier. True, I first had the thrill of an airplane ride over the city of Washington in June 1929 while the 10 members of the graduating class of old Calvert Agricultural High

School were on our trip, the climax of the four years together as classmates.

We had gone to our nation's capital for a few days as our reward to ourselves for having persevered. We had our diplomas safely in hand. The trip to Washington had become a traditional event at Calvert, and it came about for us after many cheese-and-pickle sandwiches and bowls of vegetable soup had been sold to ourselves and the members of the classes below us.

We paid our own way, you see, what with class dues and lunch sales and the like. Hotel stay was fairly inexpensive back then, as was the cost of restaurant food. While it was a big deal for us youngsters, it really wasn't. We thought it was great, though.

Getting back to that flight over the city, it cost $5 to take a ride in an open cockpit plane—a five-minute flight over the such notable buildings as the Capitol, the Library of Congress, and the White House where President Herbert Hoover and his wife then resided. The Washington Monument looked to have a mighty sharp point at the top, and the thought of landing directly on it by chance made a fellow wince.

I WAS NOT THE ONLY passenger that day: Selena Reynolds was on board, too, as was my own father, who was one of our chaperons. I foolishly stuck my head over the side and had it roughly jostled by the wind created by the plane's speed. That we landed safely is entirely evident; Selena (Mrs. Paul Mackie) and I still exchange Christmas cards and my dad lived on until 1945.

I was all of 16 then and had not the slightest notion that I would ever become a frequent flier—or that I'd ever see Mt. Ranier, if, indeed, I even knew there was such a natural monument to creation less than five hours from Zion.

Time has altered a lot of things, including our perception of how broad, and yet how narrow, the land which lies between the Atlantic and the Pacific really is—and what diverse geological wonders there are in this wondrous expanse.

THANKSGIVING IS A WEEK AWAY. As polarized as we expressed ourselves to be only last week, we are all living in this land together and have reason to be grateful that we are. One of our traditions is that we have a day proclaimed to be a Day of Thanksgiving. It's more than a day for going gunning or to a football game or to the dinner table. At least, it should be.

I'm still among those who really believe we should give thanks to God for our heritage—our freedoms, the bounty that is ours, and all the good that has gone before to make us a nation of which we can be proud much of the time. And when there are times which seem to cause us collective grief, when we make mistakes or when some of us fail to live up to what we ought to be, we somehow find a way to correct ourselves. It may take some doing, but we've managed to aright ourselves when we've had to.

We have admittedly squandered what we should have held on to from time to time, such as some good, solid values; we have misused and mistreated our natural environment. Since we know that, we must adjust our behavior and make every possible attempt we can to protect what remains and work toward replenishing that which we have destroyed or damaged. And we will surely face a day of reckoning unless we join together to tighten the belt and start working seriously on our national debt and stop holding out our hands for a free ticket.

AT TIMES WE tend to focus upon our imperfections rather than upon the blessings which have come our way. We gripe about things we could correct if we truly cared. Maybe it's good that we have some of the problems we have if those problems stir us to tackle the tasks of overcoming them.

I didn't intend to start a sermon here, and I'm not contemplating running for any office. I simply wanted to say that, in spite of ourselves, we are a great nation; and if we honestly care enough about who we are and what we are and what we want to be, we can become even greater. It's up to us—you and me. If we can send rockets into space, we can find ways of healing our national ills.

Thanksgiving is an appropriate time for us to lift up our eyes to our Creator and express our gratitude to Him for giving us the opportunity to be stewards of His creation—our portion of it. And ask for forgiveness for our abuses and for strength and courage to make amends where amends are needed: in human relationships and in our relationships with Him.

While my existence here—and yours, too—is terminal, it is also continuous; for there are those only a step or so behind us who will inherit our accomplishments and, yes, our failures. Nobody ever said that life should be one-dimensional. You see, if you stop to think about it, your life didn't start with just you—and it won't end with just you either. It gets complicated when you do stop to think, by George!

ZION, MD, MARCH 15, 1983

A Love Affair

While I have been a resident of Zion since March 1923, I have kept alive a love affair with Kent, Wicomico, and Somerset Counties down on the Eastern Shore. And that in spite of the pesky mosquitoes which could—and did, on occasion—set me afire with itching.

Now and then I am fortunate enough to meet with circumstances which set my recall in motion, and I am moved back in time and place, enjoying once again a place I called home. Some folks say it's a clear sign of aging; I dispute that by insisting that it takes a number of years to round out a lifetime and every experience is a part of that process.

Last week, two circumstances combined to stir up recollections of the three years our family lived on the edge of the Tangier Sound, down in Somerset. First, my friend, Clark Samuel, lent me his copy of *Barcat Skipper*, Larry S. Chowning's collections of "tales of a Tangier Island waterman." That started my mind churning some sixty years back in time.

Then a couple of days later, I drove out to Rising Sun to Don Amorin's barber shop to get my hair cut. There were several persons ahead of me, thereby affording me an opportunity I'd never had before—that of meeting and chatting with "Sarge" Thomas. There was a conversation going on about crabbing in or near the Chester River, and I could tell by Mr. Thomas's manner of speech that he had been born and bred down on the Shore. Sure enough, I discovered he was a native of Somerset County—the village of Champ.

Well, he and I had a good 45-minute conversation, exchanging reminiscences about Chance, Rock Creek (adjacent to Chance), Deal's Island, Dames Quarter, and other name-places below Princess Anne. Mr. Thomas, a descendant of the Rev. Joshua Thomas, known as "the parson of the islands," renewed my acquaintance with a number of my early-childhood playmates—Raymond France, Wilson and Robbie Shores, Rossie White, John Parks, Walter James, to name but a few. And our neighbors, Ira and Essie Webster who lived on one side of the parsonage, and Captain Will Kelley and family, on the other side. Mr. Thomas knew 'em all!

He remembered Dr. Simpson—and I have good reasons to remember that kind physician, too, for his care and concern saw me through a long, painful siege of rheumatic fever and once kept infection from developing after I had injudiciously kicked a pitchfork and had a multi-inch puncture wound between my toes and far into my foot. Dr. Simpson was one of the finest and kindest gentlemen I have ever known.

Tom and Watt Carew and Pete Owens, men who attended my father's church at Dames Quarter, came into the conversation. They were men whose friendship the Prettyman family cherished over many years. Watt was a lighthouse keeper.

As we talked, I explored again the cove out where Bill Carroll Todd and his family lived. That cove could well have been identical to the one Robert Louis Stevenson used as the site for the Admiral Benbow Inn in *Treasure Island*.

Talking and listening to Mr. Thomas caused me to feel that three years of my life were passing before my eyes and ears in a somewhat kaleidoscopic manner. His was the voice of the Shore, bringing back the Sound; the old wharf where steamers docked at Deal's Island; the winding oyster-shell road over the marshlands; the white sails billowing in the wind; the tall pines, whispering in the forest just an oyster-shell's throw behind the old two-story schoolhouse.

And I heard the clattering of the boards on the wooden bridge which connected Deal's Island to the mainland; the fog horns' mournful wail and the steamboats' deep-throated whistle. Yes, and the incessant whirr of mosquitoes as I pumped water into Mother's agate bucket from the well at the school-yard because the water at the parsonage was unfit for human consumption.

IT WAS ALL THERE. The tolling of the bell signaling a funeral service. The pony-drawn hearse telling us a child had died or the big, black horse-drawn one denoting the death of an adult.

I'm going back one day, even though, as Mr. Thomas and I agreed, I'll find it all changed. There'll be a feeling of homesickness and disappointment, I know. Just the same, it will be good to imagine I can hear my father say, "Time to get up, son, and meet the steamboat! Lank's coming home, and Mother already has a pan of oysters in the oven waiting for him."

Yes, time and man have conspired to change the scene and the people I once knew have moved on. But thanks, "Sarge" Thomas, for that brief journey into yesteryears. It was good for me, by George!